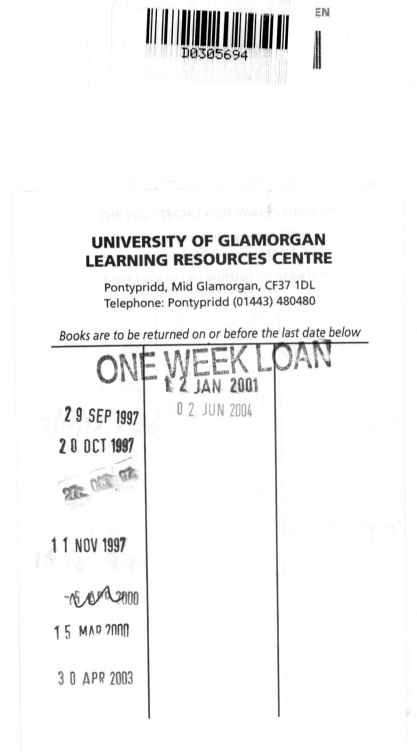

THE
BUSINESS
AMAZONS

by the same author

In Search of a Small Business Definition

THE BUSINESS AMAZONS

Leah Hertz

ANDRE DEUTSCH

First published in Great Britain May 1986
by André Deutsch Limited
105-106 Great Russell Street London WC1B 3LJ
Copyright © 1986 by Leah Hertz
Allrights reserved
Second impression June 1986

British Library Cataloguing in Publication Data

Hertz, Leah
  The business amazons.
  1. Women-owned business enterprises—Great
  Britain—Case studies   2. Women in business
  —Case studies
  I. Title
  338.7'088042   HD2346.G7

ISBN 0–233–97892–5

Phototypeset by Falcon Graphic Art Ltd
Wallington, Surrey
Printed in Great Britain by
Ebenezer Baylis & Son Ltd
The Trinity Press, Worcester and London

To my mother and my late father

Acknowledgements

I would like to thank the following one hundred and two British and American businesswomen whose frankness and generosity with information enabled me to write this book. Their achievements are an inspiration to all women and their contribution to the advancement of women will be recognised by all who read this book. I shall always be indebted to them for having allowed me to share their experiences and aspirations.

To the one hundred and two remarkable women – thank you.

British Businesswomen: Gillian V Aldam, Rosemary Askaroff, Daphne Bampton, Angela D Bertram, Adele Biss, Betty Box, Patricia Brassey, Brenda M Bryant, Irene Callender, Irene Chandler, Mrs Diane Chudley, Jennifer d'Abo, Hilda Davey, Anne Dickinson, Annabel Geddes, Dorothy Genn, Pauline Glover, Tricia Guild, Christine Heywood, Mary Hutchinson, Joan W Johnson, Lorrie Kennon, Barbara Lee, Barbara Leggate, Prue Leith, Lucille Lewin, Doris Lobl, Anthea Lyons, Dr Anna Mann, Pauline Marks, Doreen Miller, Debbie Moore, Freda Morris, Jean Muir, Zelma Myers, Sheila J Needham, Devora Peake, Reyla Pearl, Elizabeth Philip, Arlene Phillips, Judy Piatkus, Dorothy Purdew, Judy Rich, Sue Sheppard, V Steve Shirley, Christina Smith, Dorothy Smith, Wendy M Taylor, Jean Wadlow. Janice Wainwright.

American Businesswomen: Dr Carole F Bitter, Nina Blanchard, Helen F Boehm, Connie Boucher, Dorothy Bullock Heitmann, Lore Caulfield, Sheila T Cluff, June M Collier, Pamela A Crandall, Lori David, Evelyn Echols, Billye B Ericksen-Desaigoudar, Melise Erlbech, Barbara Gardener Proctor, Ellen R Gordon, Jill Hannon, C Rose Harper, Joan Helpern, Betty Ruth Hollander, Barbara W Hunter,

Helga Johnson, Dr Janice A Jones, Esther I Lawence, Sherren Leigh, Barbara M Leonard, Florence Lord Roberts, Kathleen E Martin, Marilyn Miglin, Inger McCabe Elliott, Nina Elise McLemore, Lane Nemeth, Dona O'Bannon, Benita O'Meara, Frieda Rapoport Caplan, Virginia H Rogers, Jean Way Schoonover, Diane Seelye Johnson, Rivka Seltzer, Betty R Smulian, Faith Stewart-Gordon, Ellen Sulzburger Straus, Carole Sumner Krechman, Deborah Szekely, Frances Todd Stewart, Kay E Unger, Venita Van Caspel, Lillian Vernon Katz, Julia M Walsh, Irene J Weaver, Hazel Pearson Williams, Harriete F Witmer, Lois Wyse.

I would also like to thank Marjorie Johnson who was my right-hand woman during the research and writing of this book and whose persuasive skills and diplomacy convinced these extremely busy and successful businesswomen to participate in this in-depth study; Antony Rich and Jane Birch who extracted the statistical data from the transcripts of the interviews, and Judy Chu who patiently typed and re-typed the manuscript with the tenacity and sense of mission so typical of women.

And last, I would like to thank my immediate family of Jonathan, Noreena and Arabel Hertz who did their best to be self-sufficient during the creation of this book.

CONTENTS

Introduction: Why the Amazons?

'My daughters are going to be better than sons,' was my mother's reply to the many well-wishers who hoped she would not despair and would keep trying for a son after the misfortune of conceiving three daughters in a row. Luckily for us, she didn't try for another child and, as far as her background and male-chauvinistic environment allowed, she kept her word.

In fact it is my mother who is the true superwoman, because in her determination to be equal she undertook extra duties without asking for extra privileges. Not only did she earn as much as our father, but she also cleaned, washed, cooked and sewed without seeing a contradiction between her self-image as a liberated woman and her pride in her spotless home. 'At your mother's house you can eat from the floor,' she would announce with pride at least twice a week. Our different views about women's roles in society must have begun then, when I refused to participate in the floor-washing ritual. If boys did not wash floors, I wasn't going to either.

For my mother, women's liberation was about financial and social equality, but not sexual equality. 'When your mother wants a pair of shoes, she doesn't have to ask your father for money because she earns her own,' was how she expressed her independence. The right to work and earn her living was as far as she went.

Sexual equality would have meant allowing your daughters to return home as late as the boys and condoning pre-marital sex and youthful rebellion against the roles of wife and mother, all of which was beyond her. Such behaviour made one a slut, not a modern woman. Even worse, in my wish for total equality she saw a threat that could endanger the fragile concessions women had been fighting for and were on the verge of gaining, if they could prove they deserved them. And here was I debasing the fight for women's liberation with my frivolous demands for sexual equality. I, on the other hand, failed to see why I had to prove I deserved something that should have been mine to start with.

With me as her eldest daughter the poor woman had a problem on her hands. She had introduced me to the concept of liberation and I had become addicted to it. She had brought me up to think and argue like a boy, my father had taught me how to hit back and kick like a boy, and I could not understand why my freedom was so cruelly and unexpectedly curtailed when I started to treat boys as objects of desire rather than as members of a rival gang.

The advent of sex in my life was accompanied by my mother's dramatic retreat from the campaign. Gone was the liberated mother who had brought up her daughters to be not just equal to boys but better than them. Her place was taken by a scared woman frightened by the monster she had created and could no longer control: a daughter who demanded real equality – unrestricted mental and physical freedom, a utopia where women could abandon the passive roles of the hunted and the chattel to become the hunters and the rulers. I dreamed of a world where women were aggressors, not victims.

How lonely I was in those days. The mother who had shown me the way to freedom had withdrawn her blessing before I had attained it. The mother who had taught me to strive for my just place in society, crumbled under the pressure that society put upon her and for my own safety and survival demanded that I retreat to my allotted place as a second-class citizen. She begged me to be realistic – not to underestimate the crushing power of the established order – but tired now and less strong than she had once been, she did not even try to argue rationally. She went on repeating what I had heard so many times before: 'Women don't behave like that', 'It's all right for men not to get married, but not for women', and other stock phrases in the same vein. According to my mother, I was not going to change the world and there would always be things that women could not do.

When I refused to give up my claims she accused me of obstructing women's progress. She catalogued the steady progress of women in the past forty years: how she had managed to have a high school education which had been denied her mother; how I had a yet higher education than hers; and how my daughters, if I ever settled down to have them, would go even further than me towards full equality. If I were only patient and didn't rock the boat it might all come true. But one thing I lacked was patience. I had had my taste of the good life and I was not going to settle for any scraps of equality that might be thrown my way.

———

I could not allow nature to take its course, because that course did not lead to any place fit for a woman. I reckoned that at the current rate of progress it would take a hundred years before a meaningful change in status would take place and I could not wait that long. I scorned women's rights to be hewers of wood and drawers of water. I was dreaming of a glamorous equality – of ruling mankind, not merely serving it. But I seemed to be alone with my dreams.

During my solitary protests and ineffectual rebellion as the ungrateful daughter of the women's revolution, I knew in my bones that I was right, but the evidence was all on the other side. I searched for comfort, for encouragement, for *proof* that women could be like men. Somewhere, some time there must have been such women, if only I could find them . . .

One of the things my parents constantly harped on about was that it was our duty to conquer our natures. What they meant was that any part of our character that, at best, had no positive value and, at worst, was an actual hindrance (like my own untidiness) must be eliminated, modified or exchanged. What I understood by this (I could not take the untidiness issue seriously) was that I must change the very limitations of being a woman. So that was how I, a thirteen-year-old in a small provincial town whose inhabitants were renowned for their thoroughgoing meanness, set out to defy the constraints which nature had imposed on me. I was determined that neither breasts nor menstruation were going to make me inferior to men and there was nothing that they could do that I was not going to be able to do as well.

As far as I was concerned, I was not the daughter of the two hard-working melancholic shopkeepers who nursed me when I was ill and loved me in their helpless human way, I was the daughter of that legendary tribe of women, the Amazons, who had rebelled against their predetermined role as mere breeders some three thousand years ago.

For me the Amazons were not the disfigured women of Greek mythology, who cut off their right breast because it interfered with firing a bow in battle. They were the only self-ruling tribe of women in history, living like nomads on horseback, pitching tents, grazing sheep, guarding their land against rivals, all without the help of men. They seemed more real to me than my own parents.

Years went by and the Amazons remained no more than a memory, but I continued to fight my lone battles sustained by their feats in a distant land three thousand years ago. The longing to find them and prove the possibility of their existence became the driving force of my life, and I set out on a long journey to look for them. Recently I found them: not on the military battlefields but on new fighting grounds, the commercial battlefields of the modern world. They still have the free spirit that only equals can possess though over the years they have mellowed and assumed some of the duties that their predecessors rejected. Yet, although they now look after husbands and children, they have managed to escape the drudgery of most females' existence. They are the new breed of Amazons: the business Amazons.

Publisher's Note

Without the promise of anonymity, the long and frank interviews which are the substance of this book could never have taken place. All names, therefore, are fictitious.

1 | Who Are the Business Amazons?

This title has been awarded to a hundred of the most successful women business owners in the USA and Britain. Three criteria have been used to assess their eligibility: ownership and management of at least 50 per cent of the equity of a business; employment of at least twenty-five persons; and a sales volume of at least $5 million in the USA and £750,000 (approximately $1 million) in Britain.

The search for eligible women was exhaustive, and it can be said with certainty that the hundred businesswomen on whom this study is based constitute the greater part of the present qualifying population. Finding them involved approaching all the relevant women's and general business organisations, professional and trade associations, as well as countless chambers of commerce, and the rarity of the breed soon became evident from the difficulty of locating them. In the USA the standard reply was 'There are hardly any,' and in Britain 'I did not know there were any.'

Each clue, however, was followed up relentlessly; even so most were found to be unsuitable because they fell below the required criteria. The majority were basically too small to qualify. The condition of 50 per cent ownership was introduced because it is the lowest equity stake that ensures security of ownership. Unlike an employee, even the most senior executive, a 50 per cent owner cannot be dismissed. This security absolves the owner from the competition for promotion which faces every employee. The competition-free existence is of particular value to women, who in the competitive corporate structure fall behind men. The job security, lack of personal competition and accommodating environment of their own enterprises go a long way to explain the different characteristics and attitudes of the female business owner and the female business executive.

The requirement of a minimum of twenty-five employees was

introduced to ensure that the status of a business Amazon was conferred only on businesswomen, and not on other high earners like female authors or actresses who might even own 100 per cent of a corporation, but are not businesswomen and do not have the management and decision-making problems that accompany a business.

As for the sales volume criterion, the minimum of $5 million sales volume in the USA and £750,000 in Britain were established in order to include only the most successful. The reason for the lower entry threshold for the British businesswomen was the country's smaller economy and the smaller participation of women in its management.

Because of the rigorous qualifying conditions the business Amazons' clan are to be numbered not in thousands but in hundreds. Nevertheless, for the first time, such women constitute a recognisable group, and are not isolated phenomena such as female prime ministers. Numbers confer power to influence the course of history. The success of one woman can be dismissed as an exception, the success of many establishes a pattern.

Four hundred years ago a Dutch woman, Kenau Hasselaer, was left with four children when her shipwright husband died. Needing to make a living, she took over his business and became a very successful international businesswoman. But her success had little effect on her contemporaries. Similarly, the fact that the American Rebecca Lucke owned and operated an iron mill 150 years ago, did nothing to change the prevailing order. As for the remarkable Nicole Barbe Clicquot, better known as Veuve Clicquot, a widow with a daughter who took over her husband's ailing champagne business, it took nearly a hundred years after her death before there were enough eligible businesswomen to take part in an annual competition in commemoration of her name.* In the context of their times, the achievements of these women were much greater than those of today's business Amazons, who have benefited from a changing social order, prospering economies and relative peace.

But one successful woman proves only one thing, that she is exceptional. One hundred successful businesswomen can no longer be explained away as exceptions, but must be accepted as evidence of women's abilities and competence. Because of this, the phenomenon of the business Amazons is of major importance. When a hundred women

* Currently sponsored by the Institute of Directors, the Veuve Clicquot award for the most outstanding businesswoman of the year first took place in 1973 under the auspices of *The Times*. No distinction is made between executives and owners.

of different backgrounds, age groups and marital status achieve distinction in business it suggests that thousands more could do the same. So why don't they?

Could it be that despite their differences the business Amazons have a common quality which other women lack? Could there be a factor shared by the family women who cope with husbands and children as well as with a thriving business, the single businesswomen devoted solely to their careers, and the widows who instead of reliving past memories have found a new purpose in business? Was there something in their home background, schooling, or religion that drew them all together? Or were they endowed with specific character traits which others lacked? It is the aim of this study to find the answers to these questions.

The importance of observing the same phenomenon in two countries (the USA and Britain) rather than just one is that it makes possible the particular cultural factors of each country from the intrinsic characteristics of the phenomenon. It can also establish the spread of the phenomenon and ascertain whether it is a global or a national occurrence. Had business Amazons been encountered only in the USA, it could have been claimed that they were indigenous to that country's specific economy and/or social attitudes to business and women. But if they were found to exist also in countries with dissimilar economies and/or attitudes to business, then the phenomenon could not be attributed merely to external circumstances but would have to be explained as a result of women's inherent capabilities.

Proof of these capabilities could be found in the ownership portfolio of the women in the survey, who employed in all 23,000 persons and sold products and services to the value of $833 million and £121 million a year. The American businesswomen were by far the more prosperous and had the biggest female-owned businesses, which were headed by Sonia Kaplan's mail order firm with $100 million sales volume, and Janet Draper's electronic assembly business with 1,100 employees. The British enterprises were relatively small – not because British businesswomen were less capable but because of a smaller and less prosperous economy, a less achievement-orientated society, and the relative weakness of the women's movement. While in the USA 20 per cent of the business Amazons boasted sales volumes in excess of $30 million, in Britain only 16 per cent had a greater turnover than £3.5 million (about $5 million).

Sales volume was not the only criterion in which the American women tycoons surpassed their British counterparts. Number of employees was another. While in Britain not one of the women employed more than five hundred persons and 56 per cent employed fewer than fifty, in the USA 8 per cent employed more than five hundred persons and only 36 per cent employed fewer than fifty.

The business Amazons' ownership portfolio revealed another interesting phenomenon: the high percentage of businesses (35 per cent) which catered for women and were run by women. For example Rachel Shapiro's cosmetics firm catered exclusively for women, and employed hundreds of saleswomen. Although the businesswomen have penetrated most male bastions, from the manufacturing of screws to the electronics industry, the fact that 35 per cent of their firms were so closely linked to women indicates not only their business acumen, but also their affinity with women and the ease with which they related to them.

2 | How They Started

Not every so-called 'self-made' millionaire started from scratch. To complete the rags to riches cycle in one generation is a difficult task. Many successful business people started from some kind of vantage point. Some joined a small family business and enlarged it; others became indispensable to their employers and were given equity in their business; and some, wanting to start a business but lacking the capital or all the skills, were satisfied with minority partnership until they acquired them. In this respect the business Amazons were no exception: only 41 per cent of them were truly self-made. The rest inherited the business from their fathers or husbands, started with partners, or bought out corporations where they had been senior employees.

The qualities required in solo starters are not the same as those needed to take over established businesses and the brilliant solo starters might prove ineffective if parachuted into an established business where they had to command executives with greater knowledge and experience than their own. Thus, although it might seem a lesser achievement to take over than to initiate an enterprise, some of the most successful businessmen of our time – Paul Getty, Howard Hughes and Calouste Gulbenkian – have done just that. Yet this does not detract from their entrepreneurial status and stature. The success of entrepreneurs is judged not by how they started but by the results they achieve. For every son who expanded his father's business there are hundreds who bankrupted it.

Daddy's Daughters

For sons to continue their father's business is an accepted pattern, but for daughters to do so is rare. Only four of the present sample entered business by this route, and then only because their fathers had no sons. But the absence of male siblings, although the major reason, was not the only one, because even where there were no sons, giving a business to a daughter was rare. For a father to accept his daughter as his business heir she had to be extremely capable, and he unusually enlightened.

Harriet Hartfield, now in the construction industry, was not that fortunate with her father. She was an only child, but her wealthy entrepreneurial father did not think much of women's business potential. So when he decided to retire it did not even occur to him that she could take over, and he sold out. 'I was so hurt when he sold out without discussing it with me or suggesting that I should continue. Although I worked for him and ran a whole independent unit successfully, he could never accept the fact that a woman was cut out to be a business person.'

Harriet's father was not the exception, he was the rule. Much as most fathers love their daughters and are willing to support them in great comfort, it is difficult for them to digest the fact that they can and want to be financially independent. The fact that none of the four women who took over the family's business was British may be significant, showing perhaps that in the USA, the women's movement has been more widely effective and made it easier for women to be accepted as equals.

Why and when a father becomes ready to accept his daughter as his business heir depends firstly on his character and secondly on his attitude towards the equality of women. Of the four fathers who let their daughters take over their businesses Mr James Harper, Dorothy Harper Townsend's father, was the most open-minded. Unlike the other fathers who required corroborated proof of their daughters' abilities, Mr Harper took a gamble on his daughter's business acumen. On her twenty-second birthday he gave her and her sister an equal share in a $6 million business which specialised in the importation of household goods.

The act of giving a daughter a business is not the same as the settling of money by a rich father on a carefree offspring, because it means giving responsibilities and not leisure. Even a well-established business can collapse if not run properly. What James Harper did for Dorothy was an admirable example of how the wealthy can give their daughters an interest and purpose in life together with responsibility and the possibility of real achievement.

Not everyone would think it wise to let a twenty-two-year-old daughter take over the running of a $6 million business. Most parents in a position to follow Mr Harper's lead would opt to let their children 'work for it'. But then Mr Harper was not like most parents, and Dorothy was not like most twenty-two-year-olds. A slight figure, only 5 ft tall, she has always had the cool, efficient charm that could organise and shift whole divisions without their even noticing. In an eccentric and extrovert family where the mother was an artist, the sister an art connoisseur, and the father a flamboyant entrepreneur, her way of excelling was by being supremely methodical and reliable; qualities which her father observed and trusted. Yet this woman, known from childhood for her conscientiousness, was no shrinking violet. 'I don't think I would have gone far in employment, because I would not have been able to refrain from telling them how to run their business. I would have been out before I learned how to run a business.'

Success within the corporate structure is not a guarantee of success as an owner. And many failed executives have turned out to be successful entrepreneurs on becoming their own bosses. Thus even if Dorothy had succeeded in someone else's business it would have proved nothing about her abilities as an entrepreneuse. Realising this, her father saw no virtue in subjecting her to the frustrations of being an employee when he could offer her a business of her own. He did not misjudge his daughter. The power and the authority which accompanied her business ownership did not spoil her.

Although she was a millionairess at twenty-two, Dorothy's way of life shows none of the trappings of the idle rich. She was never a playgirl or jetsetter, and after two years married a hard-working young entrepreneur like herself and settled contentedly into the life of wife and businesswoman. Whether she ever had any doubts about her ability to run a $6 million enterprise she did not disclose, but after her four years at the helm the business is still there and thriving. Without wishing to demean Dorothy's achievements, it is hard to decide who deserves the greater acclaim: she for her obvious ability or her father for his trust and open-mindedness.

Doreen Hartman's father was more conventional. Before he was ready to risk his chain of food supermarkets to his daughter's management, she had to become a top executive with one of his competitors. Even then it was only the fact that his shops had become unprofitable, and did not fetch his asking price, that made him offer her shares in consideration of her now proven managerial skills. Yet despite the humiliation of being asked to join her father's business only as a last resort, the chance of becoming her own boss was too good to miss. She accepted her father's challenge, took over his ailing super-markets, and turned them to profit. In the seven years she has been running the business she has even managed to add three new stores to the chain. Satisfied that the dividends on his remaining equity could sustain him in style during his declining years, Doreen's father, now a widower, remarried and emigrated to Miami, leaving Doreen to run the business on her own.

Despite the happy ending – a contented father and a tycoon daughter – the fact that it took the near collapse of his business to make him take her seriously left Doreen with a residue of bitterness. Would it have taken him so long if she had been a son? Doreen has no illusions about this:

> Had I been a son I would not have needed the same kind of drive. I might not have needed an MBA, let alone a PhD. My father would have accepted me as the natural heir. I would not have needed to go off to a supermarket chain to prove myself for six years when we had a chain of our own.

Where there were sons the chance of a daughter entering the father's business were minimal; but where there were none, a father with dynastic ambitions had no choice but to consider a daughter for the succession. Like many of the business Amazons, Nancy Gardner did not realise her potential until after she had been married for twelve years and had borne three daughters in succession. She had married at eighteen, and the only hint of steel that showed then was in her dedication as a student. During her childbearing and rearing years she managed to obtain two degrees – one in mathematics and the other in modern languages. Even then she had no career ambitions; but in the light of her academic achievements her parents themselves suggested that instead of 'getting pregnant all the time' she should come and work in their thriving candy business.

So at thirty she went out to work for the first time in her life. It took seven years for her to become a fully fledged executive and to understand all the intricacies of the eighty-year-old business with its

—

$80 million sales volume. From the investment department where she started she moved to planning, and from there to the laboratories to study food technology and quality control, until bit by bit the business became central to her life. Gradually she also bought out the equity from other members of the family until she owned 58 per cent of this publicly quoted corporation and assumed total control.

Had it not been for the fact that there was a family business at hand, there is little chance that Nancy would have realised her potential. She was also unusually lucky in being encouraged by her parents in a world where even the wealthy have done so little to help their daughters.

Of the four women who continued their father's business each entered it at a different stage in her life and for a different reason. Ellis Rosen did not become a businesswoman out of choice. At the age of forty-six she lost her husband in an airline disaster, and a few months later her father died. As there were no takers for his hardware business, in which her husband had been an executive, she had the choice of letting it collapse, or trying to learn the ropes so as to support her eighty-year-old mother and her two teenage daughters in reasonable comfort.

Necessity has turned Ellis from a timid homemaker into a competent businesswoman. A typical American housewife whose only business-related activity was to entertain her husband's colleagues, she had to learn how to run a $5 million hardware business. What she found most difficult was getting used to being a leader. 'I had never thought of myself as one.' This is a common problem among women, who are still hardly ever groomed for leadership roles whereas the possibility of leadership is a part of every privileged male child's education.

The Widows

The customary advice of the family's accountant and lawyer to the widow of a businessman would be to dispose of her husband's enterprise without delay. A business, in contrast to stocks and real estate, requires active day to day management, and without leadership even a previously successful business cannot last long. Until recently widows of prosperous entrepreneurs were content to collect the insurance money and/or the proceeds of the sale of the business and remove themselves to Florida or elsewhere in search of a new spouse. But the trend seems to be changing. In the USA widows of successful businessmen are rejecting the prospect of an empty life in the sun, to deploy their hitherto unused talents in perpetuating the businesses their husbands had started but did not believe that their wives could or would continue to run.

Fourteen per cent of the American businesswomen in this study started in business by stepping into their deceased husbands' shoes without having had any previous business experience or career aspirations. Their husbands' success had allowed them the benefit of home help and plenty of free time to engage in charity and community work, but running the local charity shop was usually the apex of their commercial activity. With effectively no experience and mostly past what is considered the prime of life, they had the courage to risk a new existence and a new identity, and have even had the audacity to succeed and enjoy it. Even more incredible was the fact that they did not now feel resentful about their previous existence as mere wives. What they were ready to admit, however, was that they had acquired a taste for the new life and could not now revert to the old one.

There are various reasons why wealthy widows, who had been content to lead a life of leisure, were ready to exchange this for the harassed life of a business person. Some saw themselves as caretakers who would run the business until their teenage children grew up and decided whether they wished to continue in their father's footsteps. Others felt responsible for the veteran employees who would have had to be made redundant with no chance of re-employment; and some, like Valerie Reynolds, believed that they were carrying out their husband's wish.

At sixty-five and childless after a thirty-five-year-long marriage in which she was busy being Mrs Reynolds and not much else, Valerie found herself a widow and the sole heir to a multimillion dollar telecommunications empire which her late husband had started fifty years before, and in which she had never been involved. Although her husband had tried to get her to join the business she had steadfastly refused: 'Our style was so different, it would have been the end of a happy marriage.' So for thirty-five years Valerie waited in the wings, electing to play the role of a conventional wife rather than endanger the marriage. But when there was no longer a marriage to consider, Valerie did what he had always wanted. 'He always said, "If anything happened to me, I want you to be the president." So that's what I did.'

In the five years since her husband's death this woman, whose only work experience took place thirty years before, when she was a manageress in a catering firm, has mastered the intricacies of a highly technical and competitive business, expanded its turnover from $3.5 million to $7 million, and increased its employees from seventy-five to a hundred. Now, at the age of seventy-one, she has been offered $18 million for the business and a five-year service contract as its president. This means that at the age of seventy-six Valerie Reynolds will still be an active businesswoman presiding over a growing business. On the face of it it might seem that starting at the top is the explanation for her incredible success, but Valerie rejects this: 'People have talked about the difficulty of starting at the bottom and working up to the top. But starting at the top and working down is much more difficult. To start at the top and know less than the lowest person in the organisation is not easy, in particular as one cannot alienate anyone because you depend on them so much.'

Humility is not an acknowledged requisite for business success, but had it been, it seems to go some way to explaining Valerie's success. Everything about her is the antithesis of the common image of the brash, bossy American businesswoman. She is a small, trim, soft-voiced woman dressed in the simple but expensive elegance of a black Valentino shirt and a black skirt with just a touch of make-up. A deeply religious person, she is almost apologetic about her success, but admits she is grateful for having been given the chance to contribute to society: 'I always wanted to leave a footprint in the sand. But at the age of thirty-five or forty I realised that I was not about to write the great novel or paint the great picture, so I settled at least for not being a destroyer as far as civilisation is concerned.'

So Valerie, single until thirty, had harboured ambitions for a greater role than that of being Mr Reynolds's wife. But thirty-five years of contented marriage concealed those ambitions until even she forgot they existed. Then, at the age of sixty-five, events turned a forgotten desire into a duty: 'My contribution to society is through the business. I feel responsible for its future and the welfare of the hundred families that depend on it. This has been of paramount importance to me. I would not let all these young executives and young people down for anything in the world.'

What started as compliance with a deceased husband's wishes has turned into a reason for living. Having no close family, Valerie hates to think about the kind of life she would have led had she not had the business. At seventy-one she works between ten and twelve hours a day and has no time to feel lonely: 'It is after five o'clock when everyone leaves that I can get to do whatever I have to. So the vice-president and I sit here and work and then he gives up around seven or eight and then I will work on. I say to myself: "I'll work until ten," but then I find that it is eleven, twelve or one o'clock in the morning and I decide to go home.'

Not many people can boast of leading such a full and productive life, let alone a woman of seventy-one. Valerie was lucky, her widowhood became her rebirth; but the moral is not that if you marry an enterprising husband you finish as an enterprising widow. The moral is that women should not leave the course of their life to chance but should structure it in a way that will enable them to lead a full life, whether with a husband or without one.

It is relatively easy to keep women happy: a nice husband, a couple of kids, a few dinner parties to organise and some voluntary work to keep their conscience clear and they are contented creatures. Jennifer Kinnock Trafford was all that and more: 'I never felt an urge to get into the world and do big things. It was him who was doing the big things in life.' If her husband had not died after a lengthy illness and left her a widow at the age of fifty-seven, she would have been happy to go on the same way. 'I was happy because he was home every night. It was great to be a housewife. Don't knock it.' But her husband died and, without the main actor, the supporting actress found herself without a role to play.

Although her husband's death did not affect her financially, Jennifer refused to join the carefree, meaningless life of her widowed friends. She knew that inside the chauffeur-driven, pedicured, blue-rinsed widows was a desperation invisible to those who aspire to a life of similar luxuries. 'I was not destitute. I could have sold out and gone down to Florida and sat there with all the rich wives and got bored to death. I could have become an alcoholic and I could have felt sorry for myself. I knew too many women like that who have lost their husbands, and don't know what to do with their lives.'

At fifty-seven Jennifer was not a beauty. A short, squat motherly figure, rather hard of hearing, she was sensible enough to realise that much as she would have liked to find a new man to serve, her chances of re-marrying were dismal. So she decided to have a go at the hardware business her husband had left behind. After thirty-two years of marriage her knowledge of the business was zero: 'I knew he sold hardware and I knew he belonged to different organisations' – which is not much to go on when one takes over the running of a loss-making business with a $5 million annual sales volume. 'I did not know the business. My place, he always told me, was at home with the children.'

Thus ignorant, but loyal and tenacious as only a woman with thirty-two years of marriage behind her can be, this woman in late middle age set out to rebuild her husband's business which through his ten-year terminal illness had come to the verge of bankruptcy. She sacked the warring managers who under the leadership of her sick husband had torn the company apart, refurbished the 150,000 sq ft warehouse that had not seen a lick of paint in thirty years, and after five years at the helm has managed to halt the rot and reverse the loss-making trend. Jennifer's achievement is remarkable in particular when viewed in the context of the prevailing economic recession.

Talent is not something one can acquire at the age of fifty-seven. Jennifer's achievements since her husband's death are a clear indication that she must always have had these organisational and decision-making abilities. Yet, like an unused instrument that goes out of tune, an unused talent cannot always be revived. It is little short of miraculous that after such a time Jennifer could still awake her dormant skills. But this does not explain why she did not use her talents earlier, particularly when she must have realised that her husband's illness was affecting the viability of his business. Why didn't she at least try to help him run it during those difficult years? How could she continue with her frivolous, ladylike life, knowing that the business which had been in his family for three generations and which she was later to be so keen to preserve was disintegrating? Here is her answer:

> It was his business and he loved it, and I loved him and I had enough to eat. So I closed my eyes and ears and hoped for the best. He had cancer for ten years, and in such a state it is hard to run a business. He did not always have the strength to come down and see what was going on. I did not want to interfere, because it would have meant that I knew he could not run it any longer. His state of mind was more important to me than the business.

To let a sick person run a business into the ground in order to allow him to keep his dignity in acting the boss is a gesture of almost superhuman generosity.

But Jennifer, successful though she became, should not be taken as a model. It would be better if wives did generally take an interest in their husband's affairs and, if they become widows, it would make their widowhood less traumatic. The wife of a successful executive cannot step into his job when he dies. But the wife of an owner can. Why not take advantage of it?

—

Continuing a husband's business is not only financially beneficial, it is also therapeutic. For Cathy Simmons Randall taking over her husband's fashionable Manhattan restaurant helped alleviate the pain of her loss. His untimely death after nine years of marriage and a seven-year battle with cancer left her at thirty-five a widow with a seven-year-old daughter. Although during her husband's lifetime Cathy did not have any equity or an official role in his business, his prolonged illness and their frank discussions about the future prompted her to take an interest in the restaurant and acquaint herself with its management. By the time of his death the business had become an inseparable part of her life. 'I didn't enter the business because of the money. I would have had enough for me and my seven-year-old daughter for several years. I wanted to continue something that had meant a lot to him and a lot to me. And it was so much a part of our life that I felt that this was the natural thing for me to do.'

Not everyone has the ability to start a business from scratch, but equally the management of a going concern is no mean feat. How then have these widows, without experience and even without ambitions, succeeded where many seasoned men have failed? Pamela Carter did it by being ready to learn. As a woman, she was trained to think that others knew more than her, particularly when these others were men. Thus when, at the age of fifty-eight with six children and two lengthy marriages to her credit, she became a widow and found herself the head of an engineering business, about which she knew nothing, she was not ashamed to admit her ignorance:

> If a man told me something which I did not understand I would say, 'You have to bear with me. Repeat it.' Some people do not quite understand but they don't want the other person to know that they are as dumb as they are, so they pretend that they understand. I said to everybody, 'I do not know anything, you have an ignorant person here, but I want to learn so please repeat it.' And sometimes they would get sick of repeating it and I would say, 'Either you are not explaining it right or my brain is not thinking it right. Explain it again,' and they knocked themselves out. If you act too smart they think, 'Smart aleck.' But if you say to a man or a woman, 'I need help. I want to learn. Can you help me?' they knock you down trying to help you.

Such wisdom in handling people and getting the best out of them is not learned in business schools. This is the wisdom of a person who for years has had to humble herself in the role of a wife and a mother. This is the wisdom of a woman for which marriage is the perfect training ground.

As long as they were married there was nothing to distinguish these widowed business tycoons from other homemakers, but without their men they have become different people. Not having men to look after and to look up to, they put all they had into the business, and the results were spectacular. The $1 million restaurant which Cathy Simmons Randall took over in 1968 grew into an $18 million business by 1984. The $3 million electronics and communication corporation into which Valerie Reynolds stepped in 1978 grew into a $7 million operation by 1984; and the $500,000 chemical plant which Hilary Waldorf was left with on her husband's death in 1972 grew under her leadership into a $13 million business by 1984. These women were not caretakers or figureheads: they have proved that they were as capable as their husbands, and in some cases more capable.

Executive Buy-out

Another group of business Amazons who, like the daughters and the widows, did not start from scratch were the executives who worked their way up within an existing business and at the right moment seized the opportunity of acquiring sufficient equity to become owner of the corporation which had previously employed them. The advantage enjoyed by these women over the widows and daughters was that when they became the owners they already knew all there was to know about the running of the business. As with the daughters and the widows, those who became owners through the executive buy-out route are found only in the USA; they constitute 10 per cent of the American business Amazons.

There is no standard means for a female executive to manoeuvre herself into a position where she is either given equity, or is offered it at a lower price than its market value. This lower price is the key to the executive's transformation into an owner, because executives seldom possess the financial resources to buy the equity at the market price. What they have instead is expertise, and it is this which they try to barter for equity, because at a certain point in the corporation's existence such expertise is so vital for its continued survival or expansion that the owners are obliged to give or sell to her all or part of their holding simply to retain her with the corporation.

Because it takes longer to convince others of one's capabilities than to convince oneself, the route to ownership through executive buy-out is lengthy and the executives turned owners are rarely young. Most of the women in this survey who followed this route were in their late forties when they became owners. The exception was Lydia Eastern, who at thirty-four became a 50 per cent shareholder in the Californian travel agency which she had joined as a sales executive six years before. The travel business which Lydia joined in 1971 was an old established private firm that had started as a partnership in 1936 and became a corporation in 1958. In 1970 the original owner sold out to a multiple interest private corporation that had to rely on hired executives. Despite its long standing the travel agency was not doing particularly well, and when Lydia Eastern was brought in with the brief to increase its sales, it was doing some $3 million worth of business.

It is customary with sales people for commission to be part of their remuneration: the more they sell, the higher their income. Being a single mother, Lydia found the possibility of increasing her income through commission a great incentive, and she searched day and night for new corporate customers. Under her leadership the business which for the previous thirty-six years had been virtually stagnant began to prosper, and with it also Lydia. In twelve years she rose to marketing vice-president, general manager, senior vice-president and president; and the travel agency increased its sales from $3 million to $80 million. Along the route she collected commissions which were augmented with bonuses, and when these became excessively high she traded part of them for shares in the company. By 1977 she had accumulated 50 per cent of the equity, and thus quite simply became the owner.

Although the rise of any female executive from employee to owner must be attributable to hard work and dedication, it cannot be offered as a guaranteed route to ownership because the remuneration of an executive with equity takes place only in exceptional circumstances. Sometimes, as in Lydia's case, it is due to the realisation by the owner that through forfeiting 50 per cent of his ownership the remaining 50 per cent will become more profitable. In other situations the owners wish to sell the business and, in the absence of other buyers, are obliged to offer it to one or more of their executives at a greatly discounted value and on favourable credit terms. This was how Stevie Frederick, who had never dreamt of becoming an owner, became one at the age of forty-five.

—

As a young divorcee with three young children, and whose husband had never been able to do more than barely support himself, Stevie was always obliged to work. From a humble beginning as a secretary she graduated through work experience, night classes, and a chain of book-keeping and accounting jobs to the post that eventually turned her at the age of forty-five into the owner of a $7 million electronic component distribution business in Silicon Valley. Five years before, she had joined that company as its controller. A year later she became the general manager of the distribution division, and two years after that the vice-president of distribution. Four years after she had joined the company the owners, troubled by conflicting interests, started to look for a buyer. Stevie realised that the new ownership might mean the end of her career, and the prospect of looking for a new post at the age of forty-five dismayed her. But she never supposed for a moment that she could purchase the company that employed her. For that one would need a great deal of money, which she did not have. Having had to bring up three children on her own had left her with no reserves in the bank, let alone the millions required to buy out such a corporation.

When after six months the owners had not yet found a buyer Stevie plucked up her courage and offered them delayed payments and mortgages. Desperate to sell out, the owners agreed. The transformation of her personality was incredible: 'The biggest difference between being an employee and an owner is the sense of security. No one can dismiss me. At forty-six it is a worry not only for women. Especially with all the unemployed executives around.'

The job security of owners is not guaranteed. Bad management, which is the cause of most bankruptcies, costs failed owners not merely their jobs but also their investments; but as long as the business succeeds the owner is its absolute and undisputed king. Stevie appreciated not only the security, but the first taste of freedom of action she had experienced after thirty years in the labour market: 'I consult the people I work with but I do not have to follow their advice if I choose not to.' At an age when a great number of working and non-working women feel past their prime Stevie Frederick is at the beginning of a new career and although it will be several years before she pays off the financial commitments incurred by the purchase of the business and begins to enjoy the higher remuneration of an owner, she believes that the emotional rewards the ownership has already given her outweigh the financial risk that accompanied her entrepreneurial step.

The financial risk of ownership is great and should not be underestimated. In situations where loans are guaranteed personally by owners, and most loans are, the collapse of the corporation can be a traumatic experience. It is not just a matter of losing a job and money. It also involves letting people down and abandoning one's role as a leader. Not many business people are able to be philosophical about failure. Most of them thrive on the respect and power that ownership gives them, and when these are abruptly taken away they can develop acute withdrawal symptoms. Here age makes a difference. To the same extent that a younger body can repel disease more effectively, so a younger entrepreneur has a better chance of bouncing back. For a woman of fifty-five to take upon herself the risks of ownership after thirty-five years in the security of employment is therefore remarkable.

Joan Sheldon does not claim to possess the restlessness that typifies so many entrepreneurs, who when in employment often feel that they could do better than their superiors if only given the chance. In thirty-five years she had worked for only two corporations, both of which specialised in mailing lists. If her bosses had not sold out to a conglomerate which after two years wanted to re-sell the business and herself with it, she would have been content to soldier on as the well-paid president of that specialised subsidiary. But at fifty-five, after long years as a dutiful employee, she resented being sold off like a chattel to the highest bidder, and rebelled. Knowing that without her continued leadership the conglomerate would find it difficult to obtain a buyer, she informed them that she was not for sale. Thus when she offered to purchase the company herself, the conglomerate was co-operative and structured an amicable agreement whereby Joan became the owner, and the company itself has been a participant in her profits for ten years.

Wife and Husband Teams

Loneliness is the price business owners pay for their affluence. Despite the advice they can buy, the final decision and accountability are solely theirs. Many potential entrepreneurs gave up the chance of independence and higher financial rewards for the cosier environment of teamwork. For these more sociable souls the solution is a partnership, in which they can benefit from both ownership and joint accountability. Yet it is often overlooked that a partnership is not just for cushioning the effect of wrong decisions and failures, but also for sharing the success and profits. Consequently in a partnership the advantages of ownership are often outweighed by the disadvantage of reduced profits.

A wife and husband business team has the advantages of both partnership and sole ownership. Although the decisions and responsibilities are shared, the profits stay within the family. But then such a partnership faces other problems, because a business partnership between a wife and a husband means a twenty-four hour a day togetherness, the mere thought of which would make most married couples shudder. Nevertheless, despite the popular abhorrence of mixing business with matrimony, the majority of the business Amazons who were in business with their husbands enjoyed the arrangement, and claimed that given the opportunity to restart their business careers they would opt for the same family partnership. Indeed, teaming up with husbands seemed remarkably popular. Fifty-four per cent were involved during all or part of their business careers with their spouses. This was made up of 30 per cent in which the couples started in business together and 24 per cent where they joined forces at different stages of the business's development.

It was interesting to note that where the couples did not start together, in 79 per cent of cases it was the wife who started the business and the husband who joined when she had proven the viability of her enterprise. The explanation of why, contrary to expectations and at variance with the prevailing role norms of the sexes, a majority of the husbands joined their wives' businesses and not vice versa is not necessarily because the wives were more enterprising than the husbands, or that they had been attracted to their opposites. It is because the majority of them were married when they started in business and as such had no careers, had low earning potential, and had no immediate financial obligations, the ideal conditions for the nurture of entrepreneurs.

In business, qualifications are not a necessary requisite for success. The women whose husbands joined them after they had done the groundwork were mostly much less qualified and experienced than their husbands. The reason that it was they who started in business and not their more qualified husbands was that because of the latter's higher earning capacity and financial responsibilities they had no incentive to risk the uncertainty of business ownership, while the careerless wives had little to lose and everything to gain. Thus, paradoxical as it might sound, it was not the qualifications but lack of qualifications that encouraged the wives to start in business.

—

Switching over from employment to a business partnership with their wives was a serious step for the husbands, who therefore tended to do it gradually. First they helped after working hours and at weekends, and only later, when confident about the business's potential and their own function in it, did they break their ties with the outside world. What concerned them most were:

a the deviation from the customary male independent earning and working pattern;
b the future of the marriage as a result of the total 'togetherness';
c the difficulty of returning to the job market in the event of break-up of the business or the marriage.

Thirty per cent of husbands started a business jointly with their wives, which was emotionally much easier for the husband than joining at a later stage, because it obviated the possibility of attributing the success of the business to the wife's initial effort in which he had no part. Despite the great strides that have been achieved in equalising women and men, it is still extremely important to most husbands to be considered more capable than their wives and it is still a social stigma for a man to share his life with a wife more successful than himself. Most husbands do not encounter this problem because even when the wife is more capable, the secret is kept within the family. The problem does, however, arise when the wife becomes well known in her own right. Laura Ashley was an obvious example.

The reason why wife and husband teams are looked upon with some dread is because everyone realises that it is difficult for a man to be married to a successful wife particularly when she is successful in the same field as he is. Despite this, 54 per cent of the women were in business with their husbands, not because of any self-sacrificing quality of the husband, but because it was in the women's interest. Being in business with one's husband has certain advantages here: it disguises the female ownership which is still not an accepted fact of business life; it is sometimes the only way a wife can gain the husband's approval of her career aspirations; and it mitigates the 'clever wife' problem because the secret of her greater capability can be kept within the family and the business's success can be attributed equally to them both.

Insight into the factors that prompted husbands and wives to start in business together can be obtained from the histories of several of the women magnates. Barbara Shelensky was half her husband's age when she married a thirty-four-year-old European aristocrat who because of the war had found himself a refugee in the USA without a skill or a work permit; his undoubted charm was no substitute for their desperate need for money. So they decided to commercialise on his only asset, his fanaticism about health, which in the 1940s was not the fashionable cult it is today. The basis of their partnership was that 'He knew about fitness and I knew about work.' Their first health guesthouse was a ten-room building which four years later was traded in for a hundred-acre farm in southern California; and when that one got established, a second followed. After forty-two years in the business Barbara Shelensky's health farms, with an $8 million volume of trade and employing some 250 people, are still the most exclusive, and certainly the most expensive in the business. The Shelenskys' partnership, where the husband provided the 'front' and the wife the business acumen and work, lasted for thirty years before it was dissolved, and Barbara bought out her husband's 50 per cent stake. Having become the sole owner did not heap new burdens on Barbara: 'My husband was never part of the management so there was no problem there.'

Some fifteen years later, in the 1950s, in a provincial town in southern England, Barbara Shelensky's life story repeated itself in Hilda Bergdorf. At seventeen Hilda, a Hungarian beauty from an impoverished family, married Carl Bergdorf, twenty years her senior, a displaced Russian intellectual of aristocratic origins but without marketable skills. Hilda, too, was a great admirer of her husband's intellect; but, like Barbara, she soon realised that romance had to be fuelled by food – particularly after she gave birth to the first of her six sons. With the three-month-old baby they left Europe for domestic employment in Britain, where in consideration of accommodation, food and a small wage Hilda worked as a housekeeper and Carl as a chauffeur. Four years later, when they got to know the new country, the Bergdorfs left their domestic employment and started to manufacture babywear.

In the Bergdorfs' marriage as in the Shelenskys', it was the young wife who put into action the husband's ideas: 'Carl was very good in conceiving new marketing approaches, but it was me who was expected to go out and implement them. He had a good mind but was not an action man.' And similarly the Bergdorfs' marriage was dissolved, with the older man leaving a younger wife for a still younger woman. Hilda explains: 'After twenty-seven years of marriage I felt too tired and humiliated to fight for him. So he went.' Like Barbara Shelensky, Hilda Bergdorf bought out her husbands' share in the business as part of the divorce settlement. Both continued to run their businesses successfully on their own, long after their ex-husbands' eventual death in old age.

To an outsider, both Barbara Shelensky and Hilda Bergdorf are classic cases of young wives subjugated to older, feudalistic 'know-all' husbands who carried on with their amorous exploits while their young wives lost their youth slogging at building up a business from which the husbands were not averse to collecting more than their fair share. Yet neither Barbara nor Hilda see it that way. Business Amazons hate to feel sorry for themselves and are reluctant to admit that they have been exploited. Consequently Barbara and Hilda see their marriage and business partnerships as having been beneficial to them as much as to their ex-husbands. Despite their own greater work input, they know that without the confidence which their husbands inspired in others as well as in them, they would not have been able to do what they did.

Forty-nine-year-old Hilda and sixty-year-old Barbara refuse to speak ill of their deceased ex-husbands because they know that regardless of whether they worked harder than they should have, all they possessed – such as Hilda's white Rolls-Royce and Barbara's magnificent home overlooking the Atlantic – were a result of that business partnership with husbands who were openminded enough to realise and admit their young wives' commercial talents and allow them to use them. Barbara and Hilda were not the first and are not the last wives to work harder than their husbands but, unlike most wives, because of their indispensability to the business they could not be dispossessed of their due share. Being a business Amazon is an insurance policy that pays high dividends in the event of divorce and widowhood, as proven by Barbara and Hilda, who despite the inevitable pain that accompanied the break-up of their thirty-year-old marriages did not have much time to grieve, for if their husbands did not need them their businesses still did.

Older husbands are not typical of the business Amazons' family partnerships. Janet Draper of Mississippi is older than her husband. When they got married she was twenty-nine and he was twenty-six. For her it was a second marriage, for him the first. Both were American, both had jobs and to a certain extent also career prospects; but they were at a crossroads and when the opportunity to become business owners presented itself they seized it. They met long after her divorce at the age of twenty-one, after a marriage at sixteen to a school sweetheart who had been drafted and sent to Korea. When he returned

—

some four years later the only thing they had in common was a daughter, whom her parents brought up. She met Dan, who was to be her husband for the next twenty-one years, when both worked for a small engineering corporation, she as an accountant and he as a development engineer. In 1963, out of the blue, the corporation went bankrupt and both were left without a job. Like other employees they could have packed up and looked for other employment. However, Janet suggested that as both knew the business, she the commercial and he the technical aspects, they should take it over, particularly as the asking price was reasonable. Dan needed persuading. A slow, methodical man as suggested by his enormous physique, he takes his time in decision-making, but once decided he bulldozes on relentlessly. Once he had bought the idea he cemented the business partnership with marriage, and the Drapers spent their honeymoon sorting out the affairs of the defunct corporation they had purchased for a mere $1,500. Twenty-one years later both the engineering business and the Draper family have expanded beyond recognition. The Drapers' household includes the three sons born to Janet and Dan in addition to her daughter from her first marriage, and the business that could barely support the two of them employs 1,100 persons.

The Drapers' success is the triumph of a team, of a support system where the wife had great respect for her husband's educational qualifications, and the husband had admiration for his wife's managerial abilities. Without each other it is doubtful whether the Drapers would ever have made it to their thirty-room mansion manned by seven personal staff.

Another couple who owe their success to each other are the Blacks. Rachel Black, a bright girl from a poor Jewish home in the north of England, won a scholarship to university in 1944, when few British girls went to university and even fewer by way of scholarships. But because of the family's meagre financial resources it was decided that Rachel should abandon her scholastic dreams and settle for a job instead. The notion that Jewish parents, and in particular Jewish mothers, will make great sacrifices for their children's education seems to apply almost exclusively to their male offspring. Several Jewish businesswomen in this study, particularly in Britain, who excelled at school were discouraged from pursuing higher education on the grounds that it was not an asset for a woman. The same Jewish mothers who were ready to scrub floors in order to see their sons through medical school were not ready to do the same for their daughters.

But Rachel Black has never been easily discouraged. She did not give up her academic aspirations, and has managed to combine work with external studies at London University. Instead of getting her mathematics degree in three years it took five, but she got it and with it a job as a statistician for an international corporation. In the same year as she won her degree and her promising job, she also got married. Her husband was a craftsman jeweller but a hopeless businessman. It soon became apparent to her that a frustrated husband who felt inadequate because of his inability to support a family was no good to himself, to her, or to the marriage. So she reckoned that if she could sell his creations they could make a good living as well as have a common interest.

After two months of marriage Rachel gave up her job, the only guaranteed income they had, and set out to promote her husband's craft. The correctness of her decision was proven when in the first day of selling she earned more than she had done during a week in her previous job. From then on Rachel's life took on the familiar pattern of ascent to success as seen in the case of so many other women in the survey. She overcame such obstacles as ignorance of elementary business procedures, costing, stock control, and production techniques by sheer guts. The young woman who had just received her mathematics degree from London University understood instinctively that the success of the business depended primarily on her ability to create a demand for her husband's products, and that all other facets of business such as book-keeping, stock control, and production techniques were acquirable skills. For the past thirty-two years the Blacks' partnership has continued on the same basis of work distribution, though sales are now measured in millions of pounds. Mr Black, although no longer the designer craftsman on whom the business depended thirty-two years ago, is still concerned with the technical aspects of the production lines, and Rachel is still in charge of promotion and finances.

Husband and wife business starts are not peculiar to young couples or to the young wives encountered in the previous examples. Mature couples in their forties can also exert the energy and toughness that a business start requires. Dorothy Simmonds was forty-two years old when, after twenty-three years of marriage, she and her husband decided to start a joint business enterprise. He gave up his job as a salesman for an oil drilling equipment company and she her occupation as a homemaker. Seven years later the Simmonds employ sixty-six staff and have a sales volume of $55 million. The business which has changed Dorothy Simmonds from a housewife to a tycoon distributes and manufactures specialised equipment for oil drilling, similar to the products her husband used to promote for others as a commission salesman.

Dorothy's transformation as a businesswoman did not take place overnight. Her frustration with her scopeless role of a homemaker started long before that, during the many days when she was left alone with her three children while her husband was pursuing his equally frustrating job as a travelling salesman.

A solid, down-to-earth person in looks and outlook, Dorothy took twenty years to gather the strength to rebel. At the age of thirty-nine she turned to her husband and three children and announced her decision to enrol at a university to take a degree in accountancy. Surprisingly it was not the husband but the children, who had been used to the first-class cooking, washing and cleaning services of their mother, who resented her decision. 'My younger son was appalled at the thought that he would have to do his own laundry.' But Dorothy was unswayed. In twenty-four months of nonstop studies she gained a BSc in accountancy from Colorado University and managed to restore in herself the confidence and pride that twenty years of homemaking had eroded. The next logical step for her was to look for a job, and that was when her husband intervened and urged her to try a joint venture. He realised the asset of a partner with administrative qualifications such as Dorothy's, and whose remuneration would stay in the family, as well as the renewed interest that such a business partnership could inject into a twenty-three-year-old marriage.

A joint business career in middle age seems to be a successful formula for recharging stagnant marriages. Jane and Lewis Auerbach were in their forties and the eighth year of their second round of marriages when each of them reached a dead end in their respective careers. Lewis hated the running of his inherited chain stores selling dreary men's clothing, and Jane's career as a renowned educationalist was petering out. A joint business enterprise with Jane's untiring, enthusiastic personality and Lewis's solid business experience seemed the ideal solution. So on Jane's fortieth birthday and Lewis's forty-sixth they set out on a new business venture which they floated on the proceeds from the sale of Lewis's stores. 'Obviously there was a risk. It could easily have failed. But it was this or a continued dissatisfaction.' The gamble paid off, and instead of becoming a couple of middle-aged has-beens Jane and Lewis Auerbach have stirred up a great deal of activity. Jane is the life and soul of the fashion accessory business they

—

25

have built up, while Lewis is her moderator, the stay that anchors her to the ground and ensures that they will still be in business next year and the year after that. She is the ideas woman, the designer, the front person, and the limelight seeker; he is the solid financier and office man. At the age of fifty when other women reconcile themselves to a life of inactivity, Jane travels all over the world to sell the goods she has designed and manufactured. The business has given them not only the satisfaction of having created a $50 million empire that provides work for 250 employees, but an interesting life free of the boredom that faces other fifty-year-old couples whose only mutual creation, the children, have grown up.

The success of wife and husband business teams has always stemmed from two factors: the wife's indispensability in the business and her possession of talents complementary to her husband's. Which of the couple was responsible for what, the husband for sales and the wife for production or vice versa, was irrelevant as long as each made a different contribution. In the Auerbachs' case Jane was the ideas person and Lewis the financial brain, while in Dorothy Simmonds's case it was the opposite: she was the backroom girl and her husband the promoter. Like any successful business partnership, that of a married couple depends on the indispensability of the contributors. Only when each partner realises her or his need of the other can a partnership succeed.

Partnerships

All the reasons such as lack of finance, know-how, contacts, or confidence that prompt men to look for business partners apply also to women, but more acutely. Being pioneers in the field, businesswomen find it more difficult to raise finance or make contacts than businessmen. A commercial partnership is a complicated relationship involving a continuous balancing act between what one is receiving and what one is giving. Those contemplating entering one are warned by lawyers and accountants of the great number of failed partnerships, which like unsuccessful marriages fall prey to the partners' incompatibility. In view of this it is interesting to note that, compared with a mere 6 per cent of the American business Amazons, 26 per cent of the British ones chose this form of trading as a base for their venture into the business world. These figures are all the more significant because all their partners were males, never other women. It can only indicate that Englishwomen feel less confident in their ability to operate on their own than their American counterparts and require the patronage of male partners.

The women who started out in partnership were of two types, the initiators and the joiners. The initiators were those who conceived the idea but because of financial limitations or insufficient know-how had to part with some of their equity in exchange for financial or management skills. The joiners were in the opposite position: they were asked to join an existing business and were offered equity in consideration of their willingness to do so. Invariably they were asked to join because of their business or technical skills, not because of any financial contribution they might make.

It is interesting that of the 26 per cent of the British women who started in partnership only a minority found themselves in the favoured position of being asked to become partners. The majority were initiators who had to look for male partners in order to ensure the success of their idea.

The joiners

At the age of nineteen Debra Manham had dropped out of art school, where she had specialised in fashion design. For a year she had drifted from one job to another until she settled as an assistant designer in the lingerie company where, twenty-two years later, she was given 50 per cent of the equity. Owners do not part willingly with their equity, and had it not been for Debra's indispensability, made clear by her threat of resignation, her bosses would still have had the sole control of the company. The reason it took Debra twenty-two years to prove her worth was the classic saga of a woman who tried to combine a career, marriage, and motherhood. 'When I first started I was very very career-minded, but my social life came first. Then I had two children and they came first.' Although throughout all the changes in her marital status – from a single girl to a wife, to a mother of one, and then to a mother of two – Debra continued to work with the same lingerie company; she did not consider herself a career person and has always put her private life before her work. Only when her second child started school and she realised that she needed a life of her own did her attitude change. Then, for fear of losing her anchorage in the outside world, she had to make the necessary psychological adjustment and look upon work as a career rather than a mere source of income. 'It was a good feeling, knowing that one was needed, that they could not manage without me. But it took a long time. The reason I did not get the 50 per cent before was my being a woman and not seeing myself as a career person, but just as an earner. It is difficult for a woman to gain the confidence to ask for it. A man would have insisted on it long before.'

Debra is right. A man with her value to the company would have negotiated equity-participation long before twenty-two years had passed; but then he would also have considered himself indispensable long before that. It is women's lack of confidence in their abilities, and their undermining by the diversity of their various functions in life, that cause them to underestimate themselves, and at best be content with only a slice of the cake. 'After all,' as Debra Manham puts it, 'to get 50 per cent of an existing business is to say that one lacks the confidence to get 100 per cent of one's own.'

Judy Pike was another joiner. Her initial unhappy experience as a 49 per cent shareholder, just 1 per cent less than the magic figure which guarantees a shareholder's interests, emphasises the importance of the minimum requirement of 50 per cent ownership. After university Judy worked for several market research organisations, steadily climbing the corporate ladder until she became director of research. The managing director of that company was contemplating setting up on his own and offered Judy, who by then had excellent credentials, a 49 per cent partnership if she left the mother company to join him. On paper it sounded great, a 49 per cent stake for no capital investment. But later Judy lamented the lack of confidence that had prevented her demanding the additional 1 per cent.

Only with hindsight, after the partnership had broken up, and Judy had had to buy out her partner for much more than his share was worth because it was he and not she who owned the 51 per cent equity, did it dawn on her why, despite her strong bargaining position as the one with the client contacts, she had not insisted on a 50 per cent partnership. 'It was the upbringing I had to let men have their way. Men were always portrayed as childish creatures for whom their ego was of great importance. Whilst women, being more mature and sensible, were expected to give in in order to preserve the peace.'

Treating men like retarded children, who need to have their way lest they spoil the party, has been practised by women for too long and

—

28

always to their disadvantage. Even an educated, career-minded woman like Judy could not break the mould, and gave in to male competitors rather than face confrontation. 'My ambition was typical of females' thinking. I believed that the partnership would be more successful if he felt boss. As I knew that I was the real asset of the business I felt that it would be better for his ego to have 51 per cent.' For this Judy paid dearly and it is hoped that her example will stop other women from adopting this self-effacing but patronising attitude towards men, which only invites defeat. If women expect to be treated as equals they must treat men as equals, and not as naughty boys who never grow up.

The initiators

As Esau, the elder son, gave in to hunger and sold his birthright for a mess of pottage, business initiators who lack money or skills have to sell their equity cheaply. Phyllis Rota, the initiator of a PR business with eleven years' experience in the industry, had sufficient finance of her own. What she required from a partner were the basic skills of putting a new business into motion, and for these she was ready to part with 50 per cent of the equity. Before her transformation into an entrepreneuse her career had been typical of female executives: a university graduate at twenty-one; progressively more responsible and more remunerative executive posts with large marketing and PR corporations; marriage at twenty-nine and no obsession with future motherhood. Then, at the age of thirty-three and as a result of several job changes, personality conflicts with her superiors and encouragement from husband, Phyllis decided to go it alone. Yet, despite the top appointments she had held, she lacked the experience of how to start a business, or rather the confidence that it required. 'I was inhibited about my ability to start up a small company. I did not know the practical things, even about what your liabilities are as an employer and how to do the accounting and VAT [European "value added tax"]. So I approached Richard, who was in office equipment and whom I knew because I was a customer of his, and told him of my idea.'

They entered a fifty-fifty partnership. Richard provided the initial financial guarantees, the administrative and business experience; and Phyllis the essence of the PR business of which he had no experience. On the face of it it looks a fair partnership in which each party had a definite role to play, but on closer examination it becomes doubtful whether it was necessary for a high calibre operator like Phyllis with financial resources of her own to part with 50 per cent of her equity for someone's knowledge of administrative procedure, a skill that can be mastered by any averagely intelligent person. For a fraction of what a 50 per cent partner costs in lost profits Phyllis could have hired a top administrator, but she lacked the confidence and feared the loneliness of the sole decision-maker.

Confidence can compensate for lack of knowledge but rarely for lack of finance. Smart and confident an initiator may be, yet if she cannot raise the money required she has no option but to get a partner. Sometimes, as in Zelda Main's case, the initiator might be left with a minority shareholding because in order to keep the business going she has to exchange her equity for finance. Although a successful business-woman, and the initiator of the business at that, Zelda does not qualify as a business Amazon because she owns only 29 per cent of the equity: 20 per cent is owned by her husband, 29 per cent by a friend and 22 per cent by her parents, sister, brothers-in-law and other relatives. Although without Zelda the £5.5 million cosmetics business would lose a lot of its vitality, it would not necessarily collapse because after ten years in existence a business has its own momentum. So Zelda is wrong in thinking that the business is hers. With a minority stake of only 29 per cent she could be ousted if the other shareholders were dissatisfied with her management. Although she refuses to entertain the possibility that her family and friends could be dissatisfied with her leadership, that does not reduce the chance of its happening, as the many cases of fathers who ousted sons, and sons who denounced fathers in order to gain control of a thriving business, have proven time and again.

The events that turned Zelda from an initiator into a minority shareholder illustrate the problems encountered by women wishing to raise money for a commercial idea. At the age of forty Zelda, a London housewife whose children had grown up, became restless and, realising that the employment market had no use for wealthy, middle-class wives with no skills, she decided to go into business. 'My husband was very supportive. He thought I intended to open a boutique around the corner.' Little did he know that Zelda had grander plans in mind. What she dreamed about was the mass marketing of cosmetics, and for this she reckoned that she would require an initial sum of £40,000 (in 1972). By all normal standards Zelda was a wealthy woman. Her parents were rich, and her husband was a successful solicitor. They owned a beautiful house and took expensive holidays; Zelda did not have to work. But when for the first time in her life she needed

—

£40,000, not only did she not have it, but she did not even know where or how to get it. What she did know, however, was that without a financial track record and/or collateral, she could not ask a bank for such a sum. She had neither but she did have a loving husband.

> So when I had got it planned out, I went to him and said, 'I need about £40,000 to start.' I thought he was going to pass out. He said, 'I thought you were wanting to sign for a lease or something,' and I said, 'Oh no, I want to start this and I want to buy that.' He said, 'Well, at this stage it is a bit much to ask me to put that money up for you. But if you get half the money I will get the other half for you.'

Zelda was shocked. It did not occur to her that her husband would treat her proposition like any other financial proposition. During the sixteen years of their marriage he had always been generous to a fault. Now when for the first time in her life she asked for real money, he was treating her like a child. But she was not his child, she was his wife who could have been a wealthy person in her own right had she not waited on him and their sons for sixteen years without any thought for her own future. Strictly speaking the money was not even his: it was their money. He had made it only because she had enabled him to concentrate on his career by sacrificing her own. Alas, Zelda realised that it was impossible to turn the clock back, and that this was the penalty she had to pay for the years of dependence.

So, being the practical person she is, she set out in an ingenious manner to raise the £20,000 her husband had demanded as a precondition to his own investment of £20,000. If she could not go through the normal financial channels she was going to invent her own. She prepared a small presentation to friends and family whom she thought might have confidence in her and said to them: 'This is what I mean to do. What I need from you is to give me £1,000 for each 1 per cent of my business.' It worked. Zelda sold 22 per cent of her non-existent business to her parents, sister, and friends for £22,000. Her husband put in his £20,000 which gave him 20 per cent of the business, and she was left with 58 per cent. The £42,000 she had raised sufficed for the first six months of trading, when she experienced a cash flow crisis and was forced to sell half of her 58 per cent holding for £58,000. In total the capital Zelda managed to raise by forfeiting 71 per cent of her equity was £100,000, a pittance compared to what the shares would have fetched now that the business has reached sales of £5.5 million a year. If Zelda had managed to borrow from banks, or if her devoted husband had had more trust in her abilities, she would have kept her majority shareholding and benefited from the corporation's phenomenal growth. As it is, she is basically a top executive with a share in the business. Yet despite this, Zelda is not bitter and considers herself lucky to have achieved that much with her belated entry into the business world. She even condones the inability of banks to evaluate late entrants like her. 'How could a bank give me £20,000? I was a nobody.'

No one who has managed to build an international business organisation such as Zelda's could ever have been a 'nobody'. Women do not suddenly start to secrete an entrepreneurial hormone in middle age. That some of them manage to succeed belatedly is not proof of some miraculous awakening, but a validating of the talents they have always possessed but were prevented from using, often by those such as parents and husbands who were supposed to love them most. When they do manage to realise their potential in the business world, they are so grateful for that breakthrough that they are often not as prudent as they ought to be in safeguarding their interests. Zelda Main was so overwhelmed by her transformation from housewife to international businesswoman that she was not disturbed at being left with only 29 per cent of the corporation she had initiated. But she should have been, because it is not unknown for yesteryear's loving husband or sister to join forces against a wife in order to wrest the control of a profitable business from her hands. Yet Zelda refuses to face this possibility; such an admission would mean the collapse of her feminine world where trust and reliance are paramount.

A similar unjustified reliance on human decency was displayed by Sara Holt. Like Zelda, Sara was the initiator of a cosmetics business, but unlike Zelda she was young and single and had supported herself since she left school at fifteen, so that by the age of twenty-seven she had accumulated considerable work experience and sales commissions. Thus when she decided to start her own business she was not lacking in finance or in marketing expertise. What she was weak at, however, was office administration. Having quit school at fifteen she had a fear of paperwork, of which, in her proposed venture of importing cosmetics into Britain, there would be a good deal. The solution came in the form of her educated, elder brother to whom she offered 50 per cent of the business in consideration for its administration. The partnership between sister and brother has benefited both. In the six years of the business's existence it has reached £1.5 million sales, which in Britain is a sizeable enterprise.

—

As long as the share of the work was the same as that of the equity, which at first it was, the business's prosperity benefited both partners equally, but when Sara was obliged to part with 5 per cent of the shares in favour of an employee, it left her with 45 per cent and her brother with 50 per cent. This introduced a new element into the hitherto equal partnership: the initiator could be ousted from her own business. Sara could have prevented this imbalance quite easily by insisting that the esteemed employee whose loyalty they wanted to secure through equity participation be given 2.5 per cent from her shareholding and 2.5 per cent from her brother's. But for the sake of peace and a misguided notion that men's egos are more fragile than women's, she agreed to part with 5 per cent of her equity in favour of that employee, thus losing the control of the business which she had initiated.

Fran Andrews was more prudent about her equity stake than Zelda Main and Sara Holt. When she started her 'headhunting' company and had to attract a top male executive to join her untried business she parted with only 30 per cent of the equity. And when she realised that unless her husband had a stake in the business her meticulously balanced routine of mother, wife, and career woman might be sabotaged, she bought his support by appointing him a consultant to her company and gave him 11 per cent of the shares, leaving herself with 59 per cent and the overall control. 'As long as I am the majority shareholder the company is mine.'

The Solo Starters

Of all the ways of beginning in business, the solo starters face the most difficult task, because in addition to the inherent hardships of any business start they have also to cope with the loneliness of decision-making and responsibility. As Ulrike Jameson, who started a pharmaceutical business in partnership, has observed: 'I suppose that I could have started on my own but I was scared. I was used to working in a big lab with lots of people and had lots of support, and suddenly I was out in the world alone, with no one to discuss a problem. I couldn't see myself being able to stick it.' In view of the difficulties encountered in starting a business on one's own the fact that only 38 per cent of the business Amazons were such solo beginners did not come as a surprise.

Solo starters, like all true entrepreneurs, do not conform to a particular mould. Even their ages deviate considerably from the median, the youngest being eighteen and the oldest fifty-two. Their motives, too, lack a common denominator, except that most of them admitted to having been drifters who started in business by chance.

The youngest

Sally Harper became an owner at eighteen, Lena Gouldwin at twenty, and Sue Heathcote at twenty-one. When their contemporaries were either studying or working in nine to five jobs without responsibility or prospects, these young women were laying the foundations of business empires of their own.

Not having academic aspirations and not being expected to by her parents, Sally Harper left school at fifteen, and started to work as a receptionist, an unusual springboard for tycoonhood. If it was not Sally's first job or education that prepared her for business leadership, nor was it her home background. Although she came from a working-class family they were not poor enough to motivate her to become rich, and not diligent enough to instil in her the Germanic work ethic which possesses her. Her father was a butcher who worked for his successful elder brother, and her mother a housewife who looked after her three children, of which Sally was the eldest, and took part-time jobs like working at Woolworths. In 1958, when Sally Harper, a pretty-faced, plump girl of fifteen, was dumped on the labour market, she was no different from thousands of similar unqualified working-class girls. Yet she has made it to the top and the others did not. The secret of her success was her unusual diligence. 'I was always very industrious. Even when I was young and all my friends said: "Come on, it's Bank Holiday," I would say: "I'll go to the office and I'll meet you later." It would never be a hardship.'

With such an attitude to work Sally could not help being noticed, and within eighteen months she was made a director of an expanding employment agency. Every day during those months, when she climbed the narrow stairs to the third floor of the eighteenth-century building in Portsmouth where the head office of the employment agency was located, Sally passed the office of a driving school on the second floor below. Then one day she found out that the driving school was for sale.

Unlike most seventeen-year-olds who would not have given a second's thought to why the previous occupants had left, Sally was curious to know more. She soon discovered that the driving school was closing because it lacked business. She also discovered that besides the one room and two cars, the total fleet of the school, it also owned the head lease on the building and that her employers were sub-tenants. This meant that if she owned the driving school she would become her employers' landlord. Although the property was not a skyscraper in Manhattan but a narrow old three-storey building in Portsmouth, it was a beginning. Sally took advice from the two counsels she knew, her printing apprentice boyfriend and her butcher father. When both agreed that buying out the loss-making motoring school was a wise move, she went ahead and bought it for the grand sum of £500, which she did not possess and for which her father stood surety at the local bank.

When her employers discovered that their bright seventeen-year-old employee had become their landlord they suggested that she could do better without them. Whereupon without further ado, Sally moved down to the premises of her driving school, and put up a sign: 'Sally Harper – Secretarial Agency'. The clients she had cultivated for two years with her efficiency and friendly service were only too pleased to stop at the second floor rather than climb another floor of rickety stairs to her previous employers. Some did not even realise that Sally was no longer working for the agency on the floor above. Such was her success that within three months her previous employers had to close down, asking her to release them from their lease and offering her their office equipment at greatly reduced prices. Thus at eighteen Sally Harper became an established businesswoman.

Misogynists might view Sally's ascent as ruthless. Feminists will regard it as a tale of guts and enterprise: guts to ignore one's allotted niche in the economic and social order, and enterprise to seize opportunities and create one's own place in the scheme of things. And it continued: always on the look-out, Sally became skilled at seizing opportunities. When the first floor was vacated she moved her agency to street level, adorned the front with fluorescent lettering, and became a landmark in Portsmouth's High Street. And when the building next door came up for sale she outbid everyone else and joined it to her existing premises. With every territorial acquisition the employment agency grew and took upon itself more challenging and remunerative jobs.

Enterprise is composed of two stages: first identifying an opportunity and, second, seizing it. Failures recount endless tales of opportunities they missed. If they had only known that the driving school wanted to sell out, or that the premises next door were being auctioned, they would have done exactly what Sally did. The next stage, that of seizing the opportunity, requires courage and speed. Most people can make up their mind only after lengthy deliberation – weighing all the pros and cons. Successful entrepreneurs work much faster and with greater emphasis on the pros than the cons. The story of how Sally Harper secured a Ministry of Defence contract for a huge classified typing job, without having sufficient secretaries or typewriters, is a classic in the best tradition of enterprise.

Sally grasped naturally what graduate business schools do not always manage to explain to their elitist students: that sales are more important than production. Once she had the contract she placed advertisements in the local papers, hired typewriters from Olivetti and within twenty-four hours was set to fulfil her contract. Had she reacted like the average person, she would have expressed her doubts about her ability to execute the contract to the men from the Ministry of Defence, who would then have had no option but to look elsewhere.

Of course, Sally Harper does not have the monopoly of this kind of wisdom. Lena Gouldwin, who at the age of twenty started her own building construction business in Los Angeles, knew a thing or two about convincing others that despite her tender age and the oddity of a female in a male's domain she could deliver the goods.

Lena Gouldwin's mother died giving birth to her and she was left in the care of her carpenter father, who devoted his life to the upbringing of his only child. For him Lena was the cleverest and most capable person ever to be conceived, and had she become the first female president of the USA he would not have been surprised. He was a skilled carpenter but had no aptitude for business and though they never starved they lived on very little. His work on building sites was seasonal, and he used to wander with young Lena from one part of California to another in search of work. 'My father was a very successful carpenter. The best builder that ever existed, but he never made a dime.' He taught Lena about construction and remodelling but nothing about business. This she had to teach herself. 'My father had been in business on a two-pocket system. What came in went into the right pocket and what went out went through the left one.' By the time she had left college and tried a few jobs she was even more convinced that her only chance to become rich and compensate for the lean years was to develop skill at business.

With $1,000 she had saved she set herself up in a remodelling business, offering craftsmen for renovation jobs. Her first employee was her father, whom she placed in a better paid job than he could have found himself. After him came other craftsmen whom she hired out at a profit. The next step was to hire out a complete construction team – bricklayers, carpenters, painters, electricians, the lot. But from there to the financing of large construction projects was a lengthy and difficult progression. In the building trade Lena was dealing with tough working men, not the secretaries Sally Harper employed. These were men who insisted on their wages Friday whether she had the money or not. And when she did not know where the next $1,000 would come from it was not only a matter of the business going bust, but her skull as well.

The first five years were the toughest. She was a woman in a man's world and the men were not out to help. 'When I decided I wanted to own my own business, I wanted to do it, I was going to do it, and no one was going to stop me. Sometimes I felt that the whole world was trying to stop me. I was in a business where I was the only woman contractor in the whole of California, probably one of two in the world.' The next twenty-five years, although profitable, were still not easy: 'I was fought by every government agency, every bank, and every supplier.' Her difficulties arose principally because she was not satisfied with moderate achievements and her appetite grew with her success. 'My determination had to be such that nobody was going to stand in my way, and nobody did.' Unlike Sally Harper, whose twenty years in business have mellowed her into contentment, and who is happy with the routine of her £1.5 million business, her family, and her beautiful home, Lena Gouldwin after thirty years in business is still pushing ahead. For the $46 million business with its three divisions of construction, manufacturing, and commodities is only the beginning of the road. At fifty she feels that she has not yet reached her prime.

Having started in business at an early age has not stopped Lena from becoming a wife and a mother. At the age of twenty-eight, after securing a reasonable financial base, she married the husband with whom she has remained, and has borne three children and adopted a fourth. But it was not an easy run, neither with the husband who did not share her quest, nor with the children to whom she could not devote much time. When Lena talks about the difficulties of building up a $46 million business she is not asking for sympathy, not only because she is too proud but also because she knows that she would not get any. Ordinary people are not inclined to sympathise with single-minded individuals who have followed their aims without much regard for others, particularly when these people are women who put their

—

own needs before those of their families. 'I had to be selfish. I had decided to do what I wanted to do, simply because I wanted to do it. I never allowed my husband or my children or anyone else to take me away from what I wanted to do.'

Becoming an established businesswoman before becoming a wife and mother means that for a change the family has to adapt itself to the wife's career and not to the husband's. But this is something most people find difficult to accept. The wife who expects her husband to adjust to her career is considered an emasculator, and the husband who agrees to it is deemed a traitor to his sex. When the wife's job demands that she put her family's interest second it is customary for her to change it for a less exacting one, because on the whole the remuneration is not so large nor the job itself so satisfying as to justify the inconvenience to the husband and children. But when the wife is an owner whose business is remunerative as well as interesting the conflict between her interests and her family's becomes acute. This is why the majority of the women magnates started in business after their children had reached their teens, when they could no longer be blamed or blame themselves for putting their own interests first. It is these two tiers of values, one for men and another for women, that anger the businesswomen most. Lena Gouldwin comments: 'Men do it all the time: they put their careers before their families, but they don't feel guilty. Their conscience is clear because they claim that they provide for the family. I could say the same. I could say I did it for my children as my husband has no interest in financial matters. But I do not want to hide behind it. I did it for me.'

Outspoken, free souls such as Lena, who disdain to excuse their ambition by necessity or to hide it behind their family's financial needs, are rare even among the business Amazons, who on the whole have gone out of their way to avoid confrontation between their families and their careers, and have tailored their business activities to suit their husbands and children rather than the other way round. Sue Heathcote, who started a catering empire at the age of twenty-one, discovered that the easiest way to avoid the conflict between a business career and a family was to postpone marriage. After fourteen years as an owner and at the age of thirty-five, she decided that there was more to life than being a businesswoman, and she got married and had a child. By that time she was also ready to relax her business activities for the sake of her family's happiness.

Born in Australia to a father who was an executive with an international corporation and a mother who was a famous actress but could not even boil an egg, Sue was the only daughter of three children. Because of the mother's theatrical career and the father's managerial status the family mixed with the *crème de la crème* of Australia's new aristocracy and, although not wealthy, was quite well-off. After two years in college Sue became restless, and decided to take a year off and travel. Reaching Paris, she chose to make the best use of her stay and took a Cordon Bleu course, which she believed would get her a job in the kitchens of Maxim's. But when she found that her Cordon Bleu certificate carried little weight with the French, she settled for the less glamorous life of an au pair. Unexpectedly, at this point her father died and she had to rethink her future. The carefree daughter of a society couple had to become a self-supporting adult overnight. She abandoned her previous plan of resuming her studies in Australia and instead moved to London, where she hoped she would have a better chance as a chef. But she was unable to impress the culinary establishments of London either, and had to make do with waitressing. Not for long, however: on the look-out for the opportunity to earn more she advertised her services as a freelance cook. Soon she found herself cooking lunches for a firm of city brokers, and preparing dinner parties for wealthy suburban families.

The first five years were long and tiring. It took all that time for her to make enough to afford four full-time assistants; and all the while she was never sure that she would have enough bookings to cover the next month's rent and expenses. But from then on growth became steady. In her sixth year she opened a restaurant, in her eighth a cookery school, and in the tenth a catering division. After fourteen years she even found time to get married and start a family.

The support of the family was an important factor in the business launch of the young solo starters because, being young, they had no savings and no track record to justify a bank loan; and without some form of finance starting a business is mighty hard. Sally's father stood surety for her £500 loan from the bank; Lena Gouldwin's father offered his labour without charge; and Sue Heathcote had a small income from her late father's trust fund, as well as her mother's investment in her corporation. Although their families' actual financial support was not great in money terms, what mattered was the confidence that the young solo starters gained from their families' trust in their abilities. Although parents' moral support is not a precondition for success in business, having to fight on one front fewer made it easier for the young starters to succeed.

The late starters

In our society, where youth is associated with clarity of vision and soundness of judgement, little wisdom is now attributed to the old. Anyone who at a late age has managed to achieve what even the young find difficult to attain is felt – and rightly so – to be remarkable. A fifty-two-year-old widow who could take over her deceased husband's business and run it successfully without previous experience would be seen as especially so, for it is not customary for men or women to embark on new ventures so late in life. But when a fifty-two-year-old woman does not have any business to take over and consequently starts one herself, that is truly astounding.

As with the young starters, the number of late starters found in this survey was small. Only three of the business Amazons who started on their own were over the age of forty-four when they became owners, and all of them were lifelong career women who had a thorough knowledge of the industry they chose for their belated ventures.

Margaret Bryant and Claire Whitman were both fifty-two when they started their new businesses, Margaret after fifteen years as an executive for one of the largest British textile conglomerates and Claire after twenty-two years with the same financial brokerage firm, of which she had become vice-president. And Eva Helsing was forty-four when she became her own boss after seven years in the same investment consultancy firm.

Each of these women had her own reasons for leaving what seemed to be a secure job and becoming a late business starter. Margaret Bryant was made redundant by the textile conglomerate, which was contracting its operations, and realised that at fifty-two she was not going to be offered a similar post in what was a declining industry. Claire Whitman disagreed with her employers' business direction. Eva Helsing had no promotion prospects. Behind these seemingly different reasons was a common motive, their refusal to compromise. They knew that at their age, the chance of securing a fitting job was almost nil. Who needed middle-aged women in top managerial positions when there were thousands of young men with top qualifications chasing after relatively few jobs?

Having all their lives been working women, not homemakers, they had a clear idea of what was awaiting them as business owners, so when they decided to start on their own they prepared for the move well in advance. Once Margaret realised that within six months her fifteen years' employment would be terminated, she decided to become a children's wear manufacturer and started to attend evening classes to study production and design. The top executive with purchasing power in the millions was not shy of learning the basics of production. 'I had to go out and learn it; otherwise I would have lost everything that I would have put in.' It is often the case with executives in large corporations that their experience is very specific, whereas in order to succeed as a solo starter one has to be a Jack or Jill of all trades. The change from a top executive to an owner required some drastic adjustments. From her modern, fully carpeted and air-conditioned office on the fourteenth floor of a modern development outside London, with three secretaries and two assistants, she moved to a dilapidated Victorian building with outside washrooms and a leaking roof, no secretary and one assistant. The mink-clad executive, whose five-star hotel bills around the world had been footed by the corporation, was now wearing legwarmers to keep out the cold. Now that it was she who had to foot the bills, her view of what was essential had altered dramatically. Not many late starters would have endured such a workplace after fifteen years in the cocoon of an international conglomerate. What stood Margaret in good stead was that she was not the typical corporation product, but was at heart an entrepreneuse:

> I have always worked. I started off in insurance and was a policy checker for Lloyds. Then I went to St Paul's Institute and I learned all about insurance. When my husband decided that he wanted to be self-employed he took a shop and after a month he hated it, so I decided to give up my career and run the shop, a newsagent-tobacconist's, and after that a toy shop and a grocery business. After doing that for several years my husband decided that I was getting too involved and that he never saw me and all the rest of it. So I decided that I would retire and bought a pig farm. Actually it was lovely but after a year I got very bored. As I had no one to talk to except the young lad who used to do the cleaning, I decided that I needed a job. And that's how I got to —, where I stayed for fifteen years.

With such wide work experience, which included spells of ownership, Margaret had a good prospect of success in her new enterprise. Within a year she was earning double her previous salary and five years later, when she was fifty-seven, her children's wear business was an established name. And so it remains. As she says, 'I cannot see myself stopping – as my bank manager said, "Before seventy I cannot see you retiring." '

Claire Whitman is not sure that she will stay in the financial brokerage business for the next twelve years – that is until her seventieth birthday. After thirty-two years in the same industry she wouldn't mind a change, and envisages herself holding some public office. But until she is called upon to fulfil such a task she is continuing to run the brokerage business she started at the mature age of fifty-two. When, after twenty-two years with the same employers, she decided that the time had come to run her own business, she planned her transformation from an employee to an owner so meticulously that the chance of failure was minimal. Before announcing her departure she discussed the possibility of such a move with all her account clients and, out of 150, all but two promised to give their custom to the new corporation. In addition she secured the continued services of her personal secretaries and that of several bright financial analysts.

Yet despite what seemed to be a smooth transfer of the same commercial activities from one address to another with just slight alterations on the letterheads, the change-over from an employee to an employer was one of essence and not only of form. Whatever precautions are taken in business, risk looms constantly overhead. The 148 clients, the secretaries, and the young Turks who promised Claire to switch over their loyalty to her might have had second thoughts. Had Claire's employers offered these clients a ¼ per cent cut in their commission charges and the secretaries and the young financiers a 15 per cent raise in their salaries most of them would have stayed put. Luckily for Claire her employers felt too secure to bother.

For a time the late transformation into an entrepreneuse did not seem to affect Claire's way of life. The work was no more demanding and she did not have to alter her routine of spending the evenings with her husband and the weekends with her grown-up children. Only after a year did she begin to notice the difference. Although the financial rewards were ten times greater the decision-making was proportionately riskier, and at one time she teetered on the verge of insolvency.

Early business starters are like young mountaineers who quickly get used to the thin air of higher altitudes, while the late starters find it more difficult to adjust to the atmospheric changes after many years in the plains. It was easy for Claire to accept the higher income of the owner, but it was not so easy for her to bear the losses that are an integral part of ownership. When a wrong decision means your own downfall rather than someone else's, and a loss of money your own poverty, ownership is not the glamorous pursuit it usually seems to be. When Claire went wrong in one of her frequent speculations and was

—

on the brink of ruin, she had great doubts about the wisdom of having become her own boss:

> I got involved in some share offers which I had underwritten and out of which we were going to make a fortune, when suddenly the whole project got out of hand. For a period of ninety days it looked like it was going sour and it looked as if it would take a real miracle for it to work itself out. It was the most difficult situation I have ever been in because it involved practically everything that I had ever accumulated. If it went sour I would have been wiped out.

The miracle happened and the business pulled through, but those ninety days have left their mark on Claire. What distinguishes the owner from a top executive is that even if the executive is the head of a large public corporation and the owner the head of a small business, it is the owner and not the top executive who in a crisis faces the risk of being wiped out. For employees, business is a game of decision-making, an extension of the case studies played at business schools; and at worst a wrong decision can cost them only their job. But for the owners it is their life's work and assets that are on the line, and the older they get the more they have to lose and the less able they are to take the loss. Claire Whitman explains:

> A young man coming up with my background would have taken those risks earlier, at a lesser level of exposure. At fifty-seven everything that I had accumulated in life was on the line. If it had gone sour I literally would have been right down. I have taken all kinds of risks personally. If I had lost, let's say, $50,000 I would have been sorry, but it was not going to change my life style. I would have known that in a year or two I would have made it up. But this was different, it was going to affect my life style. It was a real experience.

The fear of losing their worldly possessions prevents young and old alike from embarking on an entrepreneurial career. However, it did not deter Eva Helsing from quitting her stable but dead-end job as a broker and, at the age of forty-four when most women are considered mentally and physically *passé*, embarking on an independent career. When, after following the typical female pattern of secretarial, clerical, and book-keeping jobs she became one of the first women to hold a broker's licence in the state of New York, she believed that her promotion would be meteoric. But she came to realise that her

—

uniqueness as a female broker was meaningful only to women's magazines, not to Wall Street's male fraternity. Calculating that she would not make it as an employee, she decided to go it alone. As a woman she had no chance of attracting the corporate clients, so instead she established herself as the guru of the small person who had only a few hundred or a couple of thousand dollars to invest. Her success has exceeded even her wildest dreams: 'It was the best thing I had done in my life. I should have done it earlier.' And her advice to other women is: 'It is never too late to hit it big in business.'

The drifters

Unlike the early starters who entered business because they were motivated by their wish to succeed beyond the entitlement of their qualifications and experience, and unlike the late starters who began in business because their position or their salary did not match their knowledge and experience, the drifters were driven by neither ambition nor frustration. Their start in business was literally accidental. Yet despite this they adapted themselves rapidly to the new circumstances until they became indistinguishable from the rest of the pack. Meeting them, it is difficult to believe that these purposeful women who travel all over the world, whose telephones ring nonstop, whose diaries are booked weeks in advance, and who look so professional that it seems they had never led a different life, were actually drifters who had neither been trained for their present role nor even intended to be what they are and where they are.

Business ownership is one of the few careers where no compliance with pre-established conditions is required. A young woman wishing to become a doctor, a lawyer, a trucker, or a seamstress would have to follow an established route. Every profession or trade has its own entry requirements: except for business ownership. This is therefore ideally suited to women who, because of their predetermined role of home-making and motherhood, find it difficult to comply with the entry requirements of most worthwhile professions. Business ownership can give a chance to purposeless dreamers and unqualified dropouts, who can become tycoons if they hit the right idea and have the stamina to see it through. Housewives who until yesterday were contentedly ironing their husband's shirts and mending their children's clothes can suddenly be inspired by an idea, perhaps sparked off by a television show, and become different women.

—

Business success, like success in all other fields, is constantly establishing new criteria. If previously it was believed imperative for a good sprinter to have long legs, a short and stocky winner would alter this assumption and open the field for other competitors of the same build. The same applies to the successful drifters. They have proven that unqualified and inexperienced women can succeed in an area which had previously been an exclusive male preserve. They have also demonstrated that motherhood is not the all-consuming, everlasting occupation it is said to be. Fifty-one per cent of the business Amazons started their businesses after they had had children, when it dawned on them that being a wife and a mother was not the totally fulfilling existence they had been led to believe. The drifters were not the only women to have discovered this truth, but unlike the majority they did not let their age or lack of experience stand in their way.

Doris Smith is a typical drifter. She does not credit herself with her success but attributes it, like all other good things that have happened, to a series of accidents. Now accidents do happen, but they tend to be incapacitating rather than advantageous. More often than not, 'accidental' success is, at the very least, the result of being in the right place at the right time. It is difficult to establish just how much Doris owed her success to chance. What is clear, however, is that, after fourteen years of marriage and with two sons aged eleven and ten, she became the owner of a health business that in twelve years has grown to employ 150 persons, including her husband and her elder son.

Nothing in Doris's preceding thirty-eight years could have indicated her future as a business tycoon. She was one of two daughters to working-class Londoners who, through the father's skills as a plumber and the mother's at wheeling and dealing, had become comfortably off but not so much as to give their children a lavish upbringing. She left school at fourteen 'with no education' and became a secretary. At the age of twenty-four she married an understanding and supportive architect to whom she is still married after twenty-six years; and at the age of twenty-eight she had her first son.

Her marriage was the end of her uneventful working life, and her initiation into the homemaking middle classes. For fourteen years she pursued the life of a well-to-do suburban housewife with its familiar routines, aided by help in the house and with an understanding husband who worked a lot abroad and did not impose much on her time or energies. In addition she had a good and close relationship with her parents and sister. The only blemish that marred this idyllic existence was Doris's obesity. From a chubby child she grew up into a chubbier young woman, and then into an obese wife and mother who weighed 210 lb. The boredom of too easy a life and a frequently absent husband only aggravated her problem until she became ill and was warned by her doctor that unless she lost weight the condition would become chronic.

Her ability to take hold of herself and lose weight was the turning point in Doris's life, as well as the foundation of her empire. The 210 lb fatty who could barely walk has become a trim 133 lb athlete able to jog ten miles daily. And, as often happens in such cases, she became a proselytiser preaching the merit of slimming to anyone who would listen. 'I was so excited with it all that it was a bit like religion. I wanted everyone to be slim and to feel as good as I did. So I started telling everybody about dieting and how they would feel better if they lost weight.' With this new-found mission in life she became a Weight Watchers instructress and despite the negligible pay of £3 a session the job transformed her life because it gave her confidence. Her ability to tell the fat, unsightly ladies who flocked to Weight Watchers that she used to look like them before she took hold of herself was worth much more than the low wages she received. Her zeal to convert the world's population into beautiful, healthy people was such that it seemed as if she feared that if she stopped for a moment, her old self would repossess her, and she would become once again the fat lady whose existence she acknowledged merely as an example to other erring gluttons. With such fervour, it did not take her long to become dissatisfied with the Weight Watchers' methods, and she began to complain about their lack of interest in the individual. So she opted out to start her own slimming clubs under the name of Weight Regulators.

The pattern of Doris's evolution from housewife to entrepreneuse was common to many of the drifters. First there was a lengthy period without work, then an undemanding and low-paid job which gave them the confidence to believe that they could do better on their own. These, coupled with a comfortable background and an idea that did not require a large capital outlay, were the basis for most of their successes.

Theories often tend to complicate what they set out to simplify. The theory of how to succeed in business is often far more complex than the reality. In Doris's case, for instance, once she had decided on her own variant of the Weight Watchers' system, she drew £60 from the bank, bought a set of scales, had some leaflets printed, advertised in the local paper, and started her Weight Regulators with a class of four people. When the ladies started to shed pound after pound of fat, the word

—

46

passed around the immediate area, and soon more customers arrived and the little hall she hired once a week became packed. The success of the first club called for the start of another, which was followed by more until she had a hundred such clubs in seventy towns and villages in England. From there the purchase of a health farm was the logical next step. Despite the rational evolution of her business activities Doris sticks to the 'accident' theory, as befits a native of a country where premeditated success is considered socially immoral by rich and poor alike. In addition the 'accident' theory has an aura of glamour and luck which the obstacle course of premeditated achievement lacks.

The tale of Rachel Shapiro is rather similar; but she wasn't fat, she had a better education than Doris, and the scene was the USA. A qualified nurse, at twenty-one she married the husband to whom she is still married after twenty-five years, and for eighteen years she stayed at home looking after her three children, who were seventeen, sixteen and fourteen when she embarked on her cosmetics business. As a drifter, she could not claim that she started in business in a methodical way but, being American, she is keen to assign her success to her own abilities rather than to chance. During the years as a housewife she experienced several bouts of discontent but these were quenched by her husband's and children's apparent need of her. After each short foray into the labour market she hastened to return to her homemaking role, not only because she felt it a duty but also because the jobs on offer were poorly paid and unstimulating. Still she did not give up. She was not exceptionally tenacious, but staying at home was becoming increasingly frustrating.

After eighteen years of looking after her family she was unwilling to return to her original profession, which entailed continuously serving others, and she felt too rusty to take up a new skill. 'Eighteen years of housework dulled my mind and blunted my instincts and I felt unable to try for a meaningful job.' Instead she applied for 'women selling to women' part-time jobs, such as those for Avon and Tupperware because, unlike Doris Smith, money was a factor in her going out to work. Her husband's earnings as a relatively well-paid engineer did not leave much for extras with three demanding teenagers. She would stick to these jobs for three to four months until she exhausted the neighbourhood and her commission dwindled accordingly. Then she would quit and keep house until her next bout of frustration.

The job that sparked her business was one of these part-time direct selling jobs, which offered women cosmetics based on natural ingredients. Having done similar selling jobs before and having evolved her

own ideas on the method of direct selling, she felt that she had it in her
to copy her employers' formula of success. At the age of thirty-nine,
after six months as a beauty consultant, she branched out on her own.
Seven years later at the age of forty-six Rachel Shapiro boasted an
annual sales volume of $7.5 million, eighty full-time employees, and
8,000 part-time beauty consultants. The way she did it sounds simple
enough. She contacted several laboratories and asked them to produce
a range of natural-based cosmetics, similar to those of her ex-
employers, and she undertook to purchase a minimum amount of
five hundred jars of each product. At the beginning her range was
limited to four items, but with increased sales she could guarantee
the laboratories more products and consequently also increased her
sales volume.

Naturally a risk was involved. She possessed 2,000 jars of cosmetics
at an average price of $2 which could net her $4,000 if sold, or lose her
$4,000 if unsold. Rachel felt confident that with her sales experience
she could dispose of 1,000 jars, which would have just about covered
her expenses. 'When your own money is at stake, and these were my
own personal savings, you somehow sell better.' In addition to her own
sales efforts she advertised for beauty consultants and offered them a
slightly higher commission than the competition. It worked: she got
enough applicants to do the selling for her, and she stayed behind to
administrate it all. 'I learned how to run an office as I went along. At
the beginning there were only a few bills and a few commissions.' Later
she took on book-keepers, clerks, and warehouse staff, and eventually
invested in a powerful computer. 'Being involved in one's work makes
it easier to study new things. I would never have believed that I could
master such complicated procedures. But I can.'

The direct selling formula with 'women selling to women' has
produced another business Amazon, Delia Lewenthal who, like Doris
Smith and Rachel Shapiro, never planned to enter business, but just
drifted into it. At thirty-five, after five years in business, Delia heads a
$10 million toy business which she regards as merely the cornerstone
of an empire. There was nothing in her background or environment to
suggest that she possessed a dormant business talent: her parents were
both employees, as is her husband who is a scientist. After a BA in
English literature she worked as a social worker for a year and then in
the city welfare department for another. After that she went back to
university to do a master's degree in child psychology and worked as a
programme initiator. Following her graduation she became a community developer for two years and a day-care centre director for the next

—

three. By that time she was twenty-eight and, after six years of marriage, she gave birth to a daughter. Motherhood cut Delia down to size. Like other university-educated career women, she had to face the simple reality that she could not resume her work because she had no surrogate mother for her daughter. Her wages were not sufficient to buy reliable help, and her own mother, to whom she could have entrusted her daughter, was a working woman herself. So she stayed at home and concentrated on the baby.

Her interest in educational toys began as the baby became a toddler and she tried to implement all the educational theories in her upbringing: 'Being a Jewish mother I had to have everything in the world for her and I said, "Well, I need to have good toys," and I went to look in the stores and they didn't exist. So I said, "Well, I'll open a toy store and will give educational demonstrations." '

Usually the distance from the conception of an idea to its realisation is great and often unbridgeable, but for Delia the route from an idea to a $10 million business was relatively short and easy. Her father, who had a life time's experience in marketing, did not think much of his educated daughter's chances as a shopkeeper and prophesied that her business would not survive to the end of the year: 'You can't just open a shop because you have a daughter and know something about educational toys. Even if you've identified a gap in the market you can't be sure that the gap doesn't exist because there isn't sufficient demand for educational toys.'

That was her father's verdict. Besides, she had no finance or sureties to guarantee the expenses of renting and maintaining a shop. So instead of committing herself to rents and stocks she decided to try home demonstrations on the lines of Tupperware. Getting the toys was relatively easy because, once located, the manufacturers were eager to supply her; and once she had the actual toys she could go out to demonstrate them. Unlike Rachel Shapiro, who was a home demonstrator herself before she started her business, Delia had no selling experience at all: 'The only time I sold something was when I was eighteen and did a Christmas stint at Macy's.' So it was a great relief to her when mothers were ready to meet her and actually buy. Looking for a better return on her time and the possibility of attracting more mothers simultaneously, she organised demonstrations in her garage, and had mothers attending in hordes. From then on it snowballed. She advertised for demonstrators, taught them the skills, and increased the range of educational toys. At present she employs five hundred demonstrators, and fifty full-time employees and thirty seasonal ones who are housed in a new complex of computerised offices and warehouse.

What makes women like Delia get up one day, and set out on their own is the realisation that they can no longer be content with a subordinate job, yet are unable to progress to a higher position because of their maternal obligations. Self-employment is the only answer: 'After two years at home I had had enough of it. I felt that I was bursting with ideas and I had to go and put them into effect. I just wanted to get out and do something. I had tremendous drive. But with a two-year-old at home I was not exactly free to undertake a meaningful job. I knew that I could no longer just work for someone else in a subordinate position. So the only way out was to do something myself.'

The inability to progress in her profession was also the reason behind Linda Bailie's embarking on a business career at the age of forty. Although her lingerie manufacturing business started accidentally, the seeds of her entrepreneurship had already been sown in her frustration as a producer and scriptwriter for the film industry. When, during a momentary depression, she craved for a pair of silk panties and could not find any, she decided to make some herself. Her reasoning from that point on was simple: if she, whose financial standing did not justify such a luxury, yearned for silk panties that cost $100 at Neiman Marcus, there must be others like her.

With this elementary but sound marketing evaluation Linda became a business owner. Whatever the outcome she had nothing to lose, because at forty she had become disillusioned with the film industry. Although she won the odd award for her documentary productions, she realised that she was not going to make it in the film world.

The film business is very difficult. I saw people around me whom I considered quite respected, talented people still having to struggle for every little job. So when something began to develop with the lingerie I seized it wholeheartedly. I wanted to have financial security. I wanted to have equity. There was never any equity in the film industry. One got tired of the inability to control one's life. I very much like to be in control. I am a controller, a manager, and not being able to control my destiny was horribly frustrating after all those years in the drama business.

Common to all drifters was their wish to reach land, but when and where the landfall was going to take place they did not know. After one year of college and numerous drama courses Linda had hung around the film studios of California for twenty years. She had taught drama, written TV scripts and commercials, produced documentaries, and written a gossip column in a Los Angeles newspaper; but she still did not have $500 to her name. When she decided to start the business, and so had to buy a roll of silk and hire a sewing machine and a machinist, she had to pawn her jewellery and ask female friends for a loan. But within two years the lingerie gamble had paid off. It bought her and her husband a fine home and luxurious holidays and, what is more, the social status and security of which the film world had deprived her. Linda discovered that as a business owner her social acceptability was greater than as a TV person. She found that 'It is easier for a woman to get into society with money than it is with the prestige of having exposure as a film producer.'

What distinguishes Linda from most of the other business Amazons is that she is one of the few self-confessed feminists among them. Yet she sees no contradiction between her feminism and making a fortune out of one of the most anti-feminist products around: frivolous silk underwear for women. Linda is not bothered by this contradiction because she believes that equality will be achieved by emulating the power base of men, of which financial success is one of the most important components.

The drifters have reached the world of business from the most unlikely occupations and ways of life. Delia Lewenthal was a social worker before her reincarnation as a toy manufacturer; Rachel Shapiro was a nurse, part-time home demonstrator and housewife before becoming a cosmetic distributor; and Linda Bailie exchanged a stagnant TV career for the manufacture of lingerie. But not all the drifters left behind them professions or gainful employment. Doris Smith was simply a fat lady who realised the business potential of slimming and built a business on that revelation.

Excessive weight was not Julie Kitson's business inspiration. Slim and athletic all her life, she found herself in one of the most unlikely female occupations, that of a stuntwoman. Julie left school at fourteen and, until the age of seventeen when she and her twin sister with their fiancés emigrated to New Zealand, she supported herself as a typist. The first night of their arrival in New Zealand they spent at a Salvation Army hostel, and in the morning Julie got a job with a detective agency by lying about her age. She started there as a secretary and was then promoted to an investigator who had to infiltrate businesses concerned about internal thefts and night clubs that were being ripped off by their croupiers.

During the week she was fully engrossed in her detective work; at the weekends she trailed behind her racing driver fiancé from one racing circuit to another until she caught the bug herself and became one of the first women to hold a licence for competitive racing driving. 'I could strip down an engine and deal with minor breakdowns myself. I have an intense love for cars.' But in addition to these manly and risky pursuits Julie did not neglect the more feminine ones, and at the age of twenty she entered a beauty contest which paved her way to a modelling career with the inevitable dreams about an acting and filming future. With these dreams came the realisation that New Zealand had nothing more to offer her, and she took the long sea voyage back to England. A week after her arrival she was in filming, not as an actress but as a stunt driver. Although her seven years in the film industry did not turn her into a star, she became an internationally acclaimed stuntwoman and took part in hundreds of adventure films of which the various James Bonds, Matt Helms, and Pink Panthers, and TV series such as 'The Saint', 'The Baron', 'The Prisoner', and 'The Avengers' were just a few. Her career as a stuntwoman came to an end when in a fight scene on top of an articulated truck that was loaded on a fast-moving train, a low-passing telephone wire wrapped itself around her neck, lifted her thirty feet in the air, and landed her on her shoulder. She was not expected to live but, being the tough woman she is, Julie recovered. However, she realised that she had to look for another career.

The seven years as a stuntwoman taught Julie a lot about the film industry, and after further investigation she decided that there was a market for the hiring out of helicopters for filming work. So at the age of twenty-seven she became the owner of a £26,000 helicopter which she bought on a hire purchase agreement, and a year later she had a fleet of three. The increased number of machines attracted many and varied jobs and the helicopters were hired out for crop spraying, the Ordnance Survey (the British government map-making organisation), live television broadcasting, police surveillance, and the supply of the North Sea oil rigs. Now forty, Julie is married with two young children and an aviation business which has expanded and prospered.

There are many tales of drifters who have touched land by becoming business Amazons. There was Ann Liddie, a divorcee who started a leisure centre because she did not know what to do with her children during the Easter school holidays. There was Lucy Curtis, a bright,

—

curly-headed Jewish girl from London, whose prosperous parents dissuaded her from going to college because they feared the influence of higher education on their plans for her early marriage and motherhood. So instead she became a secretary in a publisher's office and nurtured a dream of becoming a publisher herself. Despite the lack of encouragement from her parents and later on from her scientist husband, she has managed to survive and flourish in that risky business while raising three children and keeping a home. There was also Stella Rover, whose husband died from a heart attack leaving her with four young children, thousands of pounds of debts, and no work prospects, who found her salvation in egg farming, which not only enabled her to keep the family together but also to go on to make her fortune. The stories of women who were not selected or trained for success, but who have none the less succeeded, are among the most heartening of all.

3 | Why They Started

How someone does something can be explained by facts that are verifiable, but why someone does something cannot be that easily explained because often the doers do not know themselves. The reasons that motivated women who were not trained for any kind of achievement to embark on such an individual and risky path as business ownership are not easy to explain. The three accepted single or cumulative motives for male business starts are: the need for money; the wish to be independent; the seizing of an opportunity. This study of female entrepreneurs has brought to light additional motives unique to women.

The Need for Money

The need for money, although seemingly an obvious one for anyone who enters business, has been refuted as the motive for male entrepreneurship by several research studies. Although it was also denied by the majority of the business Amazons, for a large number it was a decisive factor. As to why and for what purpose they required the money, their reasons differed.

For some, such as Barbara Shelensky and Sonia Kaplan, who had no qualifications, no capital, and low-earning husbands, it meant survival. For Hilary Waldorf, who was provided for in her husband's will, it meant survival in a different sense: being able to maintain the standard of life to which she had become accustomed, and which she would have had to forsake if she had fallen back on the level of salary she could

54

expect as a middle-aged housewife with no experience. Delia Lewenthal and Lucy Curtis had qualifications which could have commanded them a reasonable wage but not sufficient to support a nanny and housekeeper. Thus, they too were trapped. These three reasons – survival, survival in style, and hatred of household chores – were given by most of the women for their needing the extra money which they could earn only as business owners and not as employees. Only one expressed a more aggressive motive: the wish to be rich and enjoy the power that comes with it.

Survival

The women for whom starting a business meant survival and not a mere occupation were either single women who had to support themselves or married women who had no marketable skills and whose husbands had low earning potential. For them it was often not only their physical survival that was at stake but also their marriages. For Barbara Shelensky, who at seventeen married a penniless European refugee without a work permit, starting a business was the only solution to an intolerable state of affairs whereby a thirty-four-year-old husband had to live off the earnings of a seventeen-year-old girl. 'He couldn't work because he had no permit and my earnings couldn't even provide for me, let alone for him. In addition there was also the pride of a husband who couldn't provide for his wife. So for us starting a business meant survival.'

Unlike Barbara, Sonia Kaplan could not attribute her need to work to such unusual circumstances. Her husband simply did not earn enough to support a wife and a future son. 'I started in business because I needed the money. My husband earned at that time $75 a week; I was pregnant with my eldest son, Martin, who will be thirty-one, and there was a need to earn extra money because at $75 a week we were not going to manage.'

Not being the first or the last woman who had to work in order to supplement the family's income, Sonia tried to do what countless other women in her situation do, get a job. But the sight of a pregnant woman did not encourage employers to hire her, and the part-time jobs she had been offered were not going to fill the gap between her needs and her husband's earnings. In addition, because of the pregnancy she was also losing her greatest marketable asset, her limitless energy.

Finding herself unable to get a job, she decided to try her hand at commerce. 'I needed the money. I could not get a job. So I put an advert in the paper offering these bracelets which I knew I could get hold of, if I got the money from the readers.' This advertisement, which was inserted with Sonia's last $25, was the beginning of her present $100 million mail order business.

The inability to find a job was also the reason why Genevieve Rouche started her talent agency. An eighteen-year-old child bride of a successful forty-year-old Hollywood film director, she had no need for a job. But when he died seventeen years later from drug addiction, she was left penniless and without a skill to fall back on. At thirty-five, exhausted from years of coping with sickness and failure, she was in no shape to attract another husband. She had to find a way of supporting herself. 'To put it bluntly,' she said, 'had I not hit on the idea of becoming a talent agent, I would have starved.'

Sympathetic as one would like to feel towards these particular women, the fact that they started in business because their support system failed should not be glossed over. Had their husbands been able to provide for them, these women who are today captains of industry would probably have languished in a suburban mansion or even enjoyed their role of wives and hostesses. There is nothing in their attitude to life in general or to feminism in particular to suggest that they would have striven for a career, or for the role of a joint earner, had they been fortunate enough to marry a good provider. It must, however, be said in fairness that once they realised their circumstances, they threw themselves wholeheartedly into their new role without resenting or reproaching their husbands.

The moral of the story is that the temptation of being provided for by someone else is such that even the mightiest of the Amazons would have found it difficult to resist. Most probably if men had the choice they too would have succumbed to the temptation.

Survival in style

The need for money was echoed not only by women who had nothing but also by those who wished to maintain what they had. When Hilary Waldorf's husband made her a widow for the second time in her life she was not left destitute:

I could have sold the [chemical] works. Everything is for sale from

—

a widow. The insurance money only paid for income tax obligations. I was not starving but I needed the money. Everybody needs
the money. Had I not taken over the family business, I would
have had to go to work somewhere, but at forty-eight what did I
have to offer? My experience as a hostess?

By becoming a businesswoman rather than a widow worrying about
old age and her shrinking capital, Hilary managed to sustain her
standing in the community as well as her teenage son's future
livelihood. After twelve years of widowhood she can look back and
say: 'Taking the decision to become a businesswoman was the wisest
step in my life.'

Hatred of household chores

Lucy Curtis and Delia Lewenthal, though respectively British and
American, had several things in common. Both were in their early
thirties and married to financially unambitious scientists, and both
hated household chores. This hatred was not a result of any strong
belief in women's changing role or their own destiny; it was simply lack
of physical co-ordination, which verged on incapacity. To put it
simply, they were lousy housewives. Their homes were a mess and had
they not been fortunate enough to have married gentle and undemanding men, their marriages might well have collapsed. Irrespective of
social or economic standing, and regardless of their wife's aptitude and
inclination, few men are prepared to return to a messy home after a
hard day's work. Being realistic, Lucy and Delia knew that such a state
of affairs could not last forever, and they set out to earn the money
required for the employment of domestic help. Delia explains:

> I had to get out of the house or I would have gone out of my mind.
> But my daughter was my responsibility. I couldn't just dump her
> or ask my husband to stay at home with her. What I wanted was
> someone qualified to look after children. But they don't come
> cheap. So I knew that I had to earn good money if I was to
> become free again and I knew that I couldn't earn it by being an
> employee.

Lucy had an additional complication: her eldest daughter was
disabled, and she was determined to keep her at home. So she
had to choose between dedicating herself to her daughter, to the

—

detriment of everything else, or earning sufficient money to get qualified help and enable her family to lead a more normal life. She chose the latter, started a publishing business from home, gave birth to two other healthy children, and saved herself and the marriage.

> Essentially I started in business for the money. I wanted children and I needed the money to be able to afford a nanny. I reckoned that if someone could look after your children, why should I be at home all day? I like selling things and I don't like housework. The money pays for the special help my eldest daughter requires and for the extra attention the young ones will need not to feel neglected because of their eldest sister's predicament. Had I not succeeded in business it would have been a tragedy for me, the kids, and my husband. Some women are better than others at being housewives. I am not.

Wealth and power

With the majority of the business Amazons claiming that money was not the reason they started in business, and the rest explaining themselves in a variety of other ways it was refreshing to encounter Lena Gouldwin, who admitted to wanting to be rich. 'I started in the construction business because I wanted to make lots of money, because money means power. When I came on the scene the corporate structure did not offer much to women. An executive secretary was a big deal. I couldn't find anyone to take me seriously. So I said to hell with them and I started my own business.'

Even in money-conscious America few of those engaged in the creation of fortunes admit that they did it solely for the sake of becoming rich. But Lena has never let convention bother her. To the same extent that she has no time for the hypocrisy of business people claiming a total disinterest in money she is also not ready to perpetuate the hypocrisy of high-earning women who are reluctant to admit that they earn more than their husbands. As in public matters so also in private ones, she does not believe in cover-ups: 'We have no problems about it. My husband decided very early on in our relationship that he would be quite happy if I earned $100 million.'

—

Money Was Not the Motive

Whatever view one takes of business, it is primarily about making money. Yet, although it is impossible to ignore the links between business ownership and wealth, 60 per cent of the business Amazons claimed that money was not their motivation. In itself this result is not surprising as it conforms to the findings of other studies regarding the motivations of entrepreneurs of both sexes.

A starving person might feel justifiably cynical listening to scores of well-fed businesswomen stating unabashedly that money is not the reason they are in business. The starving man might even presume to ask why they are in the money business if they do not care about money and why they continue to accumulate it if it matters so little to them. He would not be alone in questioning this phenomenon; others, including myself, have expressed their doubts. But the evidence is there.

'Actually I am not motivated by money at all,' says Mary Mead, a thirty-five-year-old millionairess whose five-year-old dance studios have become a public company. 'Money did not enter into it at all,' claims Marion Little, another young millionairess, who ploughed all her life savings into a risky venture as a conference promoter and organiser that did not make any money for the first two years. 'I took a big risk but it did not matter. The worst that could have happened was that the business could have failed. So what? I would pick myself up and put myself back into the workforce.' But then, Marion has the confidence of those who know how to make money: 'I had accumulated a fair amount of money of my own. And I threw it all into the business. I also played the stock market. The stock market was fairly good in 1978, and in 1979 I turned $40,000 into $120,000 in a very short period of time.' Wasn't it about money? Was it not really rather disingenuous to claim that 'money did not enter into it at all'?

Two types of people can afford to have contempt for money: those who can survive without what it buys, and those who know how to make it. In both cases they require a great deal of confidence, which is rarely found among first-time entrepreneurs. When successful entrepreneurs at the zenith of their careers are asked about their original motivation it is only too easy for them to ignore the money motive and substitute a more socially acceptable one. Even a woman like Laurie Richards, the merchandising magnate who needed to supplement her husband's earnings to raise her two sons, did not include this need as a motive in her decision to become a businesswoman: 'Of course you always have to work, you can always use more money, but it was not out of having to make ends meet. No.'

Independence

The craving for independence is usually felt by those who have had to survive without it and haven't enjoyed the experience. While in theory one might expect it would be people who have never lost their independence who are determined to maintain it, in fact it is mostly those who have tasted its absence who cherish it most. The 28 per cent who mentioned 'independence' as their motivation had all previously been in employment. For the widows and the ex-housewives who had not worked before, independence was not a motive.

In the context of business, independence means the ability to make decisions without requiring the approval of superiors. For male ex-employees, independence means a dramatic role reversal, from that of an order taken to an order given. For female ex-employees independence has an additional connotation. Because most bosses are male it also means independence from men; in the words of property millionairess Tricia Williams, 'I was fed up with being trodden on or trodden over by men.' Julie Kitson, in the aviation business, adds:

> I worked in a very male chauvinistic world where women are not even accepted today. They seem to think that because you are a woman you cannot do it. As they would not admit that I could run the business I said to myself that I might as well do it for myself and not for them. And that is what I did.

While a man's quest for independence is accepted as a free soul's search for full expression and the tough lone male has always gained the admiration of men and women alike, the same admiration is not extended to the tough lone female. She is either pitied or made to feel a freak, and may begin to doubt the wisdom of her choice. Daphne Glover, who has made her fortune in market research, assesses herself: 'I'm incredibly independent and in fact too much so. It is sometimes sad to think that because of it I didn't get married. I'm not worried about marriage really, but I miss the children.'

Because independence is obviously more romantic than money as a motive, the tendency is to underplay the one and overplay the other. But it is only romantics who fail to see the link between the two. Rachel Shapiro is clear on this issue:

> I started in cosmetics in order to be independent and independence means money. Independence is of the utmost importance for a woman. The way you get independent is to have your own money, and money gives you security. I can see how the women who work for us have grown since they began earning money. They start as shy housewives because, even with previous experience, after a few years at home they became very insecure. But once they earn money they develop and grow. They start to glow and they start having confidence in themselves.

Seizing an Opportunity

Not everyone who begins a business necessarily has a clear reason for doing so, let alone a plan. In fact 30 per cent of the business Amazons claimed that they got started when they suddenly became aware of a commercial opportunity waiting to be grasped. Seizing an opportunity is not an 'either-or' motive, and can well be combined with other motives. It is simply the trigger that initiates an entrepreneurial career.

Like other opportunists, Fiona Devlin did not plan to become a businesswoman. She became one because she saw a commercial potential, recognised it for what it was, and grabbed it. Before that she was a well-paid PA on Capitol Hill and enjoyed her job. One day she got a telephone call from an ex-colleague who asked her if she would like to join him in a new venture of political lobbying.

> It was really a new opportunity in my life. I was already making what I thought was very good money. So I could not have started it for money. I really did not understand how much more I could make as my own boss. I am happy to say that I have increased my income by ten, fifteen fold since I started in business. It has been

very lucrative. Now I would find it difficult to work for anyone again.

Seizing an opportunity means being the right person in the right place and time. Jane Auerbach is a good example of this:

I already had money and independence. I was very lucky because I always seemed to be in the right place at the right time. Also in my present career it was the same, it was a matter of timing. My husband inherited an unimaginative men's retail chain that was losing money, and my academic career came to a temporary halt. He wanted to sell the business, but I saw its potential and dissuaded him. Although I had never been in business, and until I was forty I was a pure academic, I saw the potential of that business and decided to have a go.

There are two types of opportunism: planned and accidental. The Amazons who ascribed their business start to the seizing of an opportunity fall into the latter class. Not only were they not expecting the chance, but they had no special training in hunting for such an opportunity. On the whole it seems that the lack of hunting training makes women more prone to accidental success than men. Fashion tycoon Kate Ullman describes the decisive moment:

It was very accidental. I never wanted to be in my own business. Most men plan their lives – but most women let things happen. They start doing something they like, something they feel is right, and then they are just deep into it. It is like a love affair. You start innocently seeing the guy a couple of times and then, without knowing how, you are hooked. If I knew what I was really doing I would never have done it.

There are always opportunities in business; either because dying enterprises and obsolete products and services need replacement, or because successful ventures create new demands that need fulfilling. Yet, despite this ever-changing market, there seems to exist an equilibrium between the number of opportunities and the number of entrepreneurs, and for every available opportunity there seems to exist someone ready to grab it. Therefore the speedy recognition of an opportunity is an essential quality for entrepreneurship. Some people are born with the instinct to recognise business opportunities, others learn it the hard way by letting some slip through. Sally Harper was one of the luckier, for she was born with that natural instinct and as a result she started her own business at the age of seventeen.

—

I was sixteen years old, and worked as a temp for a recruitment agency. Six months later they opened another branch and asked me to run it, which I did. Then one day a friend of mine who worked with me was asked by a rival agency to become a director, but she could not be bothered to go to the interview and suggested that I went instead. I thought, 'If she isn't interested I could be.' So I went and they offered me a directorship. Eventually, when they went wrong on me, I thought, 'If I could do it for them I could do it on my own.' And that was how it happened, I saw the opportunity which my friend missed.

Seizing an opportunity does not require originality. Like Sally, one can succeed in business by reproducing other people's ideas. Sally was not an originator; nor did she yearn to be independent or particularly rich. Her staff recruitment agency was a replica of the ones where she had been employed herself.

Yet by no means all opportunists lack originality. Niki Summers, who specialised in cosmetics for dark-skinned women, was an innovator. Her grasping of the opportunity, too, was far from accidental. She recognised a gap in the market and set out to fill it: 'I started in business because I saw an opportunity to provide cosmetics for black women, whom everyone had neglected. This was my motivation. It was not independence, because, being a fashion and theatrical promoter, I have always been independent.'

Each new entrepreneurial generation claims that the real business opportunities have been exhausted by previous generations. Yet the fact remains that every day all over the free world individuals discover new opportunities to start in business. It is to be hoped that, following the lead of the business Amazons, the number of women among these opportunity seizers will increase.

The Feminine Reasons

The need for money or independence, and the seizing of an opportunity, are motives which apply to both sexes. But the business Amazons were motivated by additional factors unique to women. Four of these, the 'husband', 'child', 'widow', and 'housewife' factors, related directly to women's biological and social functions; and there was a fifth, here

—

called 'altruism', which relates to their particular understanding of life.

The 'husband' factor is that of women who entered business with the sole aim of helping their husbands, and in the process discovered their own strength, capabilities, and indispensability.

The 'child' factor is that of those women who became business-women because they wished to spend more time with their children, something which was denied them by conventional employment.

The 'widow' factor is that of widows who took over the ownership and management of their deceased husbands' businesses, not for need of money or independence, but in order to continue their late husband's life's creation.

The 'housewife' factor is that of the women magnates who started in business because they were not fulfilled as housewives. Like all the feminine reasons this is a new phenomenon, a direct result of the changing role of the women in our society.

Altruism

All the reasons cited until now for the business Amazons becoming owners have one thing in common: a wish to improve their financial, social, or emotional state. In contrast, those who were motivated to enter business because of altruism did so in order to improve the lot of others.

If it were businessmen and not businesswomen claiming that they started in business in order to help others, they would be laughed at. But coming from businesswomen, about whose motivation little is known, this highly improbable reason ought at least to be given the benefit of the doubt.

When her husband died Joan Hammond took over the running of his engineering business instead of selling it, because she felt she had a duty towards the workers whose jobs would have been jeopardised if she had sold out: 'I had a high sense of duty, and immediately after paying my respects to the other widows [of the air disaster] I went to the various offices and plants and while the workers were on their lunch hour, I addressed them and told them they had job security with me.'

Like Joan, Hilary Waldorf felt responsible for her deceased hus-band's employees in their chemical works. 'There were people who had been there for over thirty-five years and were unemployable anywhere else. I couldn't just abandon them and tell them that it was the end.'

—

Similar maternal feelings were displayed by Valerie Reynolds, another widow whose decision to step into her deceased husband's telecommunications business at the age of sixty-five was influenced by her concern for the future of the employees.

Workers were not the only group to benefit. Marlene Jacobs started her own dance promotion group for those of her colleagues who were looking for a commercially remunerative outlet for their skills. 'I wanted to give other dancers the opportunity to do that type of dancing.' Eva Helsing's wish to help others was even more ambitious:

> I was working for a firm in the New York stock exchange and I found that I couldn't do enough to help the clients. I found that the brokerage house wanted to have all the client's money and equities, his life insurance agent wanted to get it all in cash surrender value, and his CPA [certified public accountant] was telling him how much taxes he owed five months too late to do anything about it. I saw so many people fractured and torn apart that I wanted to put my arms around them and make them whole financially but I couldn't do it. I couldn't handle their life insurance, which was a major mistake. I couldn't really do complete financial planning. So that frustration, when it was a hard time at the stock market and little firms were merging into big firms, made me leave a big firm and set up a little one, which was a very scary thing to do. The regulations in this country for stockbrokers are almost overwhelming. It is hard work not to violate something because there are so many rules. But I did it because it was the only way to help all those people ouside who needed help.

Being a businesswoman, for Eva, was not a matter of helping herself but of helping others. In the process she has become a millionairess, but she does not find this contradictory; and there is no reason why she should.

For years Eva had contemplated the vocation of a churchwoman so that she could bring God's message to the masses, but realising that it was easier to convince the haves than the have-nots of God's wisdom she decided that she could help humanity more by serving their financial needs than their spiritual ones. 'The only reason why at the age of forty-four I started my own business was the frustration of not helping people. You have to realise that I chose this vocation over a full-time church service.'

If it is difficult to accept Eva's declared altruism as the true reason accepted image of a business person. But then this is not the only aspect in which the women tycoons differ from their male colleagues. Women have a greater need to mask their motives, even their business ones, with benevolent intentions, simply because this is what has always been expected from them. From selfishness to selflessness, from money for themselves to money for others, the range of motives for the business Amazons' choice of vocations is surprisingly wide.

4 | Why Them?

Confronted with one hundred women who have made it to the top in a man's world, a world which prides itself on its unfeminine qualities, the obvious question to be asked is: Why Them? What did they have that other women lacked? Were they endowed with special gifts or qualifications? Or was it something in their way of life?

Formal and Informal Learning

The education of the business Amazons shows great variations. At one extreme there are those who left school at the age of fourteen, and at the other those who obtained doctorate degrees. On the whole, the American businesswomen had a better formal education than the British ones. While in the USA 86 per cent of the businesswomen had a higher education, in the UK only 14 per cent had similar qualifications.

The gap between the educational standards of the American and the British businesswomen was not only a result of the different educational systems of the two countries, but also of the different attitudes they have towards business. In the USA it is more respectable to be a business person than it is in Britain, so it tends to attract better educated people. Despite the different educational levels of the British and American business Amazons, however, no correlation between their level of education and the level or speed of their success has been found, even in the cases of the 18 per cent of American businesswomen who took degrees in business studies. Likewise no correlation was found between the subjects of their studies and the area of specialisation of their businesses. Of the 66 per cent who majored in arts subjects some ran construction, chemical, and engineering businesses, and out of the few who majored in sciences one ran a candy corporation, another a jewellery business, and a third was in ceramics.

Pre-Business Experience

If the clue to the business Amazons' success is not in their education, might it not be found in their previous occupation or training? This seems plausible, because only 19 per cent of the women started in business without having had any relevant experience. The rest had first-hand knowledge of the specific business or of the industry before they embarked on an independent career. They used their work experience in two ways. There were the 'pirates', who duplicated the exact business formula of their employers and set up in competition, and there were the 'adaptors' who made use of the knowledge they had gained during their employment by adapting it to the requirements of a different commercial product or service.

The pirates

At sixty-seven, matronly and white-haired, Ellie Leonard does not look like a pirate, or even the grandmother of one. Yet Ellie was a classic business pirate. She used the knowledge she gained in someone else's business for her own betterment and to the detriment of her ex-employers.

Ellie started her career at a travel and tour agency as a booking clerk, and finished as the manageress of one of the busiest branches. When she could no longer go out to work because of her young children, she decided to launch out on her own, working from her home. She knew personally all the agency's customers and suppliers as well as its method of operation and profit margin calculations. In other words she knew her employers' business inside out; and with this inside knowledge she contacted their main customers and offered them the same services at reduced prices. Within eighteen months she had taken

—

enough of the agency's business for it to show losses for the first time in many years.

Working for someone, learning all there is to learn, and then leaving in order to duplicate the same operation is a common business practice, which unless in direct breach of contract is usually not illegal. Even morally it is debatable whether such a deed is wrong: why should the skills a worker gains during his employment not be his own? In theory, a majority of the women tycoons considered such piracy a betrayal of confidence; but in practice they overcame their scruples. They had no other choice.

When Rachel Shapiro, after a career of part-time jobs from nursing to home selling, landed herself an evening job selling cosmetics directly to consumers in their homes, it did not take her long to realise that there was money in the formula. Six months of growing frustration with the totally inadequate direction from the company's headquarters convinced her that she could do better. Once the idea of copying her employers' business formula had taken root she continued to work for them with the sole aim of discovering their sources of supply and their methods of costing and pricing.

There is no doubt that business piracy, although no guarantee of success, can shorten the route to its attainment. Had Rachel started a business without using the same products, network of suppliers, and marketing philosophy as that of her ex-employers, she would not have had a company quoted on the stock market within seven years. Yet the achievements of Rachel and Ellie should not be underrated. Despite the apparent ease of pirating a business idea, process or client list, it is a big step from that to the creation of a viable business. The pirates may not have been innovators, but they were builders, which is a rare breed in itself.

The adaptors

These use the knowledge they have gained through their employment but do not set up in direct competition. Of the 81 per cent who use skills and knowledge gained through employment the majority are adaptors rather than pirates. There are three main reasons:

a in order to gain knowledge that is worth pirating one has to be in a top position, and regrettably most female employees are not;

b one needs 'chutzpah', which most women lack;

c women like to be able to think of themselves as nice, and feel uneasy about piracy.

The mundane secretarial jobs in which the majority of women are employed were the base for several of the adaptors' businesses. For six years Lucy Curtis worked as a secretary in a publishing firm before she felt confident enough to set out on her own. In an industry where job titles abound, Lucy was not even an assistant editor. Yet even as a plain secretary she gained sufficient knowledge and insight into the publishing trade to succeed in an industry with one of the highest bankruptcy rates of any.

Thousands of women spend their working days in boring secretarial jobs without realising the mine of information they are sitting on which, if exploited, could open a new and exciting chapter in their lives. Tricia Williams was one of the few who did realise it. After five years as personal secretary to the managing director of a chain of furniture stores she became aware of the opportunities in importing goods from the Far East. Having mastered the intricacies of letters of credit, tariff headings, customs regulations, and eastern negotiations – all without winning a proportionate elevation in her status or salary – she decided to become an importer herself. Within a short time she established such a record of efficiency that her old employers started to use her importing services, for which they were ready to pay far above what she had cost them as an employee doing the same job. Before long she also expanded into the lucrative property business.

The potential of women in commerce is astounding. If only a fraction of the millions of secretaries had nurtured the ambition to become their own boss, they would have been in an unparalleled position to learn every trick of the trade. The number of ex-secretaries in the ranks of the business Amazons is proof that, like a fifth column, they listened, observed, and took the abuse from the never-erring boss, biding their time to break away on their own. Seeing the almighty boss from close quarters, they realised that the legend was usually larger than the man. If he could make it to the top, so could they.

The originators

Evidence of a correlation between the business Amazons' pre-business occupations and the businesses in which they started is to be found in the fact that 81 per cent of them were pirates or adaptors, and only 19 per cent were originators, whose business ideas bore no relation to their previous occupation or training. The small number of originators is in keeping with females' acknowledged cautious character – it is by far the riskier course; but this very caution can be regarded as an asset and not a hindrance in business, which is after all an exercise in making money and not in exploration.

The diversity of the originators can be seen in their deviation from their pre-business occupations. Among them are an internationally acclaimed fashion accessory manufacturer who used to be a university lecturer, a renowned porcelain producer who trained as an optician, a nut and bolt fabricator who used to work as a medical researcher, and a fast food retailer who was once an insurance clerk. There are also an employment agency owner who used to be a comptometer operator before the days of electronic calculators and computers, a farmer who knew only about electrical installations, and a 'fat farm' owner whose only qualification was that she herself was once fat.

As a tribe the business Amazons, like most women, do not seek adventure for the sake of it. They do not get their kicks from gambling or unnecessary risk-taking. That so many of them minimised their risk of failure by starting in business only after studying a similar enterprise is the most convincing proof of their cautious and responsible attitude to business, which is also one of the secrets of their success. Indiscriminate risk-taking in business might be the right material for bestsellers or Hollywood movies but is the wrong stuff for good business management.

Socio-economic Background

A person's socio-economic background is acknowledged as affecting his or her development and behaviour. There is, therefore, good reason to find out whether a correlation exists between those of the business Amazons and their success in business. Of the hundred successful businesswomen the majority were of middle-class origins. More exactly, four came from very poor families, twenty-six from poor families, sixty from comfortable, middle-class backgrounds, and ten from well-off ones. It is interesting to note that the percentage of poor families was disproportionately higher in the USA than in Britain: 18

per cent American compared with only 8 per cent British. This finding
has to be qualified by the fact that several of the American businesswomen, simply because of the age they happened to be, grew up during
the Depression.

The success of those from underprivileged backgrounds is always
fascinating because it reinforces our belief in human ability and
promises all of us a chance. The rags to riches stories of self-made
businessmen have been told before; but those of self-made businesswomen have not, and the lower their origins the more fascinating the
tale. The four who came from very poor homes had all become
fatherless, though at different ages and in different circumstances.
Alice Whitmarsh, who became one of Britain's most successful film
producers, had to leave school at fifteen and go out to work despite
winning a scholarship because her father was terminally ill and her
meagre earnings were needed to help feed her younger brothers and
sisters. She recalls:

> I was mostly doing invoice checking. Horrible jobs. Routine
> things that I used to do from eight in the morning until six or
> seven in the evening. I just earned enough to pay a little bit
> towards the house bill. After three or four years working like this,
> I came up to London to look for work and I found a little
> flea-ridden room in Milton Street, off Russell Square. In the
> morning when I got up I was just covered with bed-bug bites.

Nina Dean, a leading British travel agent and a contemporary of
Alice's, was born a month after her father was killed in the First World
War, leaving her mother with no income and seven children to feed.
She says, 'I do not know a thing about my family's origins. I have never
gone into that because, being the youngest, I never knew my father and
never knew my grandparents. What I certainly knew was that we were
very poor. As long as I went to school my mother got a war widow's
pension, but it was a pittance.'

From such underprivileged backgrounds Alice and Nina managed to
elevate themselves to a position few women have achieved, and they
were not the only ones.

Sara Crandell was spared the agony of mourning her father's death
because she never knew who her father was. She was the illegitimate
daughter of a sixteen-year-old black mother, who left her when she
was four in the care of her North Carolina grandmother in order to
go to Washington for work. In her grandmother's shack where she
grew up they had neither running water nor electricity. Yet despite the

handicaps of being black, illegitimate, poor, and a single parent herself, Sara Crandell managed to build up a $20 million advertising agency.

By the rule that a hungry boxer is a good boxer, the percentage of business Amazons who originated from very poor backgrounds should have been higher, but apparently poverty is not the breeding ground for these women's commercial enterprise. It would seem that under the adverse conditions of poverty the spirit becomes so bruised that confidence in one's ability, which is the essence of entrepreneurship, is extinguished. The fact that four, however, did manage to overcome the handicap of their disadvantaged birth is not only a tribute to them but a living proof of what can be achieved and an encouragement to others.

If the very poor are not entrepreneurial material, neither are the well-off: their contribution to the ranks of business Amazons was a mere ten, of whom nine were American and only one British. Contrary to what might be expected, coming from a wealthy, well-connected family was not an advantage for a woman in business; like those who had nothing, so too those who had everything had to fight their backgrounds. Elizabeth Lyon, the only British business Amazon with an upper-class accent and whose toiletry business has an annual turnover of £20 million, found her origins were actually a hindrance: 'They did not take me seriously. They referred to me as a rich bitch playing shops. I was not expected really to go out to work, and it took me several years before my friends and family realised that I was not just a rich girl in search of an occupation.'

It cannot be dismissed as accidental that the majority of the business Amazons originated neither from poor nor from rich families but from the middle classes, because these are logically the breeding ground for high financial achievers. For children from underprivileged backgrounds financial success is an unattainable dream as they lack an identifiable model that proves such a possibility. For those from highly privileged backgrounds success is no longer a challenge. But a middle-class background is the ideal entrepreneurial hot-house. On the one hand, because the parents have reached a certain financial standing, it proves to the children that financial success is in the realm of the possible; yet on the other, because the parents have not achieved all that can be attained materially, it leaves the children ample, unfulfilled goals without the need to compete with their parents.

Parents' Employment

The business Amazons' pre-business occupation and socio-economic background were not the only factors that contributed to their success; their fathers' employment was another. It was found that the majority, 57 per cent, were self-employed, 53 per cent in business and 4 per cent in the professions. It is abundantly clear from these figures that the chances of a business person's daughter becoming a business person herself are substantially higher than those of an employee's daughter. The figure of 57 per cent becomes even more significant when it is realised that only about 10 per cent of the working population work for themselves and not for others.

It was the father's mode of employment and not the mother's that principally influenced the daughter's choice of occupation because the majority of the mothers, 51 per cent, never worked; 23 per cent worked sporadically or part-time, and only 26 per cent could be considered working women. Among these a mere 10 per cent could be described as career women, while the rest helped their husbands run the business or started to work only after the children grew up. That means that in effect 90 per cent of the daughters were brought up by careerless mothers. In the absence of a working mother, the father's mode of employment had such great influence on the daughters that even when he failed as an entrepreneur it did not deter them from setting out on their own.

Sonia Kaplan is the expansion-minded owner of the $100 million mail order business which she started some thirty years ago, and with whose achievements she is still not content. Although business was what she was brought up on, her father failed in every venture he tried. At the beginning he had a negligée business which folded, after which he went into men's suiting; when that also failed he returned to negligées; and only when this business collapsed did he admit defeat, becoming a salesman who hankered for the days when he could be a boss once again. A new chance came during the war when he tried to alleviate the scarcity of zippers by removing them from old clothes and reconditioning them. Sonia says: 'I remember working there on Saturdays, always having a bad throat from all the filth of the old clothing. It was disgusting.' Yet despite the depressing memories Sonia chose the same harassed life style, lacking in security, that she had seen at home.

—

The zipper business was not the last of her father's enterprises. The end of the war saw the end of that business. Next came a small leather goods business, which was followed by making camera cases. When Japanese competition creamed off the profits from this product he switched to expensive handbags. 'He tried. He tried so hard it was heartbreaking. He just about managed to pay off his mortgage before he died.' Having witnessed the lifelong struggle of such a failed entrepreneur would have scared most children off following a similar course, but not Sonia. On the contrary: 'The more he failed the more I was determined to succeed. That is where my drive came from.'

Sonia was not the only daughter to succeed where her father failed. In Scotland, Rachel Black, now a fashion accessories millionairess, grew up with a father whose business exploits could not even feed or dress his three daughters, yet she too disregarded his failure and adopted the same way of life:

> My father was a very, very unsuccessful businessman. We were in a constant state of financial crisis. Most of the family on both sides were extremely affluent and grew more affluent, whilst we seemed to sink in a hole in the middle. My father was a philosopher. He accepted everything that came. He was a very contented man. Content with very little. He could not understand what was the matter with his three daughters, who were all extremely ambitious.

Watching and analysing failure cannot be as educational as studying success, but there is no doubt that one also learns from negative examples. At the very least, these young women knew what they were letting themselves in for.

The Driving Force

The business Amazons are capable and forceful women yet, unlike their legendary forebears, most of them come from fairly ordinary stock. Only 12 per cent regarded their mothers as the driving force in the family and even fewer, just 5 per cent, regarded the father as the dominant personality. Parents of whom both were reckoned capable amounted to a tiny 3 per cent of the sample. On the whole the women

—

tycoons' home environment did not provide strong models to emulate. Given the rarity of mothers and even more so of fathers who managed to gain their daughters' admiration, the few who did, deserve closer investigation. Certain particular characteristics in their parents attracted their daughters' respect and admiration. In the mothers the daughters admired their drive and ceaseless hard work, and in the fathers they appreciated trust in their ability.

Of the few matriarchal dynasties, Jane Auerbach and Hilary Waldorf are typical representatives. Both were of a third generation of achieving women. Not only were Jane's grandmother and mother working women but, because her father divorced her mother when Jane was a baby and has not been seen since, the household was run by her grandmother.

> My grandmother, terrible snob that she was, used to think and say that anyone who did not work outside the home as well as inside the home was lazy and incompetent. I was never told in so many words that women had to be independent and earn their keep. I just never thought that it could be any other way, because that was the only way of life I knew. My grandmother worked. My mother worked. I would not have wanted it any other way.

The value of tradition should not be underestimated. A woman who comes from a family where the mother worked out of conviction and not merely out of necessity would in most cases tend to follow the same pattern, chiefly because it is easier than rebelling against it. The majority of the businesswomen in this study needed to be rebels, because they did not come from traditions of achieving females and had to pioneer the way.

Despite her statement that she emerged 'from a line of tough broads' Hilary's demure appearance, a little lady in a black dress and white collar, did not reveal it – nor would one have guessed that she was head of a large chemical works. Her tough, matriarchal lineage began with her widowed grandmother who, having lost most of her possessions in a chance fire, left Kentucky in 1906 and came to California. With the little money she had managed to salvage from Kentucky she started buying up properties, and through shrewd business dealings managed to put five of her children through Stanford University. Property dealing attracted several of the women magnates' mothers, as it belongs to the less demanding of entrepreneurial pursuits, and may readily be combined with motherhood and housekeeping. Nina Dean's mother, a widow with seven children, was another one saved from poverty by dealing in property. Lacking financial resources, she used to buy dilapidated houses, move into them, renovate them herself, re-sell them at a small profit and move on. 'She was a very remarkable woman. She died when she was eighty-four. She was painting a wall and fell off a ladder and broke her hip. She was very independent.'

Most daughters of capable mothers felt that their mothers were held back by their fathers and social taboos. Hilary Waldorf's father was an invalid. Nina Dean's stepfather was an unambitious trucker. As for slimming tycoon Doris Smith's father, although a hard-working man who cared for his family, he lacked his wife's drive:

> My father started his married life as a barrow boy in south London after having been unemployed during the Depression. He was a man of a great sort of love, he wanted his family to have the best, so he always worked hard. At the time they lived in two rooms but he wanted his wife and daughters to have a house, because he had been an orphan. He became a plumber, worked very hard and got it. Then came the war. When he returned home my mother wanted him to become a shopkeeper. My mother was the driving force at home. My father only wanted his family to be happy and my mother was a little restless in that. She always wanted something different to happen. She was a woman of great excitement. It was she who decided that they would have their own business, and my father said that he would have a shoe shop, because even if there was another Depression everybody had to have some shoes. My mother thought about a sweet shop or grocery shop, but he said no. Shoe shops did not appeal to my mother, so they had to compromise and they found a little hardware shop and bought that. And then they bought another one. If my father had been a man of ambition they would have got further because my mother had some drive and my father had this dedication to everything he did.

Capable women who, because of their biological and social obligations, are restricted to fulfilling themselves through their husbands are likely to become pushy wives. Alice Whitmarsh's father, who had no aptitude for business, was pushed into it by her mother who had no choice but to pin her salvation on her husband's efforts in the outside world. And he, as if to take his revenge for her constant pushing, kept going bankrupt time and again. So, having failed with her husband, she devoted her energies and ambitions to her five children. Alice remembers her:

> My mother was a most fantastic woman whom I admired enormously. She brought up five children while working the whole time. She used to sew and I would come home and she would be sitting there working day and night to make enough money to support us. She was determined that we were going to do better. She pushed us to take scholarships. She herself left school when she was twelve and had virtually no education but she taught me to read and write before I went to school, and I was the youngest of five. My mother made us. Without her we would not have had a chance.

Mothers like Alice's were in a minority. Forceful fathers were even rarer. It can only be concluded that in the case of the business Amazons it was their parents' lack of forcefulness that contributed to their daughters' eventual success.

Grooming for Success

Behind every champion is a trainer whose role is both as physical coach and spiritual mentor. He supervises the progress of the future champion's skills and watches over his state of mind, for every good trainer knows that the champion's belief in his ability to win is a crucial ingredient for success. But physical strength and agility alone do not count for much in the world of champions.

Unlike most champions, the business Amazons had to manage without any such training for success. Usually parents are the first to realise their child's potential but in the case of the women in our study only 23 per cent of parents expected their daughters to be achievers. The majority were content to see them obtain only basic secretarial skills or settle straight into the routine of family life.

It is natural for parents to want their children to lead a happy family life. Yet with sons they do not let their expectations rest at that. From them they expect more than a nondescript job leading to the cul-de-sac of marriage and fatherhood. The low expectation from daughters was less marked in families without sons where the parents were broad-minded and the daughters capable. Then the daughters received similar encouragement to that given to boys. Nevertheless, despite the high percentage of business Amazons from all-daughter families, only 23 per cent of these had been encouraged to become achievers – a sign of the deep-rooted belief that a woman's place is in the home. As for the fortunate minority who were encouraged to become achievers, they had no doubt that this contributed to their attainments. Patterns and sources of encouragement varied from family to family. In a very few mixed-offspring families, encouragement was offered to daughters as well as to sons. Niki Summers, who has made her fortune in cosmetics for blacks, came from such a rare family:

> We were just expected to be terrific. There was just no question, you had to perform, so you did. That was the way it was. We learned as kids that there wasn't anything that we couldn't really tackle and that there wasn't anything you couldn't do, and that there was nothing we shouldn't do. So I think that was maybe the start. The inculcation that if you want to do something you can do it.

Contrary to the common belief that children resent being pushed to perform by their parents, the business Amazons who were groomed for success did not resent it – even when it involved mothers who wished to relive life through their success. Grooming a daughter for success does not necessarily mean sermons about women's rights and their place in society; it can manifest itself in old-fashioned parental sacrifices which can often mean more than words. Film maker Julie Karr's mother was a simple, unpretentious Scotswoman who knew nothing of feminism. What she did know was that she wanted her daughter to have a more fulfilling life than her own and she had absolute belief in her:

> There is nothing that impresses a child more than her parents' belief in her. My mother never told me her designs for me but she gave me the feeling that I was destined for greater things than just getting married, and for this I am grateful to her. My mother did not work as such, but in order to supplement the income she took in lodgers. When they sent me on a top secretarial course I had to be funded privately; they could not afford it, but she got a part-time waitressing job and paid for it.

Among the minority of parents (23 per cent) who displayed belief in their daughters' abilities were also several sonless fathers who developed unique relationships with their daughters. Lionel Gouldwin,

Lena's father, was one of them. Her mother died during Lena's birth and her father, a carpenter who never remarried, brought her up on his own. His love for his only child was unlimited and, unable to shower her with possessions, he compensated with unbounded trust in her abilities: 'My father fully expected me to be the first woman president of the US.'

Growing up with the acknowledgement of one's abilities from the people who matter most, one's parents, is a great incentive and a tremendous strengthener of character. Stevie Frederick attributed her ability to raise three children, to gain a university degree, and to become an electronics tycoon, all while struggling as a single parent, to her father's high expectations of her. Out of his four daughters he singled out only her, and this despite the fact that she was neither the eldest, who is customarily the responsible child, nor the youngest, who is often the most indulged. She was not conspicuously brighter than her sisters, nor physically stronger; yet it was her that he selected. This feeling of having been 'chosen', and of having it in her to succeed, sustained Stevie through the difficult times. For years she tried to work out why it was she had been favoured; then it dawned on her that it was because of her name. 'My father referred to me as "Stevie my boy" and his expectations of me were tremendous. He did not expect anything from his other three daughters, just from me.'

To those who might wonder what there is in a name, Stevie Frederick would explain: 'A lot. Everything.' From her background of low-paid skilled workers, where women went out to work only because the husbands did not earn enough, daughters were no great asset. Her father was a press setter and her mother a dispatcher for a building contractor. 'Like most fathers,' she says, 'my father wanted a boy very much. They always do.' When the first daughter came along he was disappointed but not despondent. They gave her a typical girl's name, Rose-Ann, and that was that. But when the second child, who was intended to be the last, turned out to be a daughter too, Stevie's father gave up his aspirations for a son, named her Stevie, and at least half-consciously pretended that she was the son he did not have. Quite deliberately he brought up Stevie to become a tomboy. 'It was me who was expected to battle for my sisters with the neighbours' kids. It was me who was consulted about how to treat the others or what to buy.'

In her youth she hated the role her parents imposed on her, as well as her name. 'I wanted to be called Cathy, because I felt that it was a nice girly name. Alas, I was Stevie. But who knows what would have happened to me had I been named Cathy?' She would probably have become like her three sisters – the eldest is a dentist's receptionist and the other two (conceived unintentionally) are housewives. 'I don't think they are very happy. Most probably not less happy than most women. But I would have hated it. It would have been the end of me.'

To those who might think a tomboyish upbringing would confuse a girl's sexual identity, the examples of Stevie Frederick and Denise Philips are reassuring. No only did they keep their feminine identity, but they reinforced it with the strength and confidence that their male-orientated upbringing gave them. Denise's father was a lonely person to whom a family of his own meant a lot. He was adopted by a mother who died shortly after his adoption and was brought up by a succession of housekeepers and stepmothers. When in his mid-forties he married, his choice was a woman of thirty-six and it took them six years before they conceived Denise. She explains: 'I made his first real family. Nothing I would do was ever really wrong in his eyes. He would always find a good reason for me having done it. But he did expect me to do quite a lot for him as well. I was always with him on the farm. He used to take me on the back of his motorcycle and be proud that I was not scared.'

By the time her brother was born four years later, the relationship between father and daughter had already been cemented and the arrival of the son did not alter Denise's special status as her father's favourite, especially as the newborn was a sickly child who did not walk until he was five. 'Consequently father just built everything on me. Being his favourite, I never wanted to let him down.' Her subsequent success as the owner of a chain of secretarial agencies owes a great deal to his faith in her.

Most parents who groomed their daughters for success did not envisage any particular field of achievement like teaching or medicine, but gave them general encouragement. An exception was Elizabeth James's parents, who wanted their daughter to become a film star and were not ready to consider anything else, not even when she gained her doctorate in philosophy. Elizabeth's parents belonged to America's poor whites. 'We were so poor that we did not have a television set until I earned enough money to buy one. We were so poor that for the first couple of years when I started earning money, I used to spend most of my time in the supermarket buying food, because we had always so little at home.'

Being so poor that even in the land of endless opportunity they had lost their faith in their ability to improve their lot, it seemed to them that Hollywood stardom was their daughter's only salvation. So they prepared her to become a film star. To her parents' dismay she only wanted to be a scholar. Eventually, the long-legged, blonde cabaret performer completed her BA with distinctions, followed it with an MA in psychology and a doctorate in philosophy and set out on her own to become a venture capital consultant with branches all over the States.

Yet despite her parents' resentment ('They didn't talk to me for two years after I had got my PhD, because I gave up show business . . .') and the obstacles they put in her way, Elizabeth claims that while she did not favour the area of success they had chosen for her, it was the fact that they motivated her for success in one medium that gave her confidence to succeed in another.

Being groomed for success is not an absolute requirement – the fact that 77 per cent of the business Amazons managed without it proves the point – but it certainly helps.

Lack of Encouragement

The 77 per cent who were not groomed for success but nevertheless achieved it did not feel greater satisfaction for having succeeded without parental encouragement. On the contrary, most of them actually resented it. The lack of encouragement did not take the form of active opposition but of indifference, which is the worst form of discouragement. The most surprising thing was that this took place even in families where the mothers had already established themselves as career women. Hilary Waldorf, a university graduate whose mother and grandmother were both businesswomen, remarks: 'There were not any expectations that I should have a career beyond finishing college. It was not popular.' Publicist Phyllis Rota, an economics graduate whose mother was a working partner in her husband's successful enterprises, was discouraged in a more subtle way: 'Most of the hammering was about my duty to my parents. What they expected me to do for them, but not what they expected me to do for myself.'

Such indifference from career mothers towards the future of their bright daughters is a sad reminder that it takes longer than a generation to change attitudes. It took property dealer Tricia Williams forty-six years to convince her parents, and in particular her mother, who was a nurse before she married her physician husband, that as she was not going to get married her own earning power was of the utmost importance. 'Once they ceased viewing me as a source for more grandchildren, they suddenly realised that I was achieving other things – as important as a family. They never really thought about me in any context except that of a wife and mother.'

Tricia's parents like most parents were prepared to entrust their daughter's future to the hands of a stranger, their as yet unknown husband. The irony in their reading of the future was that in the end it was Tricia and not her brother, who became the big earner and it was he who turned to her for financial help. 'My mother still looks at me in total amazement. She just cannot believe that I have made it.'

Not all daughters took their parents' distrust of their potential as philosophically as Tricia. Others, such as Harriet Hartfield, were deeply hurt by it. Harriet was the talented only child of a successful father. She played the flute and the piano and had her first drawing exhibition when she was twelve. Yet, despite her being an only child and exceptionally bright, her parents did not expect much from her. 'What they wanted me to do was to have an education, get married, and be a mother.' Because of this she blames them for her early marriage at the age of nineteen and its failure after six years, leaving her with two tiny children. 'Had they given me the confidence that first and foremost I was a capable person, and not just an object for marriage and motherhood, I would not have got married so early.'

Their lack of trust in her abilities was astounding. Even when she became an architect and supervised her own construction team, she did not manage to impress them with her talents. 'My father did not even know what I was capable of doing until five years ago, when I was remodelling a health club in the street where he lived and he kept on coming and watching me directing large teams of tough construction workers. It was not until then that he really understood what I was doing.'

What hurt Harriet most was that her father could not be dismissed as a simpleton. He was an attorney and a wide-awake entrepreneur who recognised talent and ability when he saw it, except in his own daughter. When he decided to sell his hospitals in order to retire, he did not even consider offering his only daughter the chance to take them over. 'He did not think of bringing me into the business although he knew I was fascinated by it. It simply did not occur to him that a daughter could run his creation as well as he did. By the time he started to understand what I was capable of doing it was too late. The most difficult years were already behind me.'

At the age of twenty-five Harriet got divorced and for thirteen long years she brought up her children while building up an architectural business. Only then, when she had achieved stature in her own right, did she remarry. By the time her father was awakened to her ability she no longer needed his recognition, and the relationship that had deteriorated when she was thirteen, had when it had dawned on him that he only had a daughter and not an heir, could not be restored.

Harriet's parents were not the only ones who wished to see their daughter settle into married life as early as possible. There were similar reports from many of the business Amazons, particularly the Americans. Yet despite these parents' low expectations from their daughters they did encourage them to obtain a good education. This contradiction can be explained as follows: first, by ensuring their daughter's education the parents could comfort themselves that as a last resort, if their daughters failed to find a husband, got divorced, or became widowed, they would be in a position to support themselves; and second and even more important, the easier marketability of an educated daughter, who would not jeopardise the progress of an ambitious husband, or the future of bright offspring.

Wishing a daughter to be happily married and have children is not a crime. What is wrong is elevating this wish to become a woman's *raison d'être* rather than an incidental benefit. Printing millionairess Jennifer Durham's mother considered her daughter a failure, not because she was stupid or could not earn her living, but because she failed to find a husband. Moreover, she was less concerned with Jennifer's happiness than with her own humiliating status as the mother of a spinster. The refusal to consider the daughter as a person, rather than merely a female whose success is measured by her matrimonial achievements, was the cause of many of the women tycoons' late awakening to their abilities.

In contrast to many top female executives and politicians who have made it in a man's world, and who take the view that other women could do the same if they really wanted, the business Amazons were more charitable and attributed the difficulties facing ambitious women, not to their lack of resolution, but to the lack of encouragement from their parents.

—

The Feminine Factor

In trying to understand why it was that the particular women in this survey made it to the top and not others, various factors have been investigated: factors such as pre-business occupation, socio-economic background, parents' employment, driving force in the family, etc. which are also determinants in the business success of men. But unlike men, women are affected by two additional factors which, because they relate to their femininity, are here grouped together and referred to as the 'feminine factor'. They comprise the status of the daughter in the family, and the timing of the business start in relation to biological and social obligations. These factors, which have no true equivalents in a businessman's career, are crucial to a businesswoman's, because unlike her male counterpart her business activities have to fit in with her biological and social functions as wife and mother.

Status in the family

The status of the business Amazons in their families is here examined under three headings: the size of the family; the ratio of female to male children; and seniority.

Family size

Children from small families have been observed to become higher achievers than children from large families. The family size of the women in the survey is not significantly related to this finding since just 50 per cent and not an actual majority of them came from small families with only one or two children. More exactly, 17 per cent were from one-child families and the remaining 33 per cent from families with two. Obviously in such families, which might have one or two daughters, or one son and one daughter, the females were never in a minority.

Sex ratio

What was found to be more significant than the small size of a family was the sex ratio of the offspring. In a family of no matter what size, where there are no sons or they are in the minority, the daughter or daughters have a better chance of becoming high achievers. This is supported by the fact that 42 per cent of the businesswomen came from families that had no sons at all, and a further 27 per cent were from a majority of daughters, making a total of 69 per cent with a majority of female offspring. An additional 20 per cent of the families had an equal distribution of male and female siblings, which meant that the daughters were not in the minority. Only in 11 per cent of the families was the number of daughters lower than the number of sons. Thus 89 per cent of the millionairesses were the product of families without male numerical dominance. These overwhelming findings confirm that where the ratio of male to female siblings in the family is low, the females have a better chance of becoming successful.

Of the various permutations of family structures without a majority of male children – the all-daughter family, the equal son and daughter family, and the minority son family – women from the all-daughter family have the highest chance of succeeding because parents without sons are forced to change their preconceived ideas about stereotypical male and female roles.

In practice the absence of sons meant that at the basic level of everyday family life, where the first differentiation between male and female offspring took place, the daughters were not discriminated against. Consequently they were more likely to rebel against discriminatory treatment when they came across it in the outside world. Although this has not turned these women into ardent feminists, it has enabled them to aim at higher goals.

Sonless parents have to take into account the eventual reversal of the child-parent dependency roles, when ageing parents begin to depend on the adult offspring whom previously they supported. Then it will be their daughters who are their support in old age. Well-justified concern at having one day to depend on one's offspring causes such parents to assess their daughters for their capabilities, not merely for their decorative appearance or pleasant nature. In the case of Dorothy Harper Townsend, now an importer of household goods, and Doreen Hartman, supermarkets owner, the absence of sons caused the fathers to entrust the running of their businesses to their daughters. Although a transfer of business interests to a daughter is rare even in all-daughter

—

families and often takes place only as a last resort, it is unheard of where there are sons. If there exists a case where a father entrusted the management of a sizeable business to his daughter in preference to his son, one can only assume that the son must either have refused the offer, or have been mentally or physically handicapped. Doreen Hartman comments: 'Had I been a son it would have been the natural thing for me to do after college, to enter my father's business with a view to taking it over when the time came. But being a daughter, I was called in only when the business was doing so badly that I could not do worse even if I tried.'

Women are known to be their own worst enemies, chiefly because of their low self-esteem. But in the sonless families they have the best chance to develop self-appreciation because at least within the family there is no male rival. The fact that 42 per cent of the business Amazons emerged from such all-daughter families is proof of how important this is.

Where daughters were in the majority and sons in the minority (27 per cent) relationships between parents and daughters were not as clear-cut as in the all-daughter families, because the fact that parents had a male heir became an important determinant in the attitudes towards their daughters. When, for example, the father was a successful businessman who wished to perpetuate his life's creation, it was the son and not the daughter who became his automatic successor, regardless of his talents which in any case could not be properly assessed at the tender age when the father had made up his mind about the succession. This preference for sons is not specific only to wealthy fathers, but applies also to ordinary people without empires to dispose of. Such people value their sons more than their daughters if only because of the age-old expectation that it is the sons and not the daughters who will support their parents financially in old age.

Regrettably there is some validity in this belief, because until recently women had no independent earning power, and therefore could not be relied upon in this way. These fears of old age and dependence should not be underestimated, for they certainly affect their plans for their children. It is common to plan in the medium term for their daughters' future, usually ending with marriage; but their plans for their sons do not stop there. Even the most loving parents differentiate between the criteria they use in the planning of their sons' and daughters' future. They can visualise her on her graduation day, but him when he receives his professorship. They might see their daughter as an attorney, but it is the son whom they see as a Supreme Court judge. These are not bad parents who consciously elevate one child over another but practical, down-to-earth parents who accept and bow to the social and biological demands that await their daughters. Every day they see one bright, promising girl after another settle down to domesticity, dispelling any dreams her parents might have had for her. Not wanting to be disappointed, they therefore prefer not to expect from their daughters as much as from their sons.

Despite this, and although females from majority-daughter families are less likely to become tycoons than those from all-daughter families, they are more likely to achieve it than those from equal son and daughter families and from minority daughter families. This is so because they benefit from the advantage of their numerical superiority which, like all quantitative superiorities, means that although the individual can be ignored or suppressed, the group is a force to be reckoned with. As a group they can stand up to parents' favouritism towards sons and demand their due share of love, attention and financial resources, which in modern families they do not hesitate to do. Sisters have been wrongly depicted as more disloyal and jealous of each other than brothers. This is not borne out by facts because, as is often the case with young children, sex identity is the most common basis for early friendships. Little girls usually play with other little girls, and not with little boys. Even where jealousy might exist between sisters, in the face of a common enemy, whether this is a brother or anyone else, they are as likely to join forces as boys would be.

As already observed, families where daughters are in a minority are the least likely to produce business Amazons; a bare 11 per cent of the sample came from such a family. Here, daughters are usually treated either with the care reserved for delicate china dolls or with the contempt displayed towards inferior beings. Neither of these two attitudes breeds achievers. The 'china dolls', intelligent as they may be, are too fragile to take the knocks encountered in the climb towards success, and the 'inferior beings' have lost that most vital requisite for high achievement, self-confidence. Yet, despite the sterile climate that minority-daughter families provide for future businesswomen, as in all life there are anomalies, and even this infertile ground has managed to produce a few of our sample.

Seniority

This study bears out the findings of previous studies, in which the majority of high achievers were found to be the eldest children in the family, and 57 per cent of the business Amazons were firstborn children. In practical terms, what the facts about a woman's status in the family indicate about a woman's chances of becoming a tycoon is that the eldest daughters of small, all-daughter families have the best chance to make it in business.

Biological and social obligations before business start

Men and women exist in a culture which both explicitly and implicitly trains each sex for its well-defined role. Girls get married; boys get jobs. Women bear children; men provide for them. The social and biological roles allocated to females and males are clear cut. Despite the mounting concern about the changing roles of the sexes, the transformation has not yet taken place. There are a few exceptions, but on the whole, voluntarily or involuntarily, most women succumb to their biological and social obligations. Even most of the millionairesses questioned followed this established pattern and embarked on their careers only after having discharged these obligations.

The data in support of this observation are conclusive. Only 12 per cent started in business before they got married, the remaining 88 per cent afterwards. Only one quarter of the married ones (22 per cent of the whole sample) started in business before they had children, and the remaining three-quarters (66 per cent) did so only after fulfilling their biological duty to procreate.

These facts prove that despite their eventful commitment and success, they were first and foremost women and not career-minded persons. They were loyal to their biological functions and, like most other people, considered marriage and childbearing of greater import-ance than business or other career activities. Where they differed from other women was that they distinguished between their biological and social obligations. Thus they accepted their allotted biological role of childbearing, but not the social one of minding that usually accom-panies it. Once their children grew up or suitable supervision was arranged for them, they started in business. Although this route of complying with their biological duties before embarking on a career worked for them it is a risky one, because by the time most women have raised their children they have become too tame to compete in the outside world and find that they can no longer make the grade.

The safer way to combine motherhood and a business career is to establish oneself in business before getting married, or at least before

—

having children. By following this route the businesswoman ensures a financial base for herself and her children and on their arrival is able to maintain the support team of housekeeper and minder that are required if she is to resume her career without depriving her husband and the children of her attention. The few business Amazons who followed this route were convinced it was the best way. Indeed Lena Gouldwin could not envisage any other. When at the age of twenty-nine she had her first child, she had already earned enough to afford the nanny and housekeeper who enabled her to combine work with child rearing. Eleanor Michaels went even further. She claimed that had she not succeeded in her career in cosmetics she would not have become the good mother she is: 'Before I took upon myself the greatest obligation of them all, having children, I knew that I had to be a fulfilled, unfrustrated person.'

By starting in business before having children, these women managed to omit from their lives the hellish chapter of bringing up children on a shoestring, as well as the more arduous one of freeing themselves from the shackles of family life. Having managed to bypass these dismal struggles, Sally Harper discovered that bringing up children was fun. By the time she had them her employment business was established and she was spared the difficult choice between children and career. She could also afford help in the house, and as a result she enjoyed bringing up her children.

A business owner, in contrast to an employee, can arrange her timetable to suit her needs. When Sue Heathcote decided to get married and have children at the age of thirty-five after fourteen years as her own boss, she could afford to take time off and stayed at home. And when, after four months of full-time motherhood, she realised that it was not what it had been made out to be, her catering business was still there awaiting her return. After that brief experience of undiluted motherhood she organised her life in such a way that both the business and her two children received adequate attention without sacrificing one for the other.

In contrast to the 'established way', this 'right way' is not one women opt for naturally. Those who follow it require the courage to question the established order of things and fight off the accepted wisdom that their chances of marriage diminish with age and independence, and that the best childbearing years are between eighteen and twenty-six. The fear of being left on the shelf, coupled with the fear of difficult pregnancies later in life, are so potent that even today when in the western hemisphere laws have eliminated most of women's inequalities, the majority follow the 'established way' and put the fulfilment of their biological obligations before that of their own selves. Let no one make the mistake of claiming that the two are the same. For, as a man's biological function is only a small part of his essential being, so also is a woman's.

5 | The Ingredients of Success

Success is an elusive phenomenon and, as there exists no universal formula for its achievement, anyone is free to pursue it. The favourable origins of some business Amazons, who came from majority-female, middle-class, self-employed families, were not sufficient to guarantee their eventual success, but did improve their chances. What actually brought them success was not their inherited or professional background but their own personal contribution to the enterprise.

Success requires active cultivation, or it wilts before it starts to bud. Success has to be desired and dreamt about. It also has to be worked at, hard. Endless formulas may be drawn up showing that each successful person has their own unique recipe for success but knowing the ingredients that went into a recipe is not enough to duplicate the result. One also needs to know quantities and method. For one woman, hard work mixed with integrity and a sprinkling of 'guts' worked miracles; while another may swear by an equal mixture of tenacity and leadership, with a trace of good luck and good health.

If it is impossible to prescribe individual recipes for success, it is at least possible to acquaint all women with the essential ingredients. Here they are, in the order of the frequency with which they were mentioned:

1. hard work
2. tenacity
3. motivation
4. a way with people
5. leadership
6. good business management
7. integrity
8. guts
9. good health
10. common sense
11. luck

—

Hard Work

Eighty per cent of the business Amazons identified hard work as the most important element of their success. Investment broker Elizabeth James, who was raised to be a film star, puts it like this:

> I don't see how anyone can do it without working very hard, unless they have some other kind of financial support from somewhere else. Unless you just really lucked out.

On a scale of importance measured from one to ten, 10 per cent evaluated hard work as rating eight; 70 per cent as ten; and the remaining 20 per cent went off the top of the scale and gave it ten and a half, eleven or twelve.

By hard work the majority of the businesswomen meant total commitment to the business, with priority over leisure or private life. Brokerage millionairess Adele Benn: 'You have to be able to work all the hours that God made you.' Precision-engineering magnate Lois Jane Apple: 'It goes with the territory, it has to be twenty-six hours a day.' This sentiment was commonplace.

To ordinary mortals such a life might seem intolerable but the business Amazons do not separate work from life and therefore considered it no hardship. For Valerie Reynolds, a seventy-two-year-old childless widow who took over the ownership and running of her husband's telecommunications business at the age of sixty-five, hard work was a joy – infinitely preferable to spending her days on the beach or at the beautician: 'If you are enjoying it you can work long hours. Last year, except when I was away, I worked on average twelve to fourteen hours a day. I come from the old school.' Health tycoon Lisa Collier's similar work routine ought to be mentioned: she is a married woman with three teenage children but that doesn't stop her: 'Three times a week I am here at seven in the morning to teach class and get the whole place motivated, and I get out of here at six-thirty at night. Sometimes I work until midnight, because I have to work out projects that are due the next morning.'

The business millionairesses all accepted long hours as an integral part of being one's own boss. The once overweight housewife Doris Smith, now a keep fit expert, explains:

> If you want a nine to five job you have got to work for somebody

else, where at five o'clock you can close the door and go home. I have got a job that involves me seven days a week. In addition I have to be ready to sort out things on the phone twenty-four hours a day. If you think about a telephone call as work then you are handicapped to start with.

It is notable that the 80 per cent of women tycoons who mentioned hard work as the chief ingredient of success valued it even more than expert knowledge. The old adage, 'The harder I work the luckier I get' seems to have a lot of life in it yet.

Tenacity

Tenacity, which the women magnates saw as the ability to hang on when the going was bad, was considered the next most important ingredient after hard work. Cathy Simmons Randall explains:

By endurance I mean the ability to work and stick to it. Consistency. It is not just a flash of an idea but where you are ten years later. This is particularly true for the restaurant business, where restaurants have an average life of six months in New York. There are something like 30,000 restaurants including coffee shops. It is one of the businesses that usually go bankrupt because they are usually undercapitalised and everybody thinks they just need tables and chairs, and an atmosphere. If you are not tenacious you just go under.

It is all part of that total commitment voiced here by Marion Little, conferences promoter: 'You start a business and you really have to commit yourself to it. I told my husband once that if it was between him and the business it was the business, and I meant it. I am really committed to it.' Such women do not easily give up.

Motivation

Hard work and tenacity on their own are not enough: one also needs motivation – the will to succeed. Stevie Frederick, electronics magnate, says: 'I would have never gotten here without self-motivation. It is essential. You take away knowledge and skills and you can still be a successful person. You take away self-motivation and intelligence and you cannot succeed.'

Hired executives are motivated by rivalry with their peers. Owners have no such criteria to measure themselves against. Even their financial achievements cannot be compared with those of other owners because such information is not disclosed by private companies. So owners talk about self-motivation, about doing things well for their own sake. Travel agent Ellie Leonard puts it like this: 'It is the need on your own behalf to do a good job. The sole satisfaction of having done something better than anyone else. It is knowing within yourself that you are doing a good job.'

A Way with People

The business Amazons believed that in order to succeed one had to have 'a way with people', an ability to communicate one's ideas and wishes so that they were accepted by others. These others were not only employees, but also customers, suppliers and anyone else that could be instrumental to the business's success. Rachel Black: 'The most important thing is how to handle people. Whether they are your suppliers, staff, partners, or husband . . . '. Kate Ullman: 'One of the most important things is how you handle people, because if you can't they fall away from you and you get nothing accomplished. Sally Harper: 'Being able to treat everyone that you deal with with the same attitude. The girls are as important to me as the clients are.'

Of all the people who have to be handled well in order to guarantee a business's success, the employees are the most important. Without them there is no business. Many bosses have lost the race because they did not understand that to run a business one needs the good will of one's staff. For Celia Daly, furniture millionairess, the ability to handle people expressed itself in good teamwork, and the team included the boss. Here she portrays the sometimes delicate balance between employer and employee:

> Obviously you cannot have a team unless you are part of that team. If I want to be direct, and I do, then I have to expect that my

people will also have a right to say what they think. At the same time one has to remain single-minded because otherwise you have twenty-five people running the business and that does not work.

Having a way with people used to be women's only way to achieve anything because, being second-rate citizens themselves, they could not very well bully people into obedience, but had to manipulate them by understanding their weaknesses and strengths. For generations men have despised this manipulative ability and considered it a manifestation of their weakness. But in the running of a business, where having a 'way with people' is important, this 'weakness' pays dividends and results show that it is usually the manipulator and not the bully who attains better working relations.

Leadership

The needs of a business change with its size and the stage of its development. Growing and larger businesses require a more structured management than small, starting ones. The boss who does everything himself rarely evolves into a big businessman. In order to reach as high as they have, the women tycoons had to learn to delegate and inspire – in other words, to lead. Unlike hard work, tenacity and a 'way with people', leadership does not come easily to women. Even the monitors and the hockey captains of all girl schools find it difficult to lead a mixed group of males and females.

The explanation of why women are not natural leaders is primarily because they do not view themselves as leaders and their upbringing makes it plain why this is so. However, even though most of them have concentrated their talents on the more detailed functions and pride themselves on being perfectionists, the business Amazons have mastered the art of leadership, and they have done so in a distinctly feminine way. It is a style of leadership which is not taught in business schools or leadership courses because men, being in charge of business education, are not aware of its existence – and even if they are, they would probably dismiss it as unscientific. But what matters is not whether the millionairesses' leadership style is scientific or not, but that it works. An example of such a successful female leadership style is the way Lois Jane Apple, the owner of a light engineering company that employs over four hundred people in the state of New York, runs her business. She started it on her own when her four children were still young, without previous training or experience in the field of light engineering. Lois Jane does not look the typical American business-woman, let alone a business Amazon. A motherly-looking woman, she has a soft, unthreatening air, and does not radiate power waves that dazzle those around her. She runs the business according to a purely feminine philosophy – which should not be confused with a feminist philosophy, for it is often quite the opposite. Her view is:

> I can attribute my success to my enjoyment of people. My most important asset is having the right person for the right job. A corporation can grow only on the abilities and capabilities of people in the company. What is the strongest point of being a parent? You have to understand your children and understand that you guide them and you help them, but you do not force them into doing something they do not like. At least I did not. My whole philosophy was to find out the strength of the children and to go in that direction, and I apply the same philosophy to my employees. A person may be hired for one area and we see how he turns out and then move him on to something else. But once we trust him in the job he is left to do it on his own with the least interference.

Besides vision, business leadership is mainly a matter of delegation, which is not only the ability to command others but the wisdom to surround herself with the right people. Valerie Rogers maintains that: 'A business leader ought to surround herself with the best talent she can buy, give them free range, let them develop on their own, and back them up.'

When the Japanese run their industries on similar managerial lines western experts call it 'paternalism', follow it closely with great admiration, and examine the possibility of introducing similar tech-niques into their own problem industries. Yet all the time in their midst there are women who run large industries with a similar philosophy. Unlike the Japanese, they are not used as role models and no one would dream of emulating their management techniques – because, after all, what can one learn from businesswomen?

Good Business Management

For the women magnates good business management consists of three ingredients: business know-how, understanding money, and marketing. Marion Little, conferences organiser, says: 'To succeed you have to have knowledge of what you are trying to accomplish; knowledge of the product and of the service you are trying to sell; and an understanding of where you want the company to go in a year, eighteen months, five years, or ten years from now.'

Know-how

Knowing one's business is not only essential; it is also a never-ending process, especially if one wants to stay at the top. Investment consultant Eva Helsing considers: 'You need to spend a great deal of time always learning more and more. You think sometimes that your brain will just pop open because you put so much information into it. But every time you stuff in another bit of information you immediately know how to use it.'

Understanding money

Business being about money, it is only natural that understanding money is essential for good business mangement. Hotel owner Tricia Bishop says: 'Without understanding figures you cannot be successful unless you are a pure artist.' Understanding money does not mean that one has to be a financial genius, or that one requires financial training, although such training can be useful. Sue Heathcote is no financial whiz kid, but then she is in the catering business, not in offshore funds. What she knows about finance, which is quite a lot by now, she has learnt by trial and error, not through formal education. The uninitiated believe that understanding money is a science. But in most cases it is plain common sense, a quality which even women without financial training have in abundance. As long as one remembers that the bottom line matters more than the figures above it one cannot go wrong. She recalls:

—

98

Understanding money didn't come naturally to me, but over the years I have learnt that it is no good getting excited about some bargain offer that you can get a whole page in the *Standard* for £1,000 unless you are damned sure that it is going to bring in the right amount of bums on the seats in the restaurant. It is also terribly easy to lose sight of things like interest and the time it takes to get the money in. I found with many of our managers that they would have been absolutely delighted to have done £6,000 worth of business that they wouldn't normally have done, but they didn't realise that if you don't get the money in quickly, they might as well not have done the work because it eats up the profit.

To understand the basic elements of business one does not require a master's degree in business studies, nor in accountancy. Only 20 per cent of the business Amazons had formal training in finance; the rest acquired it through experience, 20 per cent by having worked as book-keepers and 60 per cent by not being too inhibited to ask their accountants stupid questions; as Sue says, 'If you pay for a service you can ask as many stupid questions as you wish.'

Marketing

Despite the glamorous mystique that surrounds marketing, and despite the fact that men tend to be marketing directors and women sales ladies, marketing and selling boil down to the same thing: finding a place for a product, service, or capital at a price. It is this ability to find customers for one's product that the business millionairesses considered essential for success. Travel tycoon Lydia Eastern puts it this way:

> The technical person can make something all day long, but if you cannot sell it, forget it. That is what the Japanese are showing us with their trading companies. We can manufacture until the cows come home, but if we can't sell it they beat us. So I think you really need sales skills. I think America does. Sales is a dirty word at school. In the sixties when the protest thing came in, profit became a dirty word too. These were the protesters of the Vietnam war and Jane Fonda, and all the kids in the campuses of

the colleges, so profit became a dirty word. People became very idealistic. They despised selling. This business is all about selling. If you don't sell enough you might as well close shop. It is a very tight business. We have low profit margins. If we do not go out to sell and sell we would be out of business.

Of the three components of good business management, an overall knowledge of the business's functions was considered the most important, salesmanship second, and understanding money third.

Integrity

Contrary to popular belief, business people *are* concerned about their public image and strive to be regarded as honest traders. Some women magnates even went so far as to suggest that without integrity one could not succeed. The importance attributed to this virtue as a requisite for success was such that some even considered it more important than hard work. Denise Philips, British employment agent, was one of these: 'You can work as hard as you like, but if you are crooked you might just as well say goodbye to it. Some people do very well when they are crooked. But one day, their day will come, and they will be finished.' And Sadie Fairweather who made her fortune in sanitation: 'I am a little bit old-fashioned but I still think that integrity is the most important ingredient.'

It is doubtful whether male entrepreneurs of the business Amazons' calibre would attribute their success or any part of it to integrity. Nowadays in industrial countries, business integrity is not left to the discretion of the individual but is enshrined in legislation, so that most business people are honest, whether they want to be or not.

Guts

Sonia Kaplan believes that for success you need guts and, being the owner of a $100 million mail order business which she started on her own, she ought to know what she is talking about.

Guts in business is similar to the guts required for scaling the Eiger or crossing the Atlantic in a single-engined aircraft. It is a matter of risk taking, confidence, and aggressiveness. The only difference is that the cost of failure is at worst the loss of one's livelihood, not of one's life. Hotelier Tricia Bishop says: 'You need a certain reckless inspiration and faith in yourself. In other words you need guts.' Cosmetics magnate Rachel Shapiro: 'You must have a positive attitude. At no time can you say, "Maybe it is going to fail." Even if you have a little fear you have to throw it out of the window, and get on with your goal. You need the guts to believe in yourself.'

Guts lends a romantic aura to its possessors, because it is a quality few people have, particularly women. Even among the women tycoons, where one might expect to find it in abundance, only 12 per cent attributed their success to it.

Good Health

The British computer millionairess Sheila Stevens says: 'You can be as smart as you like but without good health your chances to make it are diminished. There are certain stages in the entrepreneur's development when no matter how much in charge he is, if he goes sick at that critical stage he has had it.' By good health the women magnates meant not merely physical, but also mental health, which had to be of superb quality if one was to withstand the 'tremendously long hours and the tremendous stress', as cosmetics tycoon Niki Summers describes it.

Optimism was considered an essential part of good health. A pessimist would never make it in business even if she worked all the hours of the day. But when a pessimist joins forces with an optimist, as Janet Draper, the engineering millionairess, did with her husband, they made the ideal business partnership. She explains: 'The biggest thing in business is optimism. My husband is the person who if the building burned down would have said: "We will make a million dollars selling charcoal." I would probably be the one to organise it.'

Common Sense

Julie Karr, the British film tycoon, summarises the importance of common sense in this way:

> Business is about common sense and practicality, which means a basic honesty. You have to know what you are good at and what you are not good at. Recognise it and do something about it. You cannot kid yourself and pretend that you are doing something greater than what you actually do. As women were never allowed to delude themselves about their abilities or prospects they have become practical persons out of sheer necessity.

There is no doubt that women are practical creatures. They are also more honest about themselves than men because they have not been allowed to foster any illusions of grandeur. One of the reasons why women are ideally suited to business is that it requires common sense and honest self-assessment.

Luck

Luck as a requisite for success is a controversial issue. Some claim that whatever your merits, if you are unlucky you get nowhere; while others dismiss the need for luck as sheer nonsense and believe in ability and opportunity. To suggest, as it has been, that it is women rather than men who attribute their achievements to luck is to ignore the women tycoons among them, by whom luck was rated the least important ingredient of success.

Not that quite all of them discounted it. Lisa Collier is one of the 30 per cent who believes: 'You have got to have a certain amount of luck.' For years she wanted to open health farms but did not deem the time right. 'I was lucky to hit the right time when executives became conscious of the need for trim figures and exercise. It was luck, because had this change in attitude towards health not taken place, my skills in health education would not have come to fruition.'

Elsa Helsing, an outstanding financier, does not believe in luck. 'Of course I don't believe in luck. It is when preparedness and opportunity get together. If you are prepared you will have the opportunity.' She speaks for the overwhelming majority.

The Androgynous Business Owner

The attributes that the business Amazons considered imperative for success are illuminating because they reveal a mixture of masculine and feminine characteristics. For example, hard work, tenacity, motivation, leadership, and guts are established masculine traits, while a way with people, integrity, a belief in luck, and emphasis on good health would be considered feminine characteristics. As for the remaining identified ingredients for success, good business management and common sense, these would apply to both sexes indiscriminately.

Until recently the predominant view among men and women alike was that top executives had a decidedly masculine profile. Yet despite studies that have indicated a shift away from sex role stereotypes, the prevailing opinion is still that in order to succeed in business in a big way, women have to possess masculine traits. However, the women magnates have attained their success without shedding all their feminine characteristics – which is further proof of the advantages of business ownership for women, and of the error of the view that such virtues as hard work, tenacity, motivation, leadership, and guts are exclusively masculine qualities. Many women who look feminine and feel feminine possess these virtues but they tend to keep quiet about them because they fear the stigma of the virago which is attached to any female who exhibits characteristics that have been (wrongly) considered the monopoly of men.

The age of the androgyne has arrived: women need no longer hide their assertive traits, nor do they have to be ashamed of their caring ones. In business ownership they can combine both. As long as the business is profitable it does not matter whether its owner displays feminine or masculine traits, whether she is too ambitious or too concerned about human relations. The only thing that matters in business ownership is to maintain a viable business.

6 | With Husbands or Without

Unlike their legendary ancestors, most of the business Amazons have found husbands an inseparable part of their existence. When they have them they are keen to keep them, and when they don't, they are keen to find them. As there are still so few women in this position, it is not known whether their lifestyle helps to keep or find a husband. What is known is that modern career women find it difficult to combine a successful marriage with work, not necessarily because of incompatibility with their spouses, but because their career prospects and those of their husbands are often incompatible. Unlike simple homemakers, they cannot just pack up and follow their husbands to wherever their jobs take them, because they have equally important jobs of their own. Nor are they in a position to play nurse to the weary warrior on his return home, because after a day's work they are as tired as he is, if not tireder.

A woman's independent career is definitely not compatible with an institution that has been designed around the dependence of wives on their husbands, and is therefore bound to shake the foundations of that institution unless the couple are prepared to accommodate themselves to the new reality. The majority of women tycoons in this study (54 per cent) have been spared the dilemma of whether to sacrifice a husband for a career or a career for a husband by amalgamating their careers with their husbands' in a joint enterprise. Thus they have managed to combine a top career and marriage without the extensive accommodation that is required by the wives of dual wage earning families. Of the rest, 9 per cent ceased being housewives only after their husbands' death, 7 per cent started in business only after they got divorced, and 7 per cent never married. Thus a total of 23 per cent had no need to accommodate themselves to any men because for one reason or another they were unattached while they became magnates. This leaves only 23 per cent of business Amazons who maintained a career separate from that of their husbands.

Working with One's Husband

It is an accepted modern notion that for the maintenance of a happy marriage each partner should possess a certain amount of 'living space', meaning the opportunity to express and explore different parts of their personality independently from each other. Where couples do not work together this is easily achieved because they are apart for at least eight hours of the day. Consequently it is a common phenomenon for a spouse to be an ogre at work and a lamb at home, or servile at work and a tyrant at home. This schizophrenic behaviour is accepted as the norm and is one reason why the mere suggestion that husbands and wives work together is rejected outright by most couples who fear that a closer knowledge of their spouse might jeopardise an otherwise happy marriage.

Working together is bound to create an interdependence between the partners which if enjoyed can be bliss, and if not can be hell. It is remarkable that 54 per cent of the independent and self-reliant women tycoons opted for such a close relationship with their spouses. What is even more remarkable is that their working relationship had no disastrous effects on their marriage. Although 16.6 per cent of the husband and wife teams got divorced, only 3.7 per cent of them attributed the breakup of the marriage to the business partnership.

Why these strong-willed and independent women chose such a close relationship with their husbands, how they managed it, and how they overcame the inherent pitfalls of a husband and wife team is now examined in detail.

Work division

One of the secrets of a successful partnership is that each partner has a specific area of responsibility and does not tread on the other's toes. Usually such a division of duties will take into consideration the individual talents of the partners. Where women are part of the partnership, other considerations such as their maternal obligations and consequent immobility may well have to be taken into account, and as a result one might expect them to undertake the backroom duties such as finance and administration and leave the more mobile jobs like selling to their male partners.

In the case of the business millionairesses no definite patterns of male and female job allocation were found to exist. It seemed that what determined their work division was a combination of three considerations: their individual talents, which of them started the business, and the age of their children. It was usually the person who originated the business who was concerned with sales and promotion, and the one who joined with finance and administration. Where the couple had young children and the husband was a competent salesman, the wife opted for the backroom jobs; but where the business depended on the wife's selling skills the husband went out of his way to ensure that the children did not interfere with his wife's job.

The Harrises, who owned a 400-employee, London-based coat business, were a couple where the wife looked after the finance and administration and the husband took care of sales. Their case is an example where all three factors played a role in determining the spouses' jobs. The husband, who was an accomplished salesman, was also the one who had started the business and the wife, who was a natural financial controller, happened to have young children at the time. Consequently, as she put it, 'He was the foreign minister and I the chancellor of the exchequer.'

Which of the couple was responsible for which aspect of the business was not necessarily an indication of the power structure in the family. Although the tendency would be to consider the extrovert sales person as more powerful than the administrator, this was not always so where the husband was the salesman and the wife the administrator. Golda Harris, whose husband was their coat business's front to the outside world while she was behind the scenes, felt no less important than he: 'He could sell anything. But I kept the business together. Although I was the backroom girl who saw that the money came in and that the bills were paid, he would not have made the grade except for me.'

Nina Dean, who built up a successful travel business together with her husband and who at seventy, after thirty-seven years in the same business, still runs it jointly with him, found that being in the backroom did not diminish her power and influence. As with the Harrises, the Deans' division of work resulted from the partners' individual talents, the identity of the originator, and the age of the children. To start with, Nina was always interested in finance: 'I have always been good at finances. He cannot sign a cheque.' So becoming the financial director was a natural choice for her. In addition she had two young sons, and the travel business necessitated frequent journeys. Thus the combination of her personal talent for finance, the young sons, and her husband's skills as a promoter dictated that she became the backroom girl and her husband the front man.

, Yet those who mattered to the firm, both employees and suppliers, knew that without Nina there would not have been a business. Indeed, years later when her husband suffered three heart attacks in succession, it was Nina's total understanding of the business that enabled her to take over his areas of responsibility in addition to her own. 'No one who should not have known knew he was ill. I did his job as well as he.' But had she become incapacitated, Harry would have been unable to stand in for her. 'No, he could not do my job. He never took an interest in it. He hates the money side.'

The feeling that without them there would not be a business was not common to all the backroom girls. Dorothy Simmonds admitted that it was her husband's sales efforts and not her administrative ones that made their oil-drilling equipment business. 'If he does not sell the product, then I have no numbers to play with. It is his technical expertise that has made the business grow considerably in the past six years.'

But not all the wives were backroom girls. Lisa Collier is a front woman. She travels and projects her image and personality wherever she believes it might help promote her health farms, and in her absence it is her husband Hugh who stays behind to mind the children and the business.

It is often alleged that strong women can sustain a marriage only with weak husbands. Likewise, it is assumed that where a couple works together successfully, one of the partners must be dominant. When the wife is the backroom girl it is assumed that she is the weaker, but where she is at the front it is taken for granted that he must be. In the case of the women tycoons such assumptions could not be further from the truth.

The Auerbachs, both in fashion goods, are a case in point. Fifty-year-old Jane, who despite her unassertive appearance dominates any gathering within five minutes, is married to a man of the same age who for all his imposing appearance would not initiate a conversation unless spoken to – on the face of it the typical domineering wife with the weak husband. In reality Lewis is not someone who can be pushed

around. Although, true to her nature, Jane boasts about her indispensability – 'I control design, manufacturing, public relations, advertising, and the buying of raw material, and he does more of the finance
and administration' – her staff are convinced that without Lewis, who
puts the brakes on her extravagant business ideas and organises the
smooth running of the business, Jane would already have gone through
several bankruptcies. It is the partners' realisation of how much they
depend on each other's abilities that turns the marriage into an alliance
between equals, not between a strong and a weak partner.

No *private life*

The main problem about working together with one's spouse is the
erosion of the boundaries between working and private life. Business
quarrels become an inhibiting sex factor at night, and sexual impotence
at night is converted into business impotence during the day. Most
couples who do not work together cannot imagine how such a
twenty-four-hour preoccupation with work is possible, because for
them the mere thought of letting their working life spread into their
private life is appalling.

For those who liked it, it did not constitute a problem, and those
who needed a break insisted on a cut-off hour after which business was
not discussed at home. Lisa Collier, who is in the fashionable world of
'fitness', found that talking shop outside business hours enhanced her
social standing and widened her circle of friends: 'My business life
spreads into my private life, but I like it because a lot of my friends are
from my business life and they are such exciting people.' But Harriet
Hartfield, who is in construction with her husband, found that talking
business alienated their friends: 'They tell us that we have become very
boring because that is all we ever talk about now.'

Nevertheless, when an occupation is enjoyable it is natural that its
practitioners should want to extend it beyond closing hours. Dorothy
Simmonds explains:

> Our business life is our private life and our private life is our
> business life. We work most of the time, we talk business most of
> the time. I like it because we really go our separate ways so much
> of the time – as far as our duties lead us to – that we spend a lot of
> time in the evening, in the mornings and on weekends discussing
> and catching up on what the other has been doing.

But working together is more than just seeing each other during the day and talking about work during the evening. It is a twinlike existence, doing virtually everything together, even switching off together like Zelda Main: 'When you have your husband in your business you cannot just switch off on your own when you come home. We make a conscious effort to switch off together.' Denise Philips feels the same: 'If we want to switch off, we must switch off together, otherwise it is impossible. So we go on holiday where we cannot be reached by phone. Otherwise we phone every few hours to check what is happening.'

As long as both partners share the need to live the business twenty-four hours a day, and as long as the switching on and off mechanisms of both are timed identically, it must be great fun for them to work together. But in the nature of things such harmony is not commonplace. Julie Kitson and Rachel Shapiro both have to control their desire to talk business from morning to night, because their husbands are not similarly inclined. Julie says: 'I don't think I can switch off. I have been accused of being a workaholic. Even when I am indoors I am always active. But my husband needs to relax when he comes home. So he potters in the garden.'

Sam Shapiro, Rachel's husband and the financial director of her cosmetics business, feels the same way as Julie's husband. Like him, Sam needs a life away from work. Come what may, a production or financial crisis, unless the sea is rough he reserves Thursdays for fishing. At 10 a.m. he drives his Bentley to Philadelphia Harbour, changes from his dark office suit into angler's rubber boots and wind jacket, and joins his cronies for a voyage into the unknown where he cannot be reached by telephone or telex. After twenty-seven years of marriage Rachel has given up trying to change him and has reconciled herself to the fact that their temperaments differ.

Quarrels

Like all married couples and business partners the husband and wife business teams have their quarrels, but theirs have to be more ritualised and controlled. Unlike normal couples who do not work together, and business partners who are not married to each other, neither of them can return home to a sympathetic spouse and complain about their business partner, or come the next morning to their business partner and pour out their hearts about their spouse. They have to continue seeing each other during and after work and as the business is the pivot of their lives, most of their quarrels revolve around it. Unlike other couples they rarely quarrel about domestic subjects such as an unironed shirt, or which play to see. Their quarrels are usually about expansion, marketing, staff. Expansion seems to be a particularly contentious subject, because it highlights the differences between the partners' characters. Sometimes the expansionist is the wife who is held back by her husband, and other times it is she who tries to hold him back. Julie Kitson says:

> Our quarrels are basically about finance for expansion. I believe that our expansion has to remain at a sensible level without overcommitment, but my husband is less cautious. He has had some super ideas which have been very beneficial, but without me putting on the brakes he would have been out of business a long time ago.

For every example of a cautious wife and an expansionist husband, and there are many, one can provide a reverse one of the aggressive businesswoman and the careful husband. The Colliers are such a couple. Lisa has been the expansionist for whom costs are of secondary importance, while her husband has tried to balance the books after each of her extravagant purchasing trips. She says:

> We quarrel about expansion and expenses. Being the creator of this business I would like to see it grow fast. I am also less practical. My taste is very much more expensive than his. I would spend $4,000 on a wardrobe when I have a TV show. I think it is important for my type of business that I look just right. It is hard for him to see why one has to pay $1,500 for one outfit.

Nina Dean does not have that particular problem, but allows: 'We do have small differences. I am inclined to gamble more than he does. I take risks.'

To start a quarrel is easy; to resolve one without losing face is more difficult. Yet the magnates seemed to have kept their family quarrels under tight control. Being clever women for whom their marriage was important, they did not let their temporary disagreements alter the course of their lives; tough as they were, they did not hesitate to take the initiative in restoring the peace. Janet Draper explains: 'After a quarrel he sulks. So I go up to him and say sorry and tell him that he won, and he replies: "No, it is you who won." But by then we are already talking. The most important thing is not to let him sulk.'

One of the reasons why so many of the business Amazons' marriages have survived the occupational hazards of successful women has been their understanding of the social difficulties that faced their husbands. Iris Williamson, the fast-food millionairess, has been married for thirty-eight years and, although a truly emancipated woman, went out of her way to accommodate her husband's ego because she realised that being married to a successful woman was not easy for a man.

> Our quarrels stem from the fact that too many people give me more credit than I deserve and tell him, 'You really don't have to work, your wife does it all.' It is an ego-thing with him. He gets very disturbed and then tries, in turn, to compensate for it and then to put me down. That is what the argument is about more than anything. Then when I start realising why he is doing this, I just overlook it. Sometimes I do not overlook it and that is when we have an argument.

Unlike most wives the magnates are equal to their husbands, and quarrels between equals seem to lack the bitterness and frustration that accompany the usual domestic quarrels between husbands and wives. Jane Auerbach's quarrels with her husband centre on their basically different temperaments. He is a quiet, placid man who allows her bubbling, earthy personality to dominate their working world and their living environment. In her words:

> He is calmer about things than I am; he tends to allow things to go on longer than I would allow. He tends to allow people to hang themselves rather than do something about it. As I want to do things faster I also want quicker decisions. So our greatest number of arguments come in there. But basically our arguments are never more severe than we could have in public.

It is difficult to decide which of the business millionairesses' characteristics contributed most to the stability of their marriages – their tough constitution, their good nature, or their feminine good sense – for, despite the inevitable rows, nearly all these marriages have survived. Whether it was their constitution that was able to withstand the tension, their easygoing nature which did not take rows to heart, or their good sense that enabled them to see them in perspective, it is a fact that they have managed to keep their disagreements within bounds.

After thirty-five years of joint business and marriage partnership the Benns are old hands at fighting. Adele says:

> The only quarrelling we do is about the business. Very often I say: 'You know something has got to give, because the business will destroy us.' We do not quarrel about anything else. We do not quarrel about money. We do not quarrel about the kids, but we fight like cat and dog over the business. I think it is a shame. But if I don't believe in something I can't; I say: 'Yes, let us do it that way.' If I think it's wrong I dig my heels in and there is nothing that is going to make me compromise.

Naomi, one of the Benns' daughters who works with her parents in their finance business, is used to their rows: 'They have iron nerves. I could not have carried on like them. Both are tough and both want to get their way. They don't seem to mind the quarrelling. They forget it after a few minutes.'

Letting off steam by shouting at each other seems common among the business couples, regardless of their age or social background. Elizabeth Lyon, toiletry magnate, is the only aristocrat in this study and is as likely to scream when she is frustrated as any of her working-class sisters: 'Sheila, my assistant, is used to us. We shout at each other and we have the most frightful rows because we are both extroverts. But they last about three minutes and we forget all about them.' This ability to dismiss rows, to forgive and forget, was common to all the husband and wife teams whose marriages had withstood the difficulties of working together. For Denise Philips, whose accountant husband was also her employment agencies' partner, quarrelling with him was 'fun' because it gave her an opportunity to match her wits against his. Yet to her mother who observed the scenes it was a cause of great concern, because unlike her daughter she belonged to the type of woman for whom a quarrel with a husband invariably meant only one thing, his gain and her loss. Denise recounts:

> Oh, we have some lovely arguments sometimes. It is always to do with business. But we love it. My mother will look and think, 'Oh gosh, they are having an argument, they are rowing.' We will look at her and say, 'Mum, we aren't fighting, we are only arguing. We are allowed to argue like this, it is only business.' And she'll say, 'Well, it's your money, why doesn't he think you should spend it?' And I say, 'Because it's he who is advising me.' And she would say, 'But why are you paying him to advise you when you won't

take any notice of him anyway?' And I say, 'Well, that is part of the fun of it.'

Quarrelling with one's husband is not of course a requisite for a successful business team, and not all couples who work together quarrel but it is a subject that most people have something to say about.

A contribution to marriage

Despite their quarrels, the majority of the women in these wife and husband teams believed that working together enriched their marriages. Golda Harris, who until her husband's death was the female half of a Jewish couple who started in the East End of London and graduated to the prosperous suburb of Hendon, and whose thirty years of joint working and married life were characterised by endless quarrels, had no doubts in her mind that it was the business – they made coats – that kept them together and turned an otherwise difficult marriage into a viable proposition.

> Working together has made a lot of difference. When we used to visit friends and my husband met their wives, who were just housewives and not working women, he used to give me his greatest compliment. When we entered the car on returning home he would groan and say to me, 'Thank God you are not like those bloody cows.' That was his greatest compliment. What he meant was that because we were in business together he could talk to me on his level.

Working together has also consolidated the relationship of younger couples with greater demands from life than those of the Harrises. Before thirty-four-year-old Jenny Meyers became a successful fashion store owner, her thirteen-year-old marriage went through several crises and its survival seemed doubtful. But since she has become successful the marriage has improved to such a degree that for the first time she felt prepared to become a mother. She recalls: 'Before we were together in business I had six rotten years and then it got better. I stuck it out because I was too insecure to leave and I was not sure of myself and my status. But since we have been together in business it has improved our relationship unbelievably. I was even ready to consider having a child.'

Working together with her husband also seems to have cemented

Elizabeth Lyon's present marriage, which has lasted longer than her two previous ones.

> I think it is marvellous working together. Gerard and I have been blissfully happy for seven years, and he left his job two years ago because I said to him that I could not run this business without him. He said: 'You have got to be crazy. What, am I going to give up the City to come to this?' But I managed to convince him. For a bit I was very frightened because I had dragged him out of a secure and respectable job. But he is so happy and he adores it, and he said to me one day that even if he went broke, he would never go back to the City. So it proves that it works well.

Time and again the millionairesses stressed that the most beneficial aspects of working together were the common interests and the mutual respect that evolved from the business partnership. Restaurant owner Sue Heathcote would not want any other arrangement:

> I would hate it if we didn't share interests. I think it must be ghastly to have separate careers and not be able to discuss things. Let us face it, what can a doctor have in common with his lawyer wife?

Unsuccessful partnerships

It would be false to pretend that all husband and wife partnerships were harmonious. The unsuccessful partnerships were those where the husband did not pull his weight but benefited from his wife's greater contribution – in other words, where the wife felt exploited. Hilda Bergdorf, the teenage bride of a much older man who bore him six sons while building up a joint babywear business in England, resented having to do 70 per cent of the work. She recalls: 'My husband was bone lazy. He was good with the customers but he was bone idle. If I had decided to quit the business there wouldn't have been a business.'

It is not surprising that the women in this survey who tried to run a business and cope with a home and children at the same time were critical about husbands who did not pull their weight. Sonia Kaplan put up with such a husband for twenty years until she decided that she had had enough. 'I did everything – the buying and the selling and the employees and the finance. He did most of the operational aspects, such as getting the packages out.' When eventually the marriage and business partnership split up, and each got part of the business, Sonia's part flourished and became the $100 million business it is today, while her husband's foundered. She says:

> He took one business and I took the other. When I bought him out the business was only doing $1 million a year. Thirteen years later it is doing $100 million while his business was doing $4 million, and eight years later under his management he didn't have a business at all and became a realtor. I have just bought a building through him.

Of all the wife and husband teams, only two whose marriage ended in divorce blamed the business partnership for it. Another three claimed that the strain of working together nullified the benefits of their common interests. Marriage being a complex relationship, it is difficult to pinpoint the exact cause for its break-up or success. Thus any claims that the business has been responsible for the failure of a marriage have to be viewed with caution.

Although hotel owner Frieda Marks blamed the break-up of both her marriages on the business partnership with her husbands, a closer examination of the facts reveals more complex reasons for these failures. Her first husband 'came out' openly as a homosexual and left her and the kids for a younger man, and her second husband committed suicide. At any stretch of the imagination it would be difficult to suggest that a business partnership could have turned a husband into a homosexual or caused him to take his own life. Frances Roberts, whose success has been in advertising, claims in her case that: 'The split-up of the marriage can be related directly to the business. Because the marriage became a business relationship it lost the magic that holds a marriage together.' Against this it can be pointed out that after twenty-five years most marriages lose their magic whether the spouses are in business together or not.

Unlike Frances Roberts, mail order magnate Sonia Kaplan did not blame the business partnership for the break-up of her twenty-year-old marriage. What she did stress, however, was that having experienced both types of relationships – a wife and husband business partnership in her first marriage and an independent career in her second one – she is convinced that once a woman is established in business it is easier for her to run it without her husband. So, as she says, 'When I remarried we decided that we would not work together despite the fact that my present husband is also a businessman.'

Not all the critics of wife and husband business partnerships were divorcees with an axe to grind. There were also a few who, although solidly married, claimed that a business partnership with their husbands was a disadvantage to both the marriage and the business. What is illuminating, however, is that in all the instances where the wives considered the partnership with their spouses a disadvantage, the husbands had only a small equity in the business or no equity at all. Susan Willards's husband had no equity in his wife's handicrafts business and was merely her employee, Julie Kitson's husband had only 8 per cent of the equity in her aviation business, and Ulrike Jameson's had 12 per cent in her pharmaceutical company. The way Susan summarised her relationship with her employee husband was: 'We got along fine – but it was very difficult.' Julie found that: 'It can become very hostile because you tend to take the problems home with you.' Ulrike saw the business partnership with her husband as 'a disturbing factor in a marriage'. But these criticisms of wife and husband business partnerships have to be assessed in view of the husbands' small or non-existent shareholding in their wives' businesses.

Couples who work together obviously have to tread more carefully than those who do not, particularly when the business is primarily the wife's creation and the husband is only a minor shareholder in it or an employee. Had it been the wife who worked in her husband's business and not the husband in his wife's business, the difficulty of combining marriage with business would obviously have been less acute, because few wives expect to have an equal say. For most husbands being the junior partner is a blow to their ego and their accepted image as the breadwinner. Such injury to the male ego is not a recipe for a successful marriage at the best of times. Thus any claims that the business has created a strain on the marriage have to be viewed in the context of the husband's resentment of his small or non-existent equity holding, and not as a general reflection of the incompatibility of a business partnership and marriage.

The art of marriage and business partnership

Working with one's husband harmoniously is more than a feat, it is an art, and one at which the magnates in this study have excelled. Appreciating the cultural and social pressures that are piled on the husbands of successful women, they went out of their way to supply them powerful defences to rebuff attacks on their masculinity. For a start, they were smart enough to talk in terms of 'we' and 'ours' even where it was they who had initiated the business and it was they who held it together. Consequently the husband was no longer the spouse of a successful businesswoman, but a successful businessman himself. Niki Summers explains:

> I talk in terms of 'we' and 'our' although it was totally my idea and my business. But as a married woman for the past twenty-three years I can say that the greatest contribution to a woman's success is a husband who supports what she is doing and does not fight her. And you don't get it by alienating him from your business, but by involving him.

Next, even where they cared about the business more than about their husbands, they put their husbands' interests before those of the business. As a result the husbands felt that they had not lost the preferential treatment usually reserved for breadwinners. Sue Heathcote recounts:

> Before I got married it never occurred to me to stop work because it was supper time. If I had to work all night because we had a big banquet, I would go on until the job was ready. Now I couldn't possibly do that, because Rick can't go to sleep feeling happy and relaxed unless I am there, and he also likes his meals at the right time. So now I try to get back at 6.30 p.m. so that I can have an hour with him before I come back to the restaurant. In the old days I would have just worked on.

Furthermore, they were not averse to playing the role of conventional wives in public. This meant that in the outside world at least their husbands could preserve their macho image intact. Elizabeth Lyon says:

> There are conflicts between being a businesswoman and a wife. When we started in business seriously my husband said to me: 'You can do what you want providing that you also do what I want.' He likes going away for weekends and to shooting parties. He likes entertaining and he expects me to be immaculate, to cook for dinner, and to make sure the flowers are done. He is fanatical about details. This is part of the deal. In exchange he is totally supportive.

Ensuring that one's husband is credited with the business's success whether he deserves it or not, not letting him feel neglected even when it involves unnecessary extra hardship for herself, and letting him keep his macho image in front of his pals are not exactly a feminist model for the right way for a woman to establish her equality. But it certainly achieved one thing: the husband's support.

Rebels there were almost none. Of the 54 per cent who were involved in business with their husbands only Ulrike Jameson said: 'If it were a matter of losing a husband or losing a business I would have given up the husband.' And it was only she who dared to compare herself to a man and ask the question that has not yet found an answer: 'Why are women made to choose between family life and a career? No man would close a business because his wife wants him to. So why should a woman liquidate hers because of a husband? Men have other responsibilities besides their wives, why can't women have theirs in addition to marriage?'

Like the pioneering work she was doing in her bacteriological laboratories, Ulrike was trying also to pioneer a more honest and equal relationship between men and women. But meanwhile, until there appears a new breed of men who feel confident enough to consort with independent-minded women like Ulrike, future business Amazons will have to content themselves with sharing their success through a process of compromise and negotiation in the way that the majority here have done.

Knowing one's husband

To work with one's husband means to witness him screw up a deal, shout like a lunatic, and lose his nerve in a crisis without despising him and without losing one's affection for him. To work with a husband means to see his good as well as his bad side, and balancing the two. As Rachel Black says, 'As long as it is 55 per cent good – then it is good.' It also means recognising and making the most of complementary traits. Zelda Main says: 'My husband is so calm. He brings me down to earth. David has trained me, because I come from a long line of worriers. If my parents had nothing to worry about, they would worry why they had not found anything to worry about. David is fantastic, he is so cool. I am a worrier. My sons call it "the JMS", the Jewish Mother Syndrome.'

In the Mains' case the success of their business partnership was mainly because of David's coolness and Zelda's enthusiasm. In the case of the Drapers it was because of Janet's eye for detail and her husband's vision. Janet explains:

> I am careful with the little money while he is careful with the big money. I watch those pennies but I spend big money. There is good reason for that. He knows that I am going to watch him spending the pennies and I know that he is going to watch me spending the big dollars. I know that if I write a cheque for $50,000 he will look at it and say: 'What is it?' But he knows that if he signs one for $21.50 I am going to look at it and ask the same.

After eighteen years of combining business and marriage Janet knows herself and her husband inside out: 'I am stronger in my opinions. He is more subject to negotiation than I am. I will listen and he will listen. But I go out to win every battle, while he will lose a battle to win a war. He looks more at the big picture than I do. I take every day at a time.' As knowing one's enemy is essential to winning a battle, knowing one's husband is essential for a successful business partnership.

Primarily, working with one's husband means a philosophical acceptance that no two people are the same, and that just as some are smarter than others so also some like to work harder than others. Without such a stoical acceptance of human nature no partnership could survive. Rachel Shapiro admits to being a workaholic and, after twenty-six years of marriage, accepts that her husband likes his leisure. She also knows that after all these years she is not going to change him and is just thankful that he does not interfere with her twenty-four-hour day.

Some wives might find it difficult to work with their husbands, but on balance working together puts a greater strain on the husband because it undermines his dominant position as the chief earner and throws a questionable light on his capabilities. A noticeably less capable husband would be ill-advised to work with his wife. The women tycoons were aware of these difficulties and, contrary to what might have been expected, they treated their husbands with care and understanding. Only emotionally self-sufficient and capable women could bring this off.

Wives Who Earn More than Their Husbands

There exists the idea that husbands must earn more than their wives to remain the dominant partner – as if it would be a worse world if wives were not dominated by their husbands. The assumption is based on the premise that for a household to run efficiently it ought to have only one head, and it has never been doubted who it should be. Recently this long-standing earning pattern has become endangered by a small number of women who have started to earn as much as their husbands, and by a handful who earn even more.

The business millionairesses, unlike the feminists, have not set out to change the established order but only to better themselves. They were sensitive to the domestic upheavals which would result from having husbands who earned less than them, and made sure they did not get into that particular fix. This they could do because, unlike executives, owners whether in business with their husbands or on their own can determine the level of their own salaries. The married business Amazons who concerned themselves with the 'earnings issue' fell into two categories: the solo earners and the business wives. The solo earners were those married women tycoons who worked independently of their husbands, and the business wives those who worked together with them. Of these two categories, the husbands of the solo earners were more sensitive to their wives' higher earnings than those of the business wives.

The solo earners

Husbands who were in professions known to be high in social or intellectual status but poorly paid, such as scientists, were not overly perturbed about their wives' higher earnings. When the disparity first occurred, they were even proud of it. But when the pattern persisted their self-confidence ebbed. Debra Manham's husband was a pharmacist with hospital wages, which in Britain are not high. When Debra started to earn more than him in her fashion business he used to joke about it and tell friends he could retire. But when it became an established pattern Debra noticed his embarrassment, especially where the children were concerned. 'So I decided not to talk in public or in front of the children about my earnings or to imply that I earned more than him. Although he knows how much I earn, because I put the money in a joint account, we just don't talk about it.'

Fran Andrews, the boss of a 'head-hunting' agency, whose husband was an executive in a similar business, solved the disparity of their earnings differently. When hers started to exceed her husband's she gave him 10 per cent of her corporation's equity and a consultancy post. This meant that his wages were augmented by the consultancy fees, which she authorised and raised periodically to match her own income. 'I was concerned about my higher earnings so I suggested he become my consultant, for which he is paid. In this way he earns like me.'

When an employee earns less than his businesswoman wife, it could be excused as due to the inherent limitations of his career. But when a husband's business does worse than that of his wife, his lower earnings are seen as a sign of his personal limitations. Margaret Bryant, whose husband's business went into liquidation while her children's clothing business prospered, refused to discuss her success to avoid hurting his feelings.

Whether the reason why the high-earning wives treated their husbands with kid gloves was the husbands' actual resentment of their success, or whether it was only the wives' fear that their husbands might resent it, was difficult to ascertain, because in one way or another the high-earning wives endeavoured to eliminate the disparity between their own and their husbands' earnings. As a result, the reactions of their lower-earning husbands were not put to the test. It could be that if they had allowed this to happen they would have discovered that their husbands could cope with their wives' success without the anticipated trauma.

The business wives

Among the married business Amazons the issue of high-earning wives was, therefore, of importance only in the case of the solo earners and not of the business wives. For the latter the question of who earned more, they or their husbands, was of little importance because as owners it was they themselves who determined their takings, so the level of their personal earnings was not an indicator of success or failure. On the whole the earnings they allocated themselves were determined according to their tax liabilities, and if by paying the husband more than the wife, or vice versa, they could outsmart the revenue authorities they did not hesitate to adjust the level of their earnings accordingly. Where tax considerations did not apply it was usual for husband and wife business partners to be remunerated equally. Nina Dean, a leading travel agent, followed this system: 'Our salaries have always been equal. Even when I suggested that there might be a tax advantage if he took more, he did not agree and insisted we take an equal wage.' Store-owner Jenny Meyers says of her husband: 'Before he joined me he was an analyst in a City merchant bank and earned well, more than I would ever have been able to earn as an employee, but it was worth his while to join me. Now we earn the same.'

As owners have other financial criteria to measure their achievements than merely a wage at the end of the month, the husbands who worked with their wives were more concerned with equality of equity than with equality of wages. Rachel Shapiro's husband, who was an equal shareholder in their cosmetics empire, was not perturbed when his wife earned more than him. She explains: 'Now I earn more than him because I am the president of the corporation. I would say that it would not matter to my husband if I made twice as much as him. As long as he owns half the shares it does not matter to him. Because he knows and I know that it is us who decide how much each should earn. It is like buying our own competition cups and presenting them to ourselves when we do well.'

But for Susan Willards's husband, who only worked for his wife and had no equity in her handicrafts business, it was extremely important to earn more than her. As she said, 'He insisted on good pay. I never drew a pay cheque when he worked because the company was struggling, but he insisted on his pay cheques. It could have been with him because he did not have any shares in the company, but he never said so.' Without equity, what else should Mr Willards have worked for if not for good wages? For the success of his wife's business?

The Unattached

The fact that business ownership is more compatible with matrimony than employment is substantiated by comparing the matrimonial status of senior women business executives with that of the business Amazons. Not only were there many more married women tycoons (63 per cent) than married women executives (48.6 per cent), but there were also fewer divorcees among the women magnates (14 per cent) than among the women executives (20 per cent). As to single women, the disparity between the women business owners and the women executives was even greater. Of the owners only 6 per cent had never married, while for the women executives the figure was a notably high 27.6 per cent.

Only in the category of widows was there a larger proportion of owners (17 per cent) than of executives (3.8 per cent). The explanation for this disparity is simple and does not contradict the former observations. Many of the women tycoons attained this status only as a result of their husband's death, when they took over the business. Had their deceased husbands been senior executives, these wives would not have been able to take their place and would have continued to be housewives as they had always been.

Although the business Amazons had a greater commitment to marriage than their executive sisters, they seemed positively wild compared to the highly domesticated senior male executives, of whom some 93.5 per cent were married, 4.5 per cent were currently divorced and single, and only 2 per cent had never married. Widowers there were none. This low 6.5 per cent total of unattached male executives contrasts remarkably with the 37 per cent of unattached female owners and 51.4 per cent of female executives.

What was it that made male high flyers want to get married and female high flyers to stay unattached? After all, it has always been assumed that it was women who were eager to get married and men who were anxious to avoid it. So what had changed? The casual, and slanderous, explanation that successful women are unattractive to men will not do. First, there is sufficient evidence to show that it was the women who rejected the men and not the other way around; and second, such an explanation misses the effect of female financial independence on the institution of marriage.

To an extent it is true that unattached female business executives or owners find it difficult to attract suitable matches, but that is not because they lack appeal but because they are not ready to compromise their high demands from a spouse. Unlike male executives, women executives and owners do not have the same motivation to get married, because for them marriage is not going to provide the good-looking, caring, listening, cooking wife that the businessman gets in exchange for his financial support. What marriage has to offer them is usually a demanding husband who has to be pampered after a long day at work. Liberated from the most common reason that women have for marriage, financial security, they look for a male friend and companion and not just for a husband. Being financially independent, they do not have to compromise and merely get themselves hitched to a provider. In the absence of a compatible spouse they prefer to stay unattached.

Thus the fact that there are many more unattached businesswomen than unattached businessmen is not a case of the 'poor' businesswomen having had to sacrifice marriage for the sake of their careers, but of fortunate businesswomen who can pick and choose because they are free of the fear of staying unattached.

The singles

The disparity betwen the high percentage (27.6 per cent) of single female executives and the low one (6 per cent) of single business Amazons is further proof of how suitable business ownership is for women. It is simply much easier for an owner to combine a career with marriage than it is for the female executive. She can work with her husband; she can give him a job in her business, or, if he is otherwise employed and has to change his place of work, she can even follow him and start a business in a new location. In this respect there is no doubt that a female executive is much more restricted. She cannot work with her husband, she cannot offer him a job, and she can seldom follow him wherever his career dictates without sacrificing her own. Consequently, female executives' reasons for staying single are more pressing than those of the single business owners. Tricia Williams admits:

> When asked why I have never married I say that it was because I have been too busy building up my business. But it is not really true. I didn't get married because of the old boring reason of not finding the right man. But it is easier to blame it on the business than go into long stories. Somehow it is easier for people to accept a single career woman than a single homely type.

Market researcher Daphne Glover also denies any link:

> My mother tells people that I am single because of the business. It sort of provides her with an acceptable excuse. But I am sure that even without the business I would have stayed single. I have never

been dying to get married. I just haven't seen the advantage. I have almost been talked into it a couple of times, but most probably not convincingly enough.

Being single was not something that bothered the women tycoons unduly. Daphne Glover claimed: 'I do not have the burden that the married woman has to work and look after a husband. I do not have the guilt that goes with not doing everything perfectly. So I am much better off.'

What did concern them, however, was the fact that they did not have children. Sara Holt, thirty-three-year-old cosmetics businesswoman, said: 'The main reason I am trying to find a suitable man is because I want to have a family and I'm not the type of modern girl who could do it on her own.' Daphne Glover, at forty-four, was sadly past such hopes: 'The only regret I have is not having had children. Having children is different to marriage. The actual domestic part of marriage, the home building and the serving, would put me off. But I am sure I would have coped with children.'

If a woman decides to stay single and pass up marriage and motherhood, she had better be a successful career woman: although even such people do not escape the stigma of spinsterhood altogether. Sara Holt recalls: 'I got some publicity in the press and my parents were so proud of me. They showed it to all their friends as if to compensate for the aggravation of having an unmarried daughter. Also now, since my sister got divorced and returned to my mother with her three children, she started to say that it is better to stay single.' Tricia Williams had a similar experience: 'Now that I am successful my parents are proud of me. At one time there was from my mother in particular a sort of feeling that I ought to be married and have children.'

It is not only parents who were forced to admit that there were other aspects to women except being wives and mothers. Married friends, too, who had previously felt sorry for their unfortunate sisters, started to wonder who had done better, they or the single business Amazons? Jennifer Durham, a forty-five-year-old printer, confesses: 'Now that most of my friends' marriages have collapsed and they have been left to support children without adequate money or skills, they tell me how they envy me.'

The widows and divorcees

The other categories of unattached women, the widows and the divorcees, had even less incentive to get married than the single businesswomen, for they had already savoured marriage and most of them had children. It was not that remarrying was against their principles, or that they felt bitter about their previous marriage. It was just that after the independence and fulfilment they had enjoyed as business owners they could not visualise themselves as traditional wives. What shocked them most was the realisation that when it came to marriage even the successful men whom they were dating were interested only in one thing: a domesticated wife. Barbara Carpenter, head of a large industrial enterprise, recounts:

> In the past seven years since I got widowed I have gone out with several men who were charming and understanding until they offered marriage, and I expressed my wish to keep my business. This they couldn't take. As long as I was a widow it was OK for me to be a businesswoman, but as their wife they expected me to resign all my business activities and concentrate on them and the home. What they wanted me to be was a hostess and public face of a rich businessman. Obviously I could no longer go back to such a life. When I was young and didn't know better I didn't hate it, but now I couldn't become someone's live-in housekeeper.

It is unbelievable that intelligent men with grown-up children could expect a woman of a similar age and background to drop all she has created as a businesswoman for the privilege of serving them in their old age. But this is exactly what they expected. No wonder there were 37 per cent of unattached women tycoons, compared with only 6.5 per cent of unmarried male executives. By remarrying, the male executives had everything to gain and the women magnates everything to lose. Being successful did not only mean that the businesswomen had the choice of refusing to become housekeepers. It also meant that their choice of men was narrower because it eliminated all the insecure types who would be driven into impotence by the mere thought of a successful woman. Here is talent agent Genevieve Rouche on the subject:

> At first when I realised that it was becoming more difficult to date I attributed it to the fact that I was getting older, but that is not the real reason. I think that men are frightened of a successful

woman. The number of men has diminished in terms of their interest in me as a woman, in direct relation to my success. They are really frightened, not just of me when they see me, even before they know me – they don't even have to meet me and they aren't interested. All they have to do is hear the name, connect it with the fact that I am a businesswoman and they don't want to know.

Being strong women, those in this study do not have the time or the inclination for weak men, and rather than compromise they prefer to stay single. Thus it would be incorrect to say that their success made it more difficult for them to find a husband. On the contrary, it made it easier for them to avoid the trap of an unsuitable one. Market research millionairess Judy Pike explains:

> I have mixed feelings with regard to the effects of my success and my relationship with men. I find that with the exception of a few exceptional men, I am incredibly threatening to most of them. But then it is fine with me because I want exceptional men anyhow. I am not looking for a man to change my life. I like my life. What I am looking for is a man to share my life with and this is not easy.

Weak men excuse their inability to face successful women by claiming that they are hard. This allegation can be dismissed on two grounds. First, as shown by this study, such women are not necessarily harder or softer than any other women. Second, hardness or softness are not acquired, but inherent qualities. A soft woman does not become hard because she has become successful, and a hard one does not soften when she fails. Ann Liddie, a forty-three-year-old divorcee for the past nine years and a businesswoman for the past eight, is a case in point. Despite the fact that since her divorce she has become the successful owner of a London tourist centre, and is the mother of three grown-up children, she is still the same mushy person when it comes to men: 'I try not to get too involved because I am scared of my weak mental constitution. I am the type of woman who becomes a floor mat when in love. "Yes darling, no darling, whatever you want darling." At work I can be as tough as needed but in private I lose my personality. Once was enough for me. I enjoy being my own person.'

The claim that successful women are hard and therefore not easy to live with was also refuted by talent scout Genevieve Rouche's observation of the extramarital activities of men. She has observed that it was usually the men who were married to non-working women who were the greatest philanderers, not the husbands of career women. What better defence of successful women than the fact that it is mostly homemakers' husbands who play around?

Some might suggest that if this observation about the greater fidelity of career women's husbands is correct, then it might be due to these women's selection of the right husbands. But even if this is the reason for their harmonious marriages, and not the fact that they were career women, that still shows the wisdom that women gain when they lead a creative working life: they learn how to select a suitable spouse.

7 | Coping with Children

On first encounter with a successful businessman would you ask yourself whether he is married and if so, what are his wife's feelings about his success? Would you go on to wonder whether he has children and if he does, who looks after them while he is at work? And would you dare to ask whether they feel deprived because of their father's successful career? Anyone answering these questions honestly would have to say No to all of them. On meeting a successful businessman one takes it for granted that his family are supportive of his occupation and proud of his success. As to his children, and the effect of his success on them, these are not considered part of a husband's daily concerns.

Now, take the same businessman, dress him in female clothes, remove his facial hair, give him a new hairdo – in short, transform him into a businesswoman. Then notice how all your answers change. You would tend to assume that she is unmarried. If wrong you would still assume she is childless, and if this turned out not to be so, you would assume that she had messed up someone's life: her children's, her husband's, or her own. You would need a lot of persuading before you believed that she managed to cope not only with her business but a home, a husband and, in particular, her children. The reasons for your preconceived ideas about the ability of women to cope successfully with a career as well as homemaking and motherhood are not only that it is comforting for the onlooker to belittle the achievements of others, but it is indeed difficult to combine all these functions. But then the majority of the women magnates have gained entry into that exclusive clan for the very reason that they *are* extremely capable and *can* manage to combine them all.

Capability is not the only explanation of how these women have managed to combine motherhood and a career; the fact that they are owners and not employees may be an even more important factor. In contrast to an employee, the owner can arrange her timetable and surroundings to accommodate motherhood. This explains the great disparity between the number of female executives who chose to be mothers – only 39 per cent – and the women in this study of whom as many as 74 per cent are mothers. Still, a working mother has to work even if she is her own boss, and one cannot work and look after children at the same time. So, being the practical women they are, they set out to find a workable solution to the problem. Most of them (74.5 per cent), having decided that being a good mother meant being a full-time mother, delayed starting in business till their children had reached school age. The more restless ones, who could not wait, tried different solutions. Some worked from home, others took the children to their workplace, and two of them even managed to persuade their husbands to reverse roles and look after the children during their formative years. But the most common arrangement was hired help: women, some more qualified than others, who stood in for the mother while she was at work.

Working from Home

Entrepreneurs start a business from home because it saves on expenses. Mothers who work from home get an additional bonus in that they can also look after the children. This was the reason why 30 per cent of the women here took advantage of this arrangement, which is unique to the self-employed, and worked from home while their children were young. The disadvantages of this system are that unless the business-woman is highly organised the home ceases to look like a home, and despite her physical presence the children might still feel neglected because she is busy with her business affairs. Furthermore, not all businesses can be run from home: retail shops, restaurants, and heavy or chemical industries all depend on suitable industrial premises. But businesses such as publishing, travel, and insurance brokerage that basically need a desk and a telephone, can be run from home, at least in the initial stages. Other suitable types of business are farms, hotels, and health resorts, which can accommodate the family on their premises. In their efforts to start a business without neglecting their children, some of the women have also brought into the home unsuitable businesses –

toys, cosmetics, and pharmaceuticals – involving quite bulky goods that really require warehouse facilities.

For book publisher Lucy Curtis working from home was the ideal solution: she did not have to feel guilty about leaving her young children in someone else's care, and she saved on the expenses which running her publishing business from proper commercial premises would have cost. For Ellie Leonard, too, being able to run her travel business from home was a salvation. Having been a working woman all her life she postponed childbearing for fear that she would be cooped up at home in a role she would not enjoy: 'It is incredible how one doesn't think about these things at the time of pregnancy. I refused to think about staying at home. I hoped that something would sort itself out. But when the baby was there it hit me. Someone had to stay with him and it wasn't going to be my husband.'

Time and again the same reasons for working from home – being with the children and saving costs – were mentioned by these women. Furthermore, they had a way of extricating themselves from the 'great' moral dilemma of whose interests should come first, the mothers' to realise their potential, or the children's to be fed, cleaned and fondled exclusively by their mothers. Ulrike Jameson, with her pharmaceuticals business, had this in mind:

> Working from home gave me two years of breathing space to be with the kid, and sort myself out. When one decides to have a child at the age of forty-one, it isn't the same as eighteen. One feels more responsible and one wants to give more.

Rachel Shapiro stressed the practical side of her cosmetics firm:

> Working from home allowed me to keep in touch with the kids. It also gave me time to test the viability of the business. So many businesses founder because they incur too many expenses at the beginning when they don't generate sufficient income.

Although the business Amazons' reason for working from home was primarily in order to be with their children, the reality of the situation was that even when they were at home they had to delegate the minute by minute supervision of their children to hired help. After all, one cannot carry on a telephone conversation with a screaming child on one's lap. Still, the advantage of working from home was that in an emergency the mother was there and not twenty miles away. Rebecca Kemmis, a successful farmer and soft drinks manufacturer, says:

There was never a problem. We had Maisy who had been with us
for ten years and then we had Sally for some twelve years. When
the children were babies I used to go and breastfeed them between
the telephone calls, the visiting travellers and the office work, and
the nannies would change and bath them. And when they grew up
they were around the farm where they knew everyone.

Lucy Curtis, the publisher, had less permanent arrangements:

I have an au pair who lives in and a housekeeper who comes in
daily. The au pair is with the children and the housekeeper cleans
the house and cooks. But I would not have left the kids with the
au pair alone, they are too young.

In the initial stages running a business from home might be good for
the mother as well as for the children; but when the business grows it
should move out, because otherwise it encroaches on the family's
privacy, and even the children feel threatened by it. Delia Lewenthal's
toy business caused some problems:

Wherever you looked there were boxes. Closed boxes, open
boxes. My daughter's best friend was the UPS man who used to
come daily to collect the boxes for delivery to customers, and my
daughter used to help give him the boxes. There were toys
everywhere. Demonstration models, damaged returns from
customers. We could not invite friends. There was nowhere to sit.

Cosmetics specialist Rachel Shapiro was snowed under too:

The cosmetics jars and boxes were everywhere. First they filled up
the spare room and then our bedroom until they involved the
living room. The only rooms I kept them out from were the
children's. I didn't want them to feel that their territorial
sovereignty was being threatened.

The home being the joint abode of the couple, working from home
requires the husband's consent; not every husband is prepared to
return to a home strewn with toys or cosmetics jars. The explanation of
how these women obtained their husbands' consent must be the fact
that so many of the husbands held equity in their wives' businesses, and
therefore the success of the enterprise was also in their interest.

Children at the Workplace

Being the boss, the business owner can bring her children to her place of work. Not that this is always an ideal solution, but in an emergency when the au pair decides to return to her homeland at a moment's notice, or the sitter breaks her leg, it will do. The argument against this arrangement is that it might confuse the child as to why the mother, who is physically present, is unable to attend to him or her the way she does at home. Therefore such an arrangement should exist only where it suits the child's disposition and where the workplace provides a congenial atmosphere. A hyper-active child in a Fifth Avenue china shop is obviously no solution even if the mother owns the place. As to what is a suitable workplace environment for a child, that depends not only on objective but also on subjective considerations. Some mothers would shudder at the thought of having their carefully brought up suburban kids hanging around a downtown factory, while others, such as D.I.Y. tycoon Pearl White and Nancy Gardner of the candy empire, believed that a taste of real life could not harm their precious children, and let them go freely around their factories. Pearl White:

> That the surroundings were not as sterile as home did not bother me. I thought that a little bit of democracy would not harm these privileged daughters of mine. I have never thought much of uniformed nannies pushing immaculate babies in double decker prams. Sadie, our factory cleaner, has brought up four children of her own. She was marvellous. For her it was a great treat to parade around Finsbury Park and push the pram instead of cleaning the factory's loos. The girls loved it. It was funny how even babies feel that someone enjoys their company.

Nancy Gardner:

> With the fourth one it was different because I was working. I was here in the office two days before she was delivered, and I went into labour, I flew to Boston, delivered her at home, picked her up a few days later, put her in a basket, and carried her here to the factory in Chicago, and she lived here. I carried her with me wherever I went. In a basket. So she lived in this office here for the first years of her life.

Having children at their mother's workplace is more beneficial to the children than to the business, and definitely not cost effective, as invariably the person who is best suited to look after the children is also the one most needed at her job. On rainy days when they could not be taken out in the park, Pearl's daughters were put in the playpen with one of the secretaries as their minder, and later on when they went to school and refused to return with the nanny to a motherless home, Pearl arranged a television room for them in the factory. Daily at four p.m. they would be brought from school to the factory and served their tea and cookies by the canteen lady. They would watch the children's shows, and then at six p.m. mother and daughters would return to their suburban home.

Not many of the business Amazons took advantage of their owner's privileges to take their child to the workplace, primarily because they tried to separate their working life from their home life, not so much for the children's sake as for their own. They found the switch-over from the role of businesswoman to that of mother difficult, and not surprisingly; at work they had to be cool and fast, while with the children they had to be warm and slow. Although they did not find it difficult to be two different people at two different times and in two different places, they could not be both at the same time and place. To avoid this difficulty, they resorted only sparingly to their owner's privilege of bringing their children to their workplace; for example, as a last resort when they had to go on a business trip abroad and had no suitable arrangement for the children, they took them with them.

Regardless of whether it is good or bad for the child to hang around the mother's workplace, it is a fact that this arrangement is available only to business owners and not to executives. No corporation will allow its male or female executives to have their offspring crawling about all over the place, because however important they are to the corporation, there would still be the problem of where to draw the line. If this privilege were accorded to one woman executive, what about the others? And why only to women and not to widowers with small children?

When actress Lynn Redgrave breastfed her newborn baby in her own trailer on a filming location she was dismissed. But there was no one to stop Nancy Gardner breastfeeding her own baby three times every day in the head office of her $80 million Chicago confectionery corporation; Lynn Redgrave was after all just an employee, while Nancy Gardner was the owner.

Unlike businesswomen, businessmen do not need to avail themselves of the privilege of taking their children to their workplace, because the care of the children is left to their wives. Consequently most male owners emulate their executive counterparts and maintain the same 'out of bounds' attitude to the family. For them work is a sanctuary from which wife and children can be excluded by the awe-inspiring claim that 'Daddy is at work and cannot be disturbed.' Businessmen do not have to convince anyone that their children are not being neglected. But businesswomen do. Celia Daly, for one, was anxious to dispel any suggestion that her daughter suffered because of her successful career in furniture retailing: 'If she wants to have a chat she can always come and talk to me at work. She does not have to wait until I come home. I made it a rule that even at work I shall have time for her.'

Women business owners do not feel the same need for seclusion as do businessmen, or rather they cannot afford to feel such a need. They are expected to be available, if not to husbands then to children, three shifts a day. They accept this strenuous way of life and dare not complain, for fear that their licence to act as mothers and magnates at the same time might be withdrawn. A husband who becomes jealous of his wife's success, or a child who develops personality problems, is enough to jeopardise the *modus vivendi* of these businesswomen cum mothers.

Mother Substitutes

Failing the possibilities of working from home or taking the child to the workplace, the mother who goes out to work has to find a substitute who will guarantee her children's wellbeing while she is out of the house. These substitutes can vary from the full-time qualified children's nurse to the part-time student babysitter, and what determines their selection are the children's age, the mother's spending power and, above all, her views about her maternal duties.

Not all the businesswomen considered this expenditure a priority. Some, like Lois Jane Apple, with four children, preferred to struggle along without any help, investing every penny in her light engineering business. Others who could afford the best-qualified help considered childrearing an untransferable duty. Cosmetics manufacturer Eleanor Michaels says: 'I did not have my children to give them to someone else. I wanted to enjoy every aspect of taking care of them. They were first and they still are priority. So I accepted that my business would have to remain at a certain size until they grew up.'

Whatever their reason for choosing to cope alone those who took this path found it very rough going and their stories would not encourage anyone to follow suit. Nor should they. The aim of going into business is not to prove that all women are superwomen who can cope with anything and everything. On the contrary, the aim is to make it easier for them to combine work and motherhood. But to achieve this women must treat themselves with as much self-respect as men do, and not demand from themselves the impossible, of being everything to everyone at the same time.

Women who want to combine business ownership and motherhood without running themselves into the ground must accept the fact that just as they require help at work so too they require help at home; and just as they consider the service of a secretary essential, they should also regard as essential the services of a nanny or housekeeper. The idea of increasing the numbers of female business owners is not to swell the ranks of low-paid working mothers, but to create high earners who can combine motherhood and work with the dignity and ease with which men combine fatherhood and a career. Sooner or later the majority of the businesswomen surveyed here realised that unless they delegated the task of caring for the domestic needs of husbands and children, they would have to give up their business aspirations. Consequently they had to make use of one of the following four categories of maternal substitutes:

a full-time help in the form of a live-in nanny, a housekeeper, or an au pair;
b part-time help, which varied from a once-a-week cleaning lady to a regular daily, and various other arrangements with babysitters;
c special arrangements, which included grandmothers or aunts who took over the running of the house; and
d boarding schools, where the child was cared for throughout each term, thus leaving the mother free to engage in business for a great part of the year.

Full-time help

By full-time help is meant someone who lives in the house. The highest in the hierarchy of 'live-ins' is the qualified children's nurse who can be entrusted with the youngest of babies. Where the mother does not breastfeed, the nurse sleeps within easy reach of the baby and also takes over the nightly feeds. This enables the mother to sleep through the night and wake up fresh for work in the morning. Next in the hierarchy is the live-in nanny who looks after the children from the sixth month onwards. Neither of these is expected to look after the house, only after the children, which means that if the mother is to be freed from all housework, a housekeeper or a daily is also needed.

Of the live-ins who look after the home as well as the children, the housekeeper is the highest category followed, in the UK, by the mother's help, which is a British term applied mainly to foreign women who come to work as domestics; and in the USA by the maid. In the lowest category of the live-ins is the au pair, a European institution designed to enable seventeen- to twenty-seven-year-olds to study a country's language and culture by living with a local family. In consideration for part-time housework and babysitting they get free food and lodging as well as pocket money.

Only 22 per cent of the women in this survey had full-time help of some kind. Of these 78 per cent were British and only 22 per cent American. The reason so few availed themselves of full-time help was not so much the cost as a reluctance to entrust the upbringing of their children to someone else. To justify this reluctance by the conventional explanation of powerful maternal feeling is inadequate: it is at least as much a matter of habit and fashion. Those women like Elizabeth Lyon who were themselves brought up by nannies, had no qualms about repeating the pattern.

Sometimes, as with Mary Mead, it takes a crisis to expose a mother to the advantages of having someone else to look after her child. Mary, well known as a model before she became a 'keep fit' tycoon, attributes her success to the fact that she had a nurse to look after her baby; but she had to fall sick and be forced to employ help before she could justify to herself the delegation of her maternal duties.

Because I had appendicitis I had to go into hospital, and we had to get a nurse to look after my daughter. When I returned I found the baby well-fed and cheerful; I asked the nurse to stay on. I realised that all the social pressures of not handing the baby over to a nanny were not quite justified; it was actually quite nice. It was purely an accident that I took the nurse. Otherwise I wouldn't have done it, because you are pressurised by society that you should not give your child to somebody else.

There were two reasons why only a handful of the American businesswomen employed live-in help. The first was the traditional glorification of the role of wife and mother. As Juliette Marlon who is in travel put it: 'Americans are inclined to be very puritanical and very rigid in their viewpoints about raising families and we are brainwashed to believe that motherhood is the greatest thing on earth.' The second reason, apparently diametrically opposed, was the doctrinaire insistence by the women's movement that a sister should not employ a sister in a menial job. Conference organiser Marion Little doesn't mince her words: 'Making career women feel guilty about employing maids and housekeepers can block the progress of women.'

As for the women who did rely on full-time help, they could not envisage a life without it and attributed their ability to cope with family and work to such services. Cosmetics businesswoman Niki Summers speaks for most of them:

> If you are going to work you must have household help that can live with you. There is no other way I could have done it. I cannot see how any of the other women did it without live-in help. The thing that is important is to come home to dinner and sit down and be able to give your attention to your family, to listen patiently to your husband's adventure at work, and to be thrilled about your children's day at school. It is difficult enough doing it after some ten hours' work with full-time help at home. How any businesswoman can do it if she has still got to do any housework, God knows. They must have messed someone's life in the process.

There is no doubt that the glorification of the homemaker's role is intended to keep women out of positions of power and influence – safely at home. As soon as they are needed outside the home, however, whether in wartime to help the national effort, or in peacetime to improve their husband's prospects, the importance of their homemaking role is forgotten. When there are jobs crying out to be done no one argues that it would be irresponsible to leave the children. Then even husbands become convinced that children are resilient creatures. When Rachel Black's husband realised that he needed his wife to increase his fashion accessories business, he insisted on her taking full-time help arguing that she was more competent in the business than at home.

But whether it was a husband insisting they take on help or whether it was an appendix operation that required a nurse to replace the mother, the fact is that once they were out of the home, these women got hooked and dreaded the thought of going back. Fully aware of their dependence on home help, these business owners developed the highest respect for the women who enabled them to work themselves. They saw the arrangement as a work sharing partnership, where each partner carried out the task she was better at, or had time for. Niki Summers explains:

> A good manager delegates responsibility to other people, starting with help at home. The lady who says 'I would not have anyone else wash my floor' has the same attitude in business and she will not get very far because she is limited by her trust in other people. More often they may not do it as well as you would have done it, but almost as good is enough. For me, my housekeeper is one of my most important employees. Without her I could not function.

Still, let it not be forgotten that only 22 per cent of the business Amazons had such full-time help with their domestic duties. The rest became accomplished quick-change artists, at work one person, at home another. Observing how most of them conducted themselves at home, it was difficult to believe that these were the same business tycoons who at work had personal assistants, secretaries, and chauffeurs at their beck and call; who when they travelled on business stayed at the best hotels and availed themselves of the best service. The moment they returned home they changed their colours. The same woman who had three secretaries gratifying her every whim between nine and six changed at seven o'clock into a housewife eager to satisfy the individual demands of her husband and children. The desire to please and to serve was in such sharp contrast to their authoritative manner at work that one could only wonder whether by their submissiveness at home these women were trying to atone for deserting their families during the day and daring to revel in the trappings of power.

The change of personality that took place on their return home also affected the way they ran it. Only a few of them made use of their organisational skill at home, and even fewer used their wealth to make life easier. Engineering industrialist Janet Draper was the exception:

> I have seven staff in the house. A lady who comes in at seven o'clock in the morning and wakes up the kids and gives them their breakfast, and a chauffeur who takes them to school and also works in the yard. Then I have two other guys: one is a graduate horticulturist who comes in three or four days a week to look after the trees, and the other works in the yard, puts in light bulbs,

keeps the steam room going, and cleans the swimming pool. Then I have another lady who comes at two in the afternoon and cooks, and a young man who is also a butler if we need him. Then I have a twenty-three-year-old young lady who takes care of the kids. She lives in.

Most housewives would shudder at the thought of having to organise seven employees and four children, let alone do it by remote control, from London, New York, or any other place on the globe where she happened to be. They might wonder whether it wasn't as exhausting to organise as to do it oneself. But organising other people was no problem to Janet. It was what life was all about and she considered this operation a small price to pay for the luxury of enjoying herself at work as well as at home.

I don't think it's exaggerated to have all that staff at home. Remember I earn the money to pay for all this. I don't take it from anyone. I love my home and I love my kids and I don't want to become a bag of nerves and hate everyone. I want to be able to be relaxed. At work I don't want to worry each minute about my kids, and when I come home I don't want to worry about the house.

In modern times, with modern children, having help in the house does not mean that the children lose contact with their mother. Sally Harper, who began in business at seventeen by buying out a failed driving school, now engaged two live-in Filipino girls and a housekeeper as well as using the services of her own mother, and still saw plenty of her children:

I did not really miss out on bringing them up because when they were babies, I always managed to bath them before I went to work, and I used to feed them when I returned home from work. When they were toddlers I would always spend my weekends with them. I did not lead a very busy social life, and now I take them to school in the mornings and tend to keep them up late so that when I get home I put them to bed. Saturdays and Sundays we do things together: whatever we are doing we do with them, even working in the house. All my free time is spent with the children.

Present-day kids are not like nineteenth-century children who were kept out of sight and earshot. Nor are present-day mothers like their

140

own mothers and grandmothers. Even the nannies and housekeepers of today are not replicas of their predecessors. Today's children are not likely to let their mothers evade their maternal duties. Even in the rare case where the father has taken over the mothering of the children, it is still the mother who becomes involved with the feminine aspects of their lives. Toy manufacturer Delia Lewenthal is in this position:

> I have a wonderful person who looks after my daughter. But even then it is me who is involved with her needs. I don't cook. I don't clean. I have help to do all that. But it is me who goes to the school functions, and when she has a birthday I take care of sending the invitations, and phoning the mothers, and ordering the cakes. If it is a school play I get involved with her costume and her hair. And let us not talk about her health. When she isn't well she ignores my husband. Then the only person she wants is me.

Part-time help

Compared to the relatively relaxed life of those women who employed full-time help, the day to day existence of those who had only part-time help was strained and harassed. Their life was a continuously changing timetable of *ad hoc* arrangements for who would look after which child when, and who would attend to which domestic chore and where. All able-bodied members of the family were enlisted to aid the wife's efforts to combine motherhood, homemaking, and a business. Resentful husbands were sent on shopping missions. Grandmothers were blackmailed into babysitting, and neighbours were cajoled into giving the kids a lift to school. These women who were already or were soon to become members of the business elite were cooking and scrubbing before they went to work, in the evenings, and at the weekends. How with all this they still had the energy to run a business is unimaginable! Keep fit tycoon Lisa Collier recounts:

> I had three children: the youngest was just born when I started my fitness business and as I was not in a position to have meaningful help at home, I brought this au pair into our home. This meant that we had to give up a certain amount of privacy, because an au pair is not like a live-in housekeeper, they are supposed to be part of the family. They are not there to do the house cleaning – just help a bit. I still did the grocery shopping and still did the cooking. For a while I had a woman come in for half a day to

clean. But the au pair did not stop for long, just for about a month, and then she returned to her country. So that was the end of our live-in. About seven years ago I started having someone in two full days a week to do the basic cleaning, and teenagers that would come in after school to make sure that when the kids got home at three there was always someone there. I wished I could afford proper help, but I couldn't. Now I have a wonderful lady who comes in at twelve every day, and stays through five or six whenever I need her, and she also handles the car pooling for me.

Adele Benn had an even harder time:

I never had a proper live-in housekeeper. At the beginning I could not afford it and later on I did not want someone in the house. The way I coped was by never having a minute for myself. I used to run one fashion show in the afternoon from two-thirty till four, and one in the evening at eight o'clock. In between I used to dash home so that I could be with the kids for an hour or so, and check that the daily fed them and cleaned them. For the eight o'clock show I used to take them with me and have one of the dressers look after them. Sometimes it was very difficult.

But did it need to be that difficult? Lack of money and a wish for privacy, the two explanations given here for resorting to such unsatisfactory domestic arrangements, are in reality subjective reasons which result from one's priorities. Bearing in mind that unless a business is losing money it can afford the wages of a housekeeper, Lisa's plea of hardship has to reflect a choice of priorities. During the period when Lisa could not afford a live-in help her youngest daughter had private ballet lessons, and her son guitar lessons. As for herself, she still went out to buy a new outfit before each TV appearance. For Lisa these expenditures took priority over full-time help. In contrast to her, women such as fashion millionairess Linda Cartwright put self-preservation as their top priority and used their equally limited financial resources more wisely. 'I could not afford the money but I paid for the best help. I knew that if I wanted someone reliable I had to pay.' As for loss of privacy, this is a luxury the businesswoman can ill afford, and most would consider the price too high.

Special arrangements

Besides nannies, housekeepers, etc., the business Amazons have also enlisted help from parents, husbands, relatives, and older children. Some have even split their week into 'career' days and 'mother' days.

Parents and other family members were the mother substitutes most sought after but because of today's population mobility only 14 per cent of the businesswomen were fortunate enough to benefit from this most reliable form of help. Celia Daly, who had divorced two husbands by the time she was twenty-eight, and had her daughter when she was barely nineteen, could never have built up her London-based furnishing business with shops in London, Munich, Copenhagen, and Tokyo if her parents had not been there to help: 'When I had to go away my daughter would stay with my parents willingly, so I did not have to worry about how she was physically or emotionally.'

It was not only mothers but also mothers-in-law who were instrumental in these women's success. When Claire Whitman's husband was killed in an airplane crash after eight years of marriage, leaving her with four children, it was her mother-in-law who agreed to stand in for Claire and enable her to go out to work. Claire recalls:

> I struck a deal with my mother-in-law by which in consideration for her running of the home she would share in the profits of the brokerage business. Both of us did well out of this deal. I could go out to work knowing that the kids were in the best possible hands and she made a lot of money, because when I hit it big in the business she ended making good money.

Six years later Claire remarried. Her second husband was a widower with seven young children. So the household expanded to include four from her marriage, seven from his, and one joint daughter: in total twelve children under one roof, all in the charge of her first husband's mother. 'My first husband's mother continued to live with us. By the time I remarried she was getting older and we retired her, but she came in on weekends. If I was away for a week, she would supervise. She was very involved with our kids' lives. She was wonderful.'

Mothers went out of their way not only for daughters who were left to fend for themselves, but also for daughters with stable home lives like Sally Harper's. Sally has been married for thirteen years to her childhood sweetheart and lives in close proximity to her parents and sisters: a fact that has made her combined roles of mother of three and businesswoman much easier. 'My mother fetches the children from school, and takes them back to her house where they have their tea and watch the TV. They love going to her and they find her more fun than me.' Such arrangements were beneficial to all concerned. The children did not feel dumped, the mothers could relax knowing that their children were in good hands, and the grandmothers ensured a close tie with their high-flying daughters.

Another distinct breed of substitute mothers are aunts. Where it was the duty of married nieces and nephews to look after their unmarried aunts, the aunts reciprocated by looking after the children. Sadie Fairweather, who at seventy-two was the most senior business Amazon, did not find it difficult with three sons and a full-time career in the sanitation business '. . . because we have always had aunts living with us. For years we had my aunt and then we had two of my husband's aunts, so that there was always someone to look after the children.'

Among the numerous mother substitutes who assisted the business Amazons with their children, the best qualified of all, the children's natural father, was conspicuous by his absence – as if children were a woman's exclusive creation and therefore also her exclusive responsibility. What was even odder was that the women in this survey accepted it as normal. It was as if one of the ten commandments decreed that only mothers should be concerned with the rearing of children. In this milieu Delia Lewenthal's husband was the exception. His unfashionable belief that, as equal creators, fathers too had a right to enjoy the upbringing of their children enabled Delia to build up a $10 million toy business in the space of five years. Delia enthuses:

> He is an educator. He is perfect. Normally he takes care of her when I travel. He is totally supportive towards her. He takes her fishing, he takes her skiing, he is just wonderful.

In the absence of relatives ready to stand in for them, the majority of the business Amazons had to make do with housekeepers, nannies, and sitters. On the whole these arrangements, although not watertight, were satisfactory. The problem arose when both parents had to travel. When Rachel Black and her jeweller husband were confronted with this problem they decided that to leave three small children in the care of a nanny even as good as theirs would be irresponsible. So they decided to buy their peace of mind by hiring a Universal Aunt* whose task was not to work but to be in charge of the nanny and the household.

*Universal Aunts is the name of an organisation which specialises in providing experienced women such as qualified nurses, former teachers, ex-school matrons and so on for short-term supervision of children.

_____

Their fee was quite high, but they were worth every penny of it. We phoned up from southern Germany and we found to our consternation that the kids were in bed with whooping cough. By the time we got home the crisis had passed. They were on their way to recovery. The Universal Aunt knew exactly what to do, much better than we would have done. She was in fact a nurse.

That Rachel was prepared to employ the most expensive mother substitute does not prove that she loved her children more than other mothers or that she was wealthier. What it proves is her wisdom in getting her priorities right. She knew that as a mother her business success depended not only on her talents and abilities, but also on the wellbeing of her family. Not every high flyer realises that it is in the interest of a career mother to ensure for her children the best supervision that money can buy. Some, either from meanness or from stupidity, try to economise in this area and turn their children's lives as well as their own into a misery. Ellie Leonard, travel magnate, describes one such:

> I know one girl, I won't mention her name, here in Chicago earning $120,000 a year as an executive in one of the banks. Her children have been dragged out of their home every morning, and you know what the Chicago weather is like. Day in, day out, they are taken to a day care centre at seven-thirty in the morning. Those children have no idea of what home is like. The only time they are there is on Saturdays and Sundays. The mother said that she feels very guilty. 'You should feel guilty. Those children are like orphans in a storm. You are going to regret it the rest of your life.'

Boarding school

Of all the special arrangements, the one that frees the businesswoman from most daily worries and responsibilities regarding her children is putting them in a boarding school. Of the 11 per cent of business mothers who sent all or some of their children to boarding school only one-third were the products of such schools themselves. For these living without their children for the greater part of the year was normal but they did not always go along with it willingly. Elizabeth Lyon:

> I did not sent my children to boarding school in order to be a freer person. I sent them there because I was too weak to rebel. With

my class background all of my friends and all their children went and go to boarding schools. That is the tradition of the family and I have not got the courage to say this is wrong, this is not what I want.

Hotelier Tricia Bishop was also dubious:

You have two thoughts about boarding schools. I don't necessarily agree that it's good for all children. But I went to boarding school and my husband went to boarding school, and therefore it is assumed that all his children went to boarding school.

The two-thirds who had not been to boarding schools themselves had a still greater need to justify their action, to themselves and to others. Mary Mead, keep fit organiser, was one:

I was brought up in a background where you did not send your child away to school. It is very difficult to convince all my aunts that I am not cruel to this beautiful child that I have got and it was she who wanted to stay there. You find that you have to convince them all the time even though I know that it was the best thing that I could have done for her. I am always watching to see if she is happy. If suddenly it isn't right for her, then it's fine with me. She has always got a home waiting for her.

The way the business mothers compensated for the freedom they gained when their children were away at school was by devoting themselves to them during school vacations, and at visiting weekends. Unlike the full-time mothers who, by the time the holidays came round, were exhausted, the temporary mothers whose children boarded out, were fresh and eager to give their children a good time and pleasant memories. Travel tycoon Nina Dean recalls:

It made life more exciting because we looked forward to getting them out on the Sundays. And the holidays were fantastic. I was the one that always thought of different parties and different birthday cakes. For his eighth birthday I made him a clock cake. I had to be that much better than a normal mother.

Mary Mead's daughter was also a weekly boarder.

We go and see her every weekend. We stay in a hotel next to the school and she spends the weekends with us in the hotel, in an atmosphere where she has both parents available. I do not have to cook and clean. We just enjoy ourselves. In the holidays – they have very long holidays in boarding school – I usually hire a student to be a nanny so that she has someone who is bright, young, and with-it, rather than a nanny. They go to museums, plays, and the cinema.

There is no doubt that relieved of the routine of daily motherhood it is easier to be an exciting mother. Yet the value of the trade-off between a stimulating part-time mother and a tired and unresponsive full-time one is hard to establish. As there is no way of knowing whose children turned out happier, each mother should follow her own instincts as to what is best for her child.

The Difficulties

The fact that 60 per cent of the business Amazons dismissed the difficulties of combining motherhood with a career does not mean that they had it easy, but that human beings – especially women – are remarkably resilient. The apparent ease of combining a business career and motherhood was described by Nina Dean:

> I didn't find it difficult because I have always had a lot of energy, and I don't need a lot of sleep, so I used to get up in the night and do the office work. That was when the children were asleep and my husband was away.

Haulage contractor Deirdre Bovis was equally blasé:

> It's true that I worked around the clock and when one of our trucks broke down in the middle of the night, we would take out a replacement truck from the yard and drive some sixty miles until we found the broken truck and then I would help to trans-ship the load from one truck to another so that it would reach the market or the port on time. But I never thought about it as difficult. It is all a matter of energy and organisation.

Taking for granted that all the business Amazons were energetic and well organised – for otherwise they would not have become business Amazons in the first place – the fact that some had found things more difficult than others was a result of outside factors. The age of the children, the level of home help, and the degree of the husband's support were all determinants in their scale of difficulties. The younger the children, the less reliable the home help, and the lower the husband's support, the more difficult it was. Just how difficult 'difficult' can be can be guessed from the following glimpse of the early life of Sonia Kaplan, mail order expert:

> I managed with the children, but with great difficulty, despite the fact that I have always had household help. I was a screaming nervous wreck. I was like that for the first ten years. It was physically and emotionally so demanding that I was on the level of hysteria. I must have been the most unpleasant person in the world in those early years, when I had two little children – basically an unhappy marriage with a difficult husband.

An unhappy marriage is one thing, coping entirely alone is another. Lydia Eastern ran away from home at the age of fifteen and married her eighteen-year-old boyfriend; she was forced by her father to divorce him a year later when she was already mother to a son, and had a truly difficult time. Life revolved around work, the baby – and school, because Lydia realised that unless she gained an education she would not escape the gutter in which she had been dumped by the parents who had disowned her. 'There were no serious love affairs. I never lived with a man. I just forgot that aspect of life. When I first went to school I worked in the evenings. Then for seven years I went every night to college as well as on Saturday mornings.' Yet despite the difficulties, Lydia survived to tell the tale. 'I have never had welfare, unemployment benefit, child support, or alimony. I have brought up my son all by myself.' She is now owner of an $80 million travel business.

Electronics tycoon Stevie Frederick also succeeded against all odds. At eighteen she got married, at nineteen she had her first child, at twenty-one her second, at twenty-two her third, and at twenty-three she got divorced. With three babies and no husband, Stevie became the breadwinner, relying on babysitters and child care centres to mind the children during the day and taking care of them during the evenings and weekends.

Having married so young she had little earning power and had to work very hard for what she got: 'I began to work as a copy typist, worked my way up through different positions, and by staying after five o'clock and working harder I got promoted.' For years, her life was centred on work, the children and little else, till at the age of thirty-five, when they were all in their teens, she could take it no longer. She packed the children off to her ex-husband, who had just remarried, and went to college to get the education she had missed. 'There came the point when it was so confining that I knew that unless I took off and became a person and not just a mother and a worker I would lose my sanity.' This two-year fling as a student was sufficient for Stevie. Having recharged her batteries, she was back in her normal routine.

In all the cases of extreme hardship that emerged in the survey, the pattern was similar: an early marriage, young children, an early divorce. Of course single mothers with young children had the toughest time, but it was not easy for married women either. For Rita Peros who was to succeed in the chemical industry it was the never-ending physical slog that pulled her down. With six children and a home help only twice a week, she spent all her weekends and evenings doing housework, helping the children with their homework, and preparing dinners. For Nancy Lennon, too, now owner of a construction company, it was the physical burden that got her down: 'I used to work from getting up in the morning until going to bed at night.' But in Nancy's case her difficulties were partly of her own making, because she spent a lot of time she did not have on keeping a 'nice home': 'If your house is not nice you don't feel right.'

When a woman chooses to go into business she must get her priorities right, and a tidy home cannot be put at the top of the list. Sheila Stevens realised this, and in order to cope with a retarded child, a husband, and a computer business she had to sacrifice the tidiness of her home. Although, in her words, this 'degenerated to a stage which most people would find unacceptable', she did not let this worry her and it did not bother her husband either. But it worried other people and their criticism hurt not so much because they commented on the state of the house, but because they ignored her achievements and assessed her by the old-fashioned criterion that 'A woman is judged by the cleanliness of her home.' One of her critics who should have known better was a male sociologist who asked her to take part in a study of 'Economic Independence and the Modern Woman', and who afterwards wrote about her: '. . . like many women of her kind she is indifferent to the appearance of her home.'

What enraged Sheila about this was not her exposure as a slovenly housewife – about that she could not care less – but the disparity between the criteria used to judge women and men. A man's merit was not determined by the state of his home or even the cleanliness of his car. Why then a woman's?

Untidy homes are not the hallmark of the business Amazons; quite the opposite in most cases. With growing prosperity, even the most zealous among them succumbed to maids and housekeepers. Yet even with these household duties out of the way, these women had not solved all their domestic problems. The main difficulty stemmed from having to divide their loyalty between family and work. 'You get torn down the middle,' said hotelier Tricia Bishop. Lena Gouldwin, construction magnate, was similarly troubled: 'It was never the technicalities of how to cope physically that disturbed me but it was the feeling that you might not be giving the children all the attention they needed.'

The reason why it is women and not men who are torn between the demands of their families and the demands of their careers is that, despite all the talk about equality, the old male-female axis, whereby the male provides the food and the female keeps home, is still in force and is perpetuated by the myth that women are better than men at some jobs, and that men are better at others. Although in some cases this is true, it is very noticeable that there are many more jobs that women are supposed to do better than men and with which, under this pretext, they are lumbered.

As far as men are concerned, the issue of equality has been satisfactorily resolved by letting women undertake tasks which had previously been reserved exclusively for men. But the net result is that those women who adopt what used to be considered 'masculine' occupations such as banking, medicine, or the law are expected to perform these new tasks in addition to the old ones.

Like paupers who are reluctant to discard their worn-out clothes for fear that the same generous hand that gave them their new ones will take them away, so women dare not abandon their old power base for fear that those who nominated them to their new roles might as easily dismiss them. A change of regime as in Iran, a change of philosophy as in Romania,* or simply high unemployment are sufficient grounds to strip women of their newly-won rights and send them back home.

Most capable women during this interim period, when they have one foot in female territory and the other in male, encounter doubts as to

---

*Deterioration in women's rights and freedom around the world are not restricted to fundamentalist regimes such as that of Iran. The rulers of Communist Romania where women have been considered as equals, at least officially, have recently issued a directive forbidding abortions and encouraging mothers to produce more children.

---

their place and allegiance. Rachel Black, in fashion accessories, being a practical person, avoided the emotional conflict of where her loyalty lay by accepting the fact that, in spite of their apparent equality, her duties were heavier than her husband's and her life therefore tougher.

> I have to accept it, that when the chips are down, the family must come first for a woman. You cannot let your daughter be taken to hospital because she has been knocked down by a bicycle, and stay selling in the showroom. But the husband can, because it is accepted that his wife will look after the children. The wife says to the husband, 'Stay there and I'll go, and I'll phone you from the hospital.' That is accepted. But if the husband says, 'I'll go and I'll phone you from the hospital,' then everybody says, 'What an unfeeling mother.'

Besides the fact that where children require parental attention it is the mother who has to sacrifice her career, the reason women's careers are so vulnerable is that even today, when women constitute 42 per cent of the workforce, the right to work is seen primarily as a man's and not a woman's right. When unemployment is discussed, the subject is never those women who have lost their hard-won financial independence and have been forced to throw themselves on their husband's mercy, but the poor men whose self-esteem is at risk because they are no longer the providers.

When, regardless of the level of financial remuneration, society considers a husband's career more important to him than his wife's career to her, it is also taken for granted that in a crisis it is she who has to sacrifice her career for him and not he for her. Thus it is not only the children who come before a woman's career, but also the husband. The prevailing attitude regarding children is too ingrained in our culture to change in the foreseeable future. But should the husband's interests too have priority over the wife's?

Where children are concerned mothers have no option but to sacrifice their careers; where husbands are concerned, however, they do have the option of sacrificing them. Yet none of the women in the survey took up this option. In order to keep the marriage going, they let their husbands' careers take first place. Unlike the feminists, the business Amazons set out to achieve individual success, not to reform society, so when they come across inequalities they do not stop to fight them, but look for ways to accommodate or circumvent them. Had Rachel Black insisted that her career was as important as her husband's, the marriage would not have survived for thirty-three years.

Being the realist she is, she has accepted the inequalities between the sexes as inevitable and hopes that life will spare her most of them.

> A conflict of interests is looming for the businesswoman. For example, in our business 80 per cent of the selling for the whole year is done in two exhibitions. Each exhibition provides us with orders for six months. Two years ago, a week before the exhibition, my husband was taken to hospital with thrombosis. The show had to go on. So I went to the hospital in the morning, then rushed to the exhibition, and at eight p.m., when the show finished, I went back to the hospital. This was possible because both the show and the hospital were in London. Now imagine if the show were in Paris and my husband was in hospital in London, would I have been able to carry on in the show in Paris? Never. I would have sent a substitute to Paris and stayed in London to visit my husband. I would have had to. But had it been me in the hospital, I am sure he would have gone to Paris. He would have been concerned and he would have phoned twice a day, but he would have still gone and not because he doesn't care about me, but because it is assumed that a man's job comes before his family. The logic behind this is that he shows his love and appreciation of his family by working for them. And who do I work for? For myself? A husband whose wife is in hospital cannot turn to his customer and say, 'I am sorry that I cannot give you my attention because my wife is in hospital.' No one expects him to be there next to her. But if I continued to serve the customers whilst my husband was in hospital, they would say, 'Aren't you in the hospital?'

Accepting the facts of life is not the same as liking them. It simply means facing up to a 'no option' situation without deluding oneself that a change is imminent. Being helpless to alter one's circumstances is humiliating and the moment of full realisation of their importance is the point at which people begin to hope for miracles. The miracle that toy magnate Delia Lewenthal prayed for was to be given a wife:

> If I could only have a wife, it would solve all my problems. Men have wives. Why can't a woman have a wife? She will do all the house chores like a live-in help but she will also give emotional support to the child. A wife who would prepare the child's birthday and make the invitations with her and I will just appear at the party. She would also judge my mood when I return home

tired from work and wouldn't bother me until I had had a drink and had rested for half an hour. It would work beautifully if husbands would be content to stay at home. Role reversals are wonderful. But I do not think it will work because nobody is content to stay at home. The reason why most women stay at home is not because they like it but because coping with work and home is hell. No one asks a man to do it, do they?

With all these difficulties, was it really worth it? Sonia Kaplan's answer is Yes. 'So many women go through similar hardships and much worse, without having much to show for it at the end of the day.' At least in Sonia's case her $100 million mail order business, her two sons who work with her, and her successful second marriage are fair compensations for the hard time she had. Lydia Eastern, too, a single parent married at fifteen and compelled to divorce a year later when she had a son, has no doubt about it: 'It was difficult, but I knew that I had taken the chance to succeed. Had I taken an easier course, like not studying in the evenings in addition to working and bringing up my son, it might have been easier in the short term, but not in the long run.' With Lollobrigida looks, an $80 million travel business and a handsome grownup son, the only item that is missing from the successful family picture is a husband, an omission which after twenty-four years on her own Lydia intends to correct. 'I still hope to get married one day. But this time on my terms, as an equal.'

It is not only the single mothers who had no option but to fend for themselves who did not regret the difficulties. Married women whose husbands were willing to support them in style accepted the difficulties as a low price. Nina Dean reckoned: 'Between rotting at home and waiting for my husband to return from work – any difficulties were worth it.' Hotel owner Susanna Barnes agreed: 'It gave me a sense of worthwhileness. That I was a person to be reckoned with and not just a wife.'

The Guilt of Working Mothers

Working mothers are expected to feel guilty because it is assumed that their children cannot receive the same care and attention as those of housebound mothers. This guilt cuts across economic and social barriers so that the cleaning lady whose children return from school to an empty house and the rich businesswoman whose children are collected from school by the chauffeur, fed by the housekeeper, and tutored by the governess, are equally affected.

Like most of society's rules, those regulating child care are based on the capabilities of the average woman, and neither exempt nor acknowledge those with exceptional abilities. Even without going to work most housewives find their children a handful, so it is assumed that mothers who combine work with child care must be neglecting their children. Needless to say, there is no proof of this. No scientific study has been able to correlate the relationship between quality and quantity of maternal care, and the ratio between a child's wellbeing and the number of hours his mother spends in the home remains an open question.

Distinguishing between the cleaning lady who works out of necessity and the business Amazon who works from choice, society is readier to absolve the cleaning lady, for nothing is more abhorrent to the guilt promoters than mothers who work to satisfy their needs rather than those of their children. But guilt, like fear, is only a limited deterrent. It is enough to observe the pleasure the smoker gets from smoking, the fat man from eating, and the mountaineer from climbing to realise that pleasure is an even more potent force than fear. Similarly, feelings of guilt have not deterred the businesswomen from pursuing their particular form of pleasure.

There are three ways to eliminate guilt: by eradicating its causes; by learning to live with it; by rejecting it. Most working mothers unable to take the constant barrage of guilt opt for the elimination of the cause and cease to work. But not the business Amazons. With or without guilt feelings they pursued their careers.

Not guilty

The great majority (76 per cent) of the women in the survey refused to feel guilty. They justified their part-time motherhood on several grounds.

The absence of a guaranteed formula for successful upbringing was cited by engineering tycoon Janet Draper: 'You never know if you have been a good parent or not until they are grown. So I do what makes me and them feel good. And I hope the kids turn out OK.'

The lack of a convincing correlation between full-time motherhood and children's wellbeing was hotelier Susanna Barnes's reason: 'I believe that healthy neglect – and I don't mean detrimental neglect – helps them to be themselves. I spent an awful lot of time without anyone and I survived it – so did they.'

Or business was simply considered a superior calling, as by Linda Cartwright, millionairess fashion designer:

> If you are really obsessed with what you are doing, then it helps you not to feel guilty about neglecting the child. Of course if you are not 100 per cent with the child, you are neglecting it 50 per cent of the time. But as I am obsessed by what I do, I don't allow the guilt feelings to rise and take over.

But the revelation that a working mother need not feel guilty about her children did not always come early or easily. How they eliminated their guilt feelings varied according to individual circumstances. Some refused to be superwomen, for example restaurateur Cathy Simmons Randall:

> Women have to decide what they want without feeling guilty about it. If they decide to have a career they should not also decide to breastfeed their children and tear themselves apart – because you cannot change a baby's diapers yourself, feed it yourself, and have a big job outside.

Others restricted their guilt feelings to certain occasions. Toy specialist Delia Lewenthal, for instance:

> I only feel guilty about one trip a year. I have to go to Europe for almost a month every year, and I tear myself into shreds over it. I send her presents and I phone every day. But other than that I don't feel guilty about three or four day trips.

Still others, like Anne Liddie, whose business career began with a leisure centre inspired by her own children's needs, realise that children have a life of their own.

> Sometimes I felt guilty. I felt that I should talk to my kids more and then I would go home and say, 'Let's have supper together.' And they would say they were going out. And I'd sit there feeling really glum. Until I realised that children have a life of their own and that their need for parents took up only a small part of that life.

One way or another these women found ways of coping that did not entail giving in and giving up.

Guilty

Human nature being what it is, a few of the women (24 per cent) enjoyed the cake and then regretted having eaten it. When people have an option to avoid feelings of guilt by eliminating a certain activity, yet do not take advantage of this option, one must wonder why. There was no need for any of them to feel guilty about their families. They could have stopped working, or they could have stopped feeling guilty. Their having chosen to maintain both their careers and their guilt, suggests that they considered feeling guilty something worth preserving: proof that their business pursuits had not destroyed their female natures.

The 24 per cent who did feel guilty about their children fell into four categories:

a those who had no reason to feel guilty;
b those who felt guilty only about the emotional neglect of their children;
c those who felt guilty in retrospect; and
d those who had been made to feel guilty.

Those who had no reason to feel guilty were the ones who started in business when their children were already in their teens. The fact that they could still feel guilty after having put in twelve years of full-time motherhood shows how irrational these feelings were.

Zelda Main started her cosmetics business when her sons were in their teens. Until then she had not worked, and had excelled in all domestic pursuits. Why should such a woman feel guilty? Is it because women are so insecure in their new role that they are ready to atone for crimes they have not committed?

Emotional neglect is an easy crime of which to accuse oneself and working mothers who want to feel guilty often fall back on this. When they were poor they could not provide for all their children's material needs, now they are rich they must be letting them down some other way. It is as if it is impossible to be a mother without feeling guilty; and as if it is only the mother who can provide for a child's emotional needs.

It is restrictive enough that only women can give birth and only women can breastfeed. There is no reason why reading a book to a child, or taking him or her to the zoo, should be an exclusively feminine occupation. There is also no reason why only the mother should feel guilty. For the most part the children have fathers too. Why should their upbringing be entrusted solely to their mothers? Lena Gouldwin was no single parent; she was married to the same man for twenty years; and yet, despite the fact that she was the bigger earner and he the one with more free time, she was the one who felt bad.

> My guilt is a big thing. My children found out at a very early age how to lay guilt on me. When I had to go away on a business trip my daughter would suddenly say, 'We have a piano recital; I was hoping you could be there, all the other mothers are going to be there.' They specialised in guilt traps. As a woman you probably feel a great deal more guilt than if you were a man. That has always been a problem with me.

It is also quite usual to feel guilty in retrospect, for maternal guilt is one of those diseases that have a long incubation period. Sometimes it can erupt when the cause for guilt no longer exists. Jay Simpson, for instance, who runs a large plant manufacturing food additives, says:

> At the time I did not feel guilty. Amongst working-class people we did not talk about guilt. But I think the fact that I was a businesswoman told the tale. I think my daughter grew up a little bit frightened of me. I think it was the way that I said things. I just had to look, I never had to touch her. But I don't think that I realised what was happening at that time. Only now when I watch her with her own children do I see the difference in the way she is bringing up her children and the way I brought her up, and I feel bad about it.

There are other ways in which mothers are made to feel guilty. Since the revival in Hitler's Germany of woman's traditional role – *Kinder, Küche, und Kirche* (children, kitchen, and church) – surprisingly little has changed on the feminine front; and this despite the publicity that the women's movement has received, and despite a greatly equalised legal system. A recent survey found that 69 per cent of American women still considered motherhood and homemaking a woman's prime occupation, proving that despite the obvious improvement in women's social and legal status, the essence of a woman's function in society has not changed. It is therefore no wonder that the few nonconformist women are made to feel guilty not only by men but also by their conforming and powerful sisters.

The aim should not be to change the wishes of the 69 per cent of womanhood who are perfectly entitled to be traditional housewives, if that is what they want, but to make sure that the minority who have chosen a different life style are not made to feel guilty about it. One of the sad ironies of the situation is that it is a direct product of women's liberation. As long as women were seen as ignorant and feeble creatures, they were discouraged from spending time with their children, especially their sons. Going back from Victorian times to ancient Greece we find that the Greeks had special male servants and tutors to bring up their sons. In Victorian Britain all middle-class children had nannies and governesses and the French sent their children away until they could be introduced into civilised company.

If, as it seems, 'staying with the children' was not a maternal behaviour pattern throughout history, how is it that nowadays, when women have become equal as never before, they accept that staying with the children is their exclusive responsibility? Illogical as it might sound, this resulted from the liberation of women. The same liberation that allowed them education, the vote, and career opportunities has also shackled them to the kitchen and the children.

By becoming better educated and higher earners they became a threat to men in areas where men had held exclusive rights. It was imperative to halt their advance before they should change the accepted order of society by blurring the separation between male and female functions, and finally, perhaps, making men redundant. The trick that halted the advancement of women was brilliant in its simplicity and effectiveness. Women were told that since they were now so well educated they could be entrusted with the exclusive upbringing of their children. Furthermore it was impressed on them that, since they were in possession of that invaluable commodity, knowledge, it was their moral duty to ensure its transfer to their offspring. In their gullibility women swallowed the bait. Even those who could well afford help with their children immersed themselves with missionary zeal in this new vocation, of improving the quality of the human race.

The ploy succeeded beyond men's wildest expectations. In one sweep, by flattering their wives that they were the only persons suitable to look after their joint creation, men have stopped women from advancing themselves, and eliminated their most threatening competitors. In addition they have also got the best possible nannies for their children. They have thus ensured that the earning of money, one of the few roles they know how to perform better than women, has remained largely a male preserve. Once the bright and educated women who could threaten their hold on the economy were safely locked up in the home, men had the lion's share of the economic realm.

It is no longer possible to go on paying lip service to women's liberation and join the chorus of interested parties who hail achievements that have not been achieved. The fact is that where it really matters, in the economic and political citadels, there are almost no women. They are not there because the top female brains that could have penetrated these strongholds have been brainwashed into believing that it is more important to read fairy tales aloud to two-year-olds, or to prepare gourmet dishes for their husband's business friends. What is also undeniable is that, irksome as 'house detention' may sometimes be, it is usually less demanding than taking part in the combats that go on outside.

It has been said before and it is being said again that regardless of the reasons, if women are content to remain in confinement when they have the choice of opening the door and walking out, their choice should be respected. Our concern must be with those who are not content, yet are scared to step outside because they have been indoctrinated with the guilty fear that their own self-fulfilment will inevitably lead to their children's unhappiness. These women must be made aware that a mother's love is not to be measured by the number of hours that she spends with her children. If physical proximity were the criterion for parental love, most fathers would rate as hating their offspring, for the time they spend with them is minimal.

If fathers' love is not measured by the time they spend with their children, why should mothers' love be measured differently? Do fathers possess some faster acting chemical catalyst than mothers? Can they give their children the same love and attention in a fraction of the time? Marlene Jacobs does not think so. An outstanding publicist, she believes that mothers too can achieve good relationships with their children without spending twenty-four hours a day with them. Marlene does not have to acquaint herself with the latest socio-psychological studies about the effect of a mother's work on her children's wellbeing. As a mother she is sensitive enough to her daughter's feelings.

I don't actually feel guilty, I feel that everybody that knows my daughter Jennifer knows that she is a happy, secure child. Next door there is a little boy who is with his mother all the time and he is a nervous, miserable child. So I don't believe it's the amount of time the mother spends with the child. It's the relationship. But society makes you feel very guilty because you don't spend all your time with your children.

Working mothers like Marlene resent the pressure put on them by psychologists and all males, by their own housebound sisters, and by the media. The way they are made to feel guilty is subtle but effective. To start with, it is assumed that because the mother physically carried the child, her relationship with it is more important than the father's. This can never be disproved because there are not enough husbands who have reversed roles with their wives and stayed with the children. Consequently most studies deal with the effects a mother's work has on her children, and not with how their father's work affects them. It is surely obvious though that it would be the person who physically attended to the child that the child would need most.

Marlene is not an intellectual; she is a hard-working mother who has built up a business in promotion and publicity, and has little time for or understanding of the feminists' exposé of the politicisation of motherhood. But the implications of the continuous new 'discoveries' concerning the child's need for its mother do not escape her. Instinctively she senses that whatever these 'discoveries' discover implies criticism of women like her who want to combine a career with motherhood.

Only the other day there was something on the radio about no matter what the birth is like, they should not take the babies away from their mothers, because those first few hours and those first days are vital. When you hear something like that, you start feeling bad, you start asking yourself if you are doing the right thing. You start feeling guilty.

The most horrible thing that can be done to working women is to turn their children against them, by letting them think that the only good, loving, and caring mothers are those who stay at home. For years caterer Iris Williamson was made to feel guilty by her daughter: 'Why aren't you at home when I come from school? Why aren't you like the other mothers?' Now the daughter is a mother herself and behaves just as Iris did.

Older children go on expecting service from their housebound mothers not because they need it but because it is nice to be waited upon. Dorothy Simmonds, who became a leader in oil drilling equipment, thought that when she was thirty-nine, her children old enough to manage without her, she could go to college and get a degree. She announced her decision and the children were horrified. It meant they would no longer receive the high quality service they were used to.

> How it hurt. I thought they would be proud that at the age of thirty-nine I still wanted an education. I thought they would feel that after twenty years of living only for them, I was entitled to a life of my own. But no, what they were concerned about was that they would have to do their own laundry. So I put a big sign above the washer, giving cleaning instructions how to use the machine, so that everyone would know how to wash his own clothes.

Preaching the child's exclusive and continuous need for its natural mother to an audience of bored middle-class housewives will not do much harm. But preaching the same message to working-class women who can ill-afford to stay at home is positively immoral, because not only does it deprive them and their children of an improved standard of living, but it loads them with guilt.

The Issue of Domestics

Postulating the same way of life for all classes is unfair and dangerous. For the middle-class woman whose husband earns enough to own two cars, devoting herself to her children in her sunswept open-plan house with a swimming pool in the yard, and a daily cleaner to relieve her of the hard work, might be enjoyable at least for a time. It is not the same thing for an unmarried mother whose home is a 10-ft square, flea-infested room with a shared kitchen and bathroom.

The social injustice of the situation is blatant. So what is one to do? If one recommends to an unprivileged mother that she stays with her children, one condemns her to added misery. Yet if one reserves such advice for the affluent classes one breaches the rules of human equality. The solution is not that difficult, particularly if one accepts that the dictum that it is best for a child to be looked after by its natural mother should not be applied indiscriminately. The solution is in increased numbers of good, government-aided day care centres for the needy, and an end to the propaganda that children suffer if for forty hours a week they are cared for by others.

An example of the ridiculous extremes of the 'looking after your own child' doctrine was recounted by travel organiser Juliette Marlon, who was a member of a Women's Help Welfare Committee in Sacramento. The committee was made up of wealthy, leisured sub-urban wives. Its aim was to help uneducated unmarried mothers, mostly from minority groups, to train for a job of some kind, so that eventually they would be able to support themselves and their children. Yet its members refused to set up day care centres where the children could stay while their mothers went out to work, because they claimed that it was an affront to the idea of the family in general for mothers to leave their children and go out to work. As a result, these unmarried mothers were sent back to rot in their airless rooms with no other hope than to live on welfare handouts forever.

Why? Because a group of high principled ladies thought it right to apply the tenet of 'each mother to her child', to those for whom the results would be calamitous. Had they asked these young mothers what they wanted, they would have been surprised to learn that they would have chosen a day care centre for their children, and the freedom of being separated from them for eight hours a day. But they did not ask these women what they wanted because they did not want to face the truth that the very custom of 'looking after your own child' was a practice that could not be transferred to every woman.

In countries like the USA and Britain the pressures to make women feel guilty about not living solely for their children are subliminal. There are no laws that demand it, and no financial incentives for mothers who stay at home. The pressure is applied subtly. Women's libbers, for instance, condemn the employment of maids and house-keepers as not becoming to womanhood, when there are many women who could not do anything else or even prefer working in a luxurious apartment to toiling in a polluted factory that endangers their health.

A lot of nonsense is talked about the demeaning role of domestic servants. It is time for this issue to be aired properly. Why should it carry a stigma to work as a domestic? Housework, looking after children included, is a job like any other job, and if the pay is good there is no reason why it should be considered an inferior occupation. It is appreciated that in the past, when this kind of work was miserably paid, one could justify its low status and the maids and housekeepers who left it for factory work were right to sell their labour to the highest bidder. But things have changed. The majority of women who require home help are themselves working women. Industrial jobs have not proven to be women's salvation, and the rise of unemployment coupled with advances in technology have eliminated many low-paid female jobs. The argument that keeping house for a working woman is not demeaning, but the equal of any other job, is based on two grounds. First, this is not the same as working for a lady of leisure; and second, it is comparable to working as the personal assistant of a male director.

Keeping house for a working mother is similar to nursing an invalid, as both are prevented from performing certain physical functions, one because of her physical disability and the other because of her physical absence. Thus the housekeeper of a working woman is her helper and not her inferior. Furthermore, because the working mother is prevented from being in two places at once, she is totally dependent on her stand-in and is therefore bound to pay her well and treat her with respect.

It seems to be accepted that there is a discrepancy between the degree of unpleasantness of an unpleasant job when it is carried out for oneself, and for someone else. For example, take the washing of soiled diapers (a job so classically nasty that people are now prepared to go to some expense to avoid it by the use of disposables): when the maid washes them it is supposed to be demeaning, but when the owner of a $20 million business handles them she is expected to find fulfilment in it, because it is her own baby's excreta. Soiled diapers do not go through a metamorphosis, they remain the same whoever is dealing with them. If it is admitted that they are smelly and unpleasant to handle, then they are unpleasant for the mother as well as for the maid. But if it is agreed that a child's excreta is a manifestation of the Lord's creation, then the maid as well as the mother should treat the soiled diapers with the respect they deserve. What one cannot have is two different criteria for the same phenomenon.

If the running of a home has been analysed and found to be a demeaning occupation then, on the grounds that every person should clean up his or her own mess, it could have been argued that the mother and not the maid should perform it. With housework thus acknowledged as a soul destroying job, mothers who wanted to bail themselves out would have to entice others to replace them with high financial rewards. The mother substitutes would have been compensated for the unpleasantness of their job in the same way as (at least in theory) miners and garbage collectors are compensated for theirs. And just as no one suggests that each householder should remove his own trash, so also it cannot be argued that each wife should clean her own home.

But the present attitude to domestic work is not that. When wives perform it, it is a worthwhile occupation, but when paid labour carries it out it is demeaning. The incredible thing about these double standards is that no one even tries to disguise or justify their transparent hypocrisy.

The double standards that govern domestic work do not apply only to the person who does the job but also to the person it is done for. Consider the illustrious job of personal assistant. When an unattached female dresses smartly for a married family man, smiles at him for eight hours a day, tidies his desk, arranges for his sauna, cheats on his behalf by telling people he is out when he is in, and generally tries to fulfil most of his needs, her job is essentially that of a servant; but it is dignified with a high-sounding title. When the same service is rendered to a working mother at her residential address rather than at her office, the job description is 'housekeeper', which has the connotation of a servant and not of a personal assistant. But in essence there is no difference between the two jobs: both aim to assist an employer who has a lot on his plate.

When domestic staff deserted the homes of leisured nineteenth-century ladies in favour of dusty mills, they changed the social pattern of society and forced women to take greater control of their lives. For this they are owed the gratitude of society. But times have changed, and the grimy factories have not proven the salvation women expected them to be. The jobs are boringly repetitive, the pace exhausting, and the pay poor. In view of this, shouldn't the merits of domestic work, where the pace is slower, the work more varied, and the surroundings more pleasant, be reassessed? It is not suggested that such employment would suit everyone but those who found industrial work unsatisfactory should be offered an alternative, and should not be made to feel inadequate for choosing it.

For those career women who have not deprived themselves of home help, no justification of the system should be necessary. But there are many whose life would have been vastly eased had they not adopted the mistaken teaching of 'liberal' women. Lingerie manufacturer Linda Bailie was active in a Los Angeles women's group which, among other good causes, tried to help underprivileged women who had no commercial skills and therefore no prospect of useful employment. Being a businesswoman who employed housekeepers, Linda suggested that one of the ways to help these women was to train them as housekeepers. She tells what happened next:

———

The committee objected to my proposal as vehemently as if I had suggested turning these women into prostitutes. They claimed that it was an affront to the dignity of mankind to expect somebody to come into your house and clean it for you. I was horrified. I never looked on myself as a bad person because I had help in the house. I looked at it always the way I look at people who help me at work. I cannot do everything myself, so I delegate and pay for their help.

Besides losing jobs for those who need them, portraying domestic employment as degrading reduces the number of entrants into the professions and creates an actual shortage of talent. Women who have the potential to break into the outside world are prevented from doing so. Like Moses on Mount Nebo they see the promised land but cannot enter it.

Opposition to career women who dare to make their lives easier by resorting to mother substitutes has united three most unlikely allies: men, homemakers, and feminists. The men want to keep the women servantless to eliminate competition. The homemakers, posing as the legitimate guardians of all children, proclaim that they are needed there to prevent neglect. The feminists are determined to prevent the employment of sisters in domestic chores.

This unholy alliance between 'left' and 'right', conservatives and progressives, men and women, all aiming to make career women feel guilty about their children, is shameful. High achieving women deserve better. They already have enough on their hands: daily encounters with males who regard them as inferiors, husbands whose egos have to be constantly massaged, and children who are made to question their mothers' love. The last thing they need is for other women to gang up against them.

The Amazonian Children

How the business Amazons coped with their children was only one side of the mother-child relationship. How their children coped with their mother was the other. It has commonly been taken for granted that they must have been deprived. How else could the propagandists of children's exclusive need for their mothers promote their views? But were the children deprived? Did they fare worse than those of mothers who had no other interests than the upbringing of their children?

The world of business is not like that of show business or politics, and attracts little media attention. Consequently, despite their success, the women in this survey were not celebrities and their children experienced no conflict between their mothers' public and private image. The majority of these women started in business after their children had reached school age, so that their children's early years were no different from those of any other children. Rose Kraus, who owns several radio stations, is an example of such a mother: 'I took eight years off to raise my children. I think women have to take some zigs and zags in their careers. Especially at the time when the children are really young.'

Later on, until their early teens, what differentiated the Amazonian children from others, was that their mothers were not at home when they returned from school, and that they were not always present at school functions. In total only 19 per cent of the survey's women were confronted with such complaints, and not necessarily from all their children. Sometimes, as with the daughter of travel-firm owner Lesley Trance, the grudge appeared only years later when she was about to become a mother herself and told Lesley: 'I hope you will have more time for your grandchild than you had for me.'

How should such complaints be assessed? Are they to be taken as a manifestation of the children's suffering or of their awakening to the fact that they are different? The 81 per cent whose children did not complain explained their adjustment in terms such as: 'The children didn't know anything different.' Hence it seems that at least some of the children's complaints have to be discounted because they originated from the comparison between their own and other mothers' behaviour, not from genuine deprivation. When a mother has a good relationship with her children, the fact that when they return from school they meet the housekeeper or the sitter instead of her is not going to make them resentful. But when in addition the home environment is strained, her absence from home takes on a more sinister meaning.

In the same way as parents assess their children's traits and adapt themselves to them, so also children have quite a clear idea about their parents' make-up and adjust themselves to it. The expectations of a businesswoman's child from his mother are different from those of a housewife's child. To the same extent that the latter would feel uneasy with an Amazonian mother, so the Amazonian child would find it difficult to adjust to a mother who waited on him, interfered with his privacy, and nagged about his homework. When Niki Summers, cosmetics millionairess, started to question her role as an Amazonian mother and feared that the children might have been deprived of companionship, she discussed the matter openly with them.

> I have asked them and I have analysed it with them, and they said that sometimes when they came home from school they would have liked to have seen me. But they said that the thought of having all my energy channelled towards them was so dreadful that they were glad I worked. They said: 'If all you had to do was to think about us, we couldn't stand it.'

For children to expect mothers to be at home when they return from school, but not fathers, is not the expression of an innate need for the mother, but the result of the habit of seeing the mother and not the father at home. Where this habit has not been established, the children view the mother's work as they do the father's and, to the same extent that they do not hate him for returning home only in the evening, so they also do not hate the mother. For the majority of housebound mothers these facts of life are not easily digestible, because they undermine their way of life and the justification of their sacrifice.

Janet Draper's children knew only one type of mother, a working one. At weekends and during school vacations they would visit their parents' enormous engineering assembly plant and observe them in their managerial roles. When one day, on one of those rare occasions when Janet was fed up with work, she came home and told her children that she was tired and intended to retire, instead of being pleased that from now on their mother would be a mother like all other mothers, they became worried. Janet says:

> They looked at me with bewilderment and asked, 'What are you going to do, aren't you going to make any more money? You cannot retire, because all you know is accounts receivable and gushers.' And I said, 'I am going to stay home and play with you.' They laughed and said, 'You don't know how to play.' So I said, 'Sure I do, test me.' They consulted each other and the seven-year-old, the youngest one, said, 'OK, let us roll the garbage cans.' At this I gave up and said, 'You've got me. I don't retire. You are right. I don't know how to play.' They enjoyed it. But for a moment they were really concerned about having to change their way of life because of my decision to retire and stay at home.

The impression that as strong women the business mothers had to be tough parents is incorrect. On the contrary, because they were aware of their impressive image they went out of their way not to be over-powering where their children were concerned. Travel organiser Lesley Trance remarks:

> I have always had to be more tactful with my children than any of my non-working girlfriends. Especially when they were grown up and the issues were more serious – because automatically they take it for granted that you are a strong, powerful woman, trying to get your way. So with the children I had to be extremely soft and understanding.

In the final analysis, these mothers were convinced that pursing their business careers had no adverse effects on their children; and to the sceptics they show their trump card, the fact that 63 per cent of them had one or more of their children working with them.

8 | Matriarchal Bosses

It is widely believed that female bosses are bitches. It is said that they are petty and unyielding, that they are jealous and halt the progress of other women; in effect, that they behave like former slaves who are now on top. Whether this unflattering image is justified, or whether it is no more than malicious slander, will now be examined.

Are Female Bosses Bitches?

The norms of morals and behaviour are not absolute values, and the definitions 'good', 'bad', 'a bitch' are not absolutes: they are relative descriptions derived from comparisons. From this it follows that the portrayal of female bosses as self-seeking bitches must have been arrived at by contrast with male bosses who have been found to be generous, reasonable, open-minded and fully willing to promote their rivals.

'You find them, I'll work for them free' was how scores of employees of both sexes greeted this conclusion that if female bosses were bitches, then male bosses were angels. In reality no bosses, male or female, are angels. So how and why did the myth about the bitchiness of female bosses originate? As no studies measuring the niceness or nastiness of bosses have been carried out, or ever could be, the stereotype can have no scientific basis. However, smoke indicates fire and in the absence of scientific support it has to be assumed that the unflattering reputation of female bosses owes its origins to three groups: male executives, female employees, and male employees.

For the purpose of understanding why female bosses are deemed to be hard and unrepresentative of womanhood, a distinction has to be made between female executives and female owners. But when the three groups joined forces to tarnish the image of the female boss they failed to make this distinction between the female executive who threatened their status and prospects and the female owner with whom they were not in competition.

The arrival of the female executive on the corporate scene threatened male executives because it exposed them to a new type of competitor whose tactics were different to their own; it was also the end of their exclusive dominance. One of the last bastions of male supremacy, the corporate structure, crumbled, and women, formerly restricted to the area of employees only, began to climb over the wall. Men who previously derived a crucial sense of their masculinity from the nature of their job now had to look elsewhere, and when the search failed they knew whom to blame: their emasculating female competitors. By denying the feminine attributes of their female colleagues and describing them as ogresses and bitches, male executives both tried to diminish them and to discourage other women from following in their footsteps. In such unwelcoming surroundings the newly arrived female executives had only one defence: to survive through sheer toughness – hence the reputation for hardness. Female employees, too, were unsettled by the arrival of their executive sisters, who would treat them as equals in terms of gender and withdraw the allowances that male bosses made for the 'weaker' and 'less intelligent' sex. As for male employees, having a woman boss was the ultimate degradation; now they were not superior even to women.

This unflattering portrayal of female executives, intended to lower their standing in the corporate structure, also stuck to female business owners. The reason was simply the greater number and visibility of the female executives, so that these and not the female business owners became the representatives of all businesswomen. Yet, despite their joint, false image, women business owners are a different breed.

The biggest difference between the two is that, however senior, the executives are still employees whose promotion and even survival depend on someone else. Although this contrast also exists between male business owners and male executives, the fact that the woman executive's survival generally depends on a male superior makes the contrast between the female business owner and the female executive more acute.

Operating not within male territory but parallel to it, female business owners do not compete with men and their interests do not conflict (except in the obvious case of rival firms). Being their own bosses, they also have no need to prove their superiority to other women, for their ownership puts them on a higher footing from the start. Having the power to hire and fire, they need not resort to the kind of underhand techniques that are attributed to female executives; they can be straightforward and relaxed in their relationships with their collegues and employees. They do, however, have a job to do and they adopt the leadership style which they believe will achieve the best results.

The women in this study rejected the suggestion that they might be hard bosses: demanding – yes; hard – no. Fifty-four per cent saw themselves as demanding, 26 per cent as reasonable, and 20 per cent as soft.

Demanding Bosses

The 54 per cent of bosses who described themselves as demanding saw their style of leadership in such terms as these: 'I am a hard taskmaster.' 'I am a dictator, difficult and demanding.' 'I would not like to work for me.'

The most common reason given by them for being demanding was their desire for perfection. To quote Eileeen Geermie, who owns a $12 million gift business: 'I like perfection, whether it is in the execution of a design, setting a table, or preparing a speech. I will not compromise.'

Aiming to be popular leaders, they did not rely merely on their ownership for the legitimisation of their leadership, but sought their employees' endorsement. They set personal examples of commitment and skill, and acknowledged the efforts of their followers in several ways. Ellie Leonard (annual sales $5 million): 'I don't ask my employees to do anything I would not do myself. If the floor needed cleaning I would clean it.' Frances Roberts (annual sales $55 million): 'I am more demanding with myself than I am with anyone else. I answer the telephones, I make the coffee. I pick up the dishes after lunch. There isn't anything that I won't do.' Barbara Shelensky, in health farms: 'I have done every job that I have asked people to do, so I know how long it takes and I know what to expect.' Harriet Hartfield architectural builder: 'I can do almost anything that I ask someone to do. So I know that it can be done. No one can fob me off by claiming that it can't be done better.' Such readiness to perform any job is rarely encountered among executives, who can be extremely sensitive about status.

The women tycoons in the survey remunerated good work with good pay and considerate treatment: 'I am strict but we pay well.' 'We pay above the market price.' 'I am always there to talk. If they have a problem the door is always open.' Being able to perform most jobs, and treating one's employees fairly were considered by the 'demanding' business Amazons to constitute good management. What they did not regard as good management was the mixing of personal sympathies with business leadership. In business, the job took priority over the person, even if that person was themselves: 'I do not tolerate illness, lateness, or going out to shop.' 'I do not carry lazy people.' 'I am out to get the job done, not to be liked.'

A consequence of being a demanding boss is that it makes one appear ruthless. For a male boss ruthlessness (real or imagined) is a sign of masculinity. For a woman boss, a reputation for toughness is not an advantage. Although it is associated with capability and smartness, it suggests the loss of a certain softness which is often mistaken for true femininity. Consequently only women who are confident of their femininity can take the attribute of 'tough' in their stride: 'I am either loved to die for or am hated.' 'Reps are terrified of me.'

Some businesswomen, such as Nina Dean, the *grande dame* of the British travel industry, were amused by their tough public image. In Nina's case this came to light when a director of IATA (the airline regulatory body), who did not know her personally, came to her after a lecture and said, 'I have been most impressed by your presentation and the great respect you are given in the industry. For the life of me I cannot believe that you are the devil that everyone was telling me you are.' Others, like farmer and soft drinks manufacturer Rebecca Kemmis, felt rather upset, because they did not see themselves as tough. She says, 'It sometimes upsets me when people say, "Mrs Kemmis is tough." I am only tough when people are unfair. I sincerely believe that I am a rather considerate person. Most of my staff have been with me for years.'

Women, who on the whole are brought up to look upon themselves as soft and caring, are bound to find it difficult to come to terms with the fact that business success requires different qualities. Ideally they would have liked to get the results that tough bosses achieve, without compromising their image of nice, considerate people. But as Stevie

Frederick, electronics components distributor, has discovered, this is impossible. When one has to show results, one cannot always be nice. This does not mean that one becomes a bitch. Time and again the businesswoman differentiated between being tough and demanding, attributes which they did not mind, and a bitch, a description they resented. Stevie Frederick explains:

> To be tough is one thing, to be a bitch is another. A bitch is petty, spiteful, and insecure. Tough is to have your priorities right. I am tough but in no way am I a bitch.

Nevertheless, despite acknowledging the need to be tough and despite admitting to having mastered this art, the need to be considered feminine kept the business Amazons from wholehearted commitment to toughness. Even hardy operators like market researcher Daphne Glover tried to convince themselves that beneath the hard facade there was a soft heart: 'The girls in the office are used to me now, they know that one's bark is worse than one's bite, but outsiders must be horrified. Sometimes the painter has been here and I bet he thinks: "That old bag, I won't work for her for anything in the world."'

Soft Bosses

Despite the fact that 20 per cent of the business Amazons defined themselves as soft, it is questionable whether such a creature as a soft boss exists. The terms are contradictory, because in order to be a boss one has to value results above relationships, and in order to be soft one has to value relationships above results. The question of whether it is possible for a boss to be soft is not merely hypothetical. Hardware millionairess Jenny Kinnock Trafford, who became a businesswoman after she had lost her husband, had to ask herself the same question. Was it possible for a boss to be nice? Her friends warned her that it was not.

> A friend of mine who had been in business for some fifty years said to me, 'You can't be a sweet, nice lady and run a business. You have got to be a mean son of a bitch.' I said, 'I can't be that way.' He said, 'Yes, you can, because if you don't people will step

on you. They kick you around and take advantage of you and steal from you. You have got to go in and be as mean as you can be.' It isn't as bad as he said it would be, but I had to stop being a nice lady.

Like Jenny, health expert Doris Smith also started with the intention of being a friendly boss but discovered that in business one could not afford to be too soft. In her words:

> I try to fit both roles of friend and boss but it doesn't work. You can't be a boss and a friend at the same time, you have got to be one or the other. Having learnt my lesson, I am trying to create a comparatively relaxed atmosphere. We believe that if you make it a nice environment for the staff they will work better and probably stay a little bit longer. Unfortunately there are always the few odd people who will abuse it. On the whole I am maybe a bit too soft.

Not being a soft boss does not mean that one cannot be a good boss. But in their eagerness to prove to themselves as well as to others that their occupation has not detracted from their feminity, these particular businesswomen adopted the feminine attribution of 'soft', which they definitely were not, instead of the neuter description of 'good', which they most probably were. Their mistaken self-identification as 'soft' stemmed from their mistaken interpretation of what a soft boss stood for. For them being soft meant remunerating their employees well, and taking a personal interest in their welfare. Although concern for one's workforce is commendable, in the existing climate of labour relations it is not a sign of softness, but a necessity.

For an employer to refer to herself as 'very benevolent' because she paid some veteran employees for time lost through sickness, when it is obvious that the motive was to ensure their continued dedicated service, demonstrates either extreme naivety or an extreme need to see oneself as a nice person. Rachel Black describes a related incident:

> I had an employee phoning me last night to give me the result of the X-rays which I had arranged for her at the hospital because her doctor would not send her, and I asked her to let me know how it was, and she did. And I have arranged for her to see my specialist next Thursday. She came to me and said: 'Mrs Black, can you help?' I am very maternal. I think it is very important.

Construction magnate Lena Gouldwin sees herself in the same light: 'If anyone is in trouble here they know my door is always open. I really mean it. I am very aware of people's personal problems and I take an interest in them.'

The remuneration of good work with good pay is not, of course, practised only by female employers; but involving oneself with employees' personal welfare is more typical of them than of male employers. This is not because they enjoy such intervention more than men, but because they are in greater need of harmonious relationships. Thus it seems that the reason so many of the women referred to themselves as soft bosses, when it was apparent that they could be as hard as nails, was a recognition of their need to operate in an environment where they were loved and respected. Hitherto such a need for harmonious relationships would have been considered incompatible with successful business ownership, chiefly because it might jeopardise objective decision-making. But the fact that these very successful women have managed to combine good results and harmonious relations with their employees demonstrates that they have hit on a unique leadership style. Frances Roberts claims:

> I run my business the way I run my home. I think the best preparation for being a boss is to be a mother, and the staff are like my children; we have birthday parties, we have surprises, and we have treats: we have a lovely life together. If you look around you will see that it is very relaxed, looking very homelike. I decorated this with our art director using a professional decorator and it is just the way we feel, our attitude towards ourselves.

Had Frances not been the successful owner of a $55 million advertising agency with 175 employees, her suggestion that motherhood was the best training for being a boss, and that employees should be treated like one's children, would have been dismissed as a joke. Just as the western business world considers the hugely successful Japanese management style is unique to Japan and cannot be transplanted, so it may come to be accepted that women have a unique management style that cannot be emulated by men. Once a boss is equated with a mother and employees with children, the 'soft boss' syndrome becomes easier to understand.

Fair and Reasonable Bosses

Only 26 per cent of the business Amazons considered themselves fair and reasonable – that is not too hard and not too soft – knowing from whom to demand more effort and when to ignore a mistake. This did not mean that they were not demanding but 'fair' and 'demanding' were not mutually exclusive qualities. A boss was fair if she both gave and took. From employees, the 'reasonable' woman boss expected two things: high standards of work and honesty. From themselves, they expected to hire the right people and to appreciate these people's efforts.

The emphasis on a high standard of employees stemmed from the realisation that without competent employees even a brilliant boss gets nowhere. Nina Dean explains: 'I appreciate that not everyone is capable of performing to my standards. Some people do try their best, but if their best is not good enough for me, I will get rid of them. It isn't fair on me or on them.' It seems that for these women employers fairness did not include making undue allowances, and definitely did not preclude ruthlessness.

Employees' dishonesty is a sensitive subject with all owners, for in addition to depleting their personal wealth, dishonest employees expose their owners' vulnerability: the worst thing that can happen to a boss is to be 'taken for a ride', something that happens only to fools. Talent agent Genevieve Rouche says: 'If I ever find out that someone lied to me or stole from me that it is. They are out.'

Honest and able employees make it easier for a boss to be reasonable and fair and choosing the right employees in the first place is of crucial importance. Here, everyone's priorities are different. Investment consultant Eva Helsing's was the employee's ability to work independently, while Sheila Stevens, in computers, set greater store by a pleasant personality. Janet Draper wanted employees in her engineering firm who were ambitious: 'There is a fine line between ambition and greed. I don't like greedy people, and many times I have hired the needy rather than the greedy but I have been generally sorry.'

Having hired the right people, the business Amazons considered it an indispensable part of being a fair and reasonable boss to show appreciation. But while most large employers show their appreciation mainly by wage increases, the women tycoons added their personal touch. Health farm proprietor Lisa Collier gives this example:

> I am a very aware boss. Little things, like when someone is cleaning a window, I stop by for a second and say: 'That looks really nice. I like what you are doing today.' So I treat my employees more like a family and a team than just people who are on the payroll.

Hotel owner Susanna Barnes continues on the same theme:

> I am told that as one's business grows one has to change one's management technique into a more formal one. It might be necessary but I don't like it. As long as I'm here I prefer to adopt a more personal approach. I have a good word for everyone. These are people who have been with me for years. When I take visitors around I make sure to introduce them to the staff and praise their contribution to the company. My son, who is a business school graduate, doesn't like it.

The fact that these women set great store by good relations with their employees did not mean they were ready to compromise in their demands from them. In toy manufacturer Delia Lewenthal's words: 'You are perfectly free to make mistakes here. People do it all day long, but not the same mistakes.'

Temper and Temperament

Despite working in one of the most unladylike occupations, the majority of the business Amazons tried to behave like ladies. But not all of them found their self-imposed ladylike behaviour easy to keep up. Nancy Lennon protests: 'Mothers have a breaking point. Mothers also have needs.And as children cannot expect perfection from their mothers, so workers cannot expect it from their bosses.' Showing impatience and giving voice to frustrations are two of the deadliest sins a would-be lady could commit, and these were the two that the businesswomen tried to keep under tight control. With regard to impatience, they failed abysmally: 83 per cent of them admitted to being impatient. In not vocalising their frustration they were more successful, as only 24 per cent admitted punctuating the smooth course of their leadership with the occasional unladylike yell. Linda Cartwright, in fashion: 'I never shout. It doesn't suit me. Some people find shouting enjoyable. I don't. I find it upsetting.' Doreen Hartman who owns food supermarkets: 'No screaming or yelling. I cannot remember any time when I have lost my temper and screamed and yelled.'

If they saw shouting as too masculine a way for them to express disssatisfaction, how did they express it? Doreen Hartman: 'I cut people off and say: "No negotiations." This is the way it should be done.' Elizabeth James, the cabaret performer who became a finance consultant: 'I show my displeasure by talking very quietly. It is almost a whisper. Those who work with me know what it means.'

Had these women added to their vocal control the cardinal virtue of patience, they would have been saints and therefore quite unsuited to the pursuit of business. Fortunately there also existed a minority (24 per cent) that was less controlled and more representative of the business fraternity. Julie Kitson, helicopter magnate, admits: 'I am not ashamed to shout. I can be very adamant and very direct. I am extremely blunt. Not rude. I am very blunt and very direct about things. Then everybody knows where they stand with me.'

Before castigating the 'shouting' Amazons for detracting from the dignity of businesswomen, it ought to be remembered that shouting is indicative of confidence – the confidence to display one's feelings publicly. Few people, and even fewer women, are in a position to disregard the accepted norms of behaviour. Therefore the existence of a handful of 'shouting' Amazons indicates that businesswomen are on their way towards feeling at home in the business world. Ulrike Jameson, pharmaceuticals millionairess, is one such:

> I shout and I don't have any hangups about it. It might be unladylike but it is not unfeminine. And I have never tried to be a lady. To be a woman is exciting, to be a lady is a bore. Now that I am successful, my top people are trying to make the perfect boss out of me. What a bore. I am expected to be sweet and kind, the whole bullshit. I'm not supposed to have any emotions. If somebody drops $10,000 of products I am supposed to be very quiet about it and not scream. I can't. I am not yet that successful. Maybe when $10,000 stops having a meaning to me I shall manage to smile and say, 'Oh, what a shame', and walk on.

One of the boss's prerogatives is to demonstrate her annoyance in a visible and audible manner. An employee's fit of temper may cause his dismissal, but an employer's will merely raise some eyebrows. The fact that the bosses did not generally take advantage of this 'perk' can be interpreted either as a new leadership style peculiar to women, or as a newcomer's lack of confidence which will disappear with time. It will only be possible to tell which when more women join the club.

Women as Financial Controllers

Business achievements are measured in terms of money. Business leadership is not merely a matter of controlling people but also of controlling money. Of two business partners having equal equity, one of whom is a natural leader, the other a financial expert, it is usually the latter who has greater control. Being aware of this, it is no accident that 84 per cent of the business Amazons ensured they held the final financial control, the signing of cheques – for, however one looks at it, signing a cheque means expenditure and not signing one means preventing expenditure.

Although the authority to sign cheques gives the signatory the ultimate power over any business decision, not all bosses are keen to sign cheques in person. Some have no eye for detail and are likely to sign anything that is put in front of them. Others feel that signing cheques implies a petty kind of mind, overconcerned with detail and incapable of vision or broad policy decisions, the type of mind that is so often attributed to women. The reason why 84 per cent of those in the survey did not mind being seen like this and insisted on signing their company's cheques, was not that they feared others' dishonesty (against which precautions can be taken) but because it gave them a greater understanding of what was going on. Bridget Hutchinson who is in the high-level employment business explained:

> This is the time when I can discover where the money goes to. I query the price of raw materials. I ask to see last month's prices and if higher, instruct the buyer to shop for better prices. Signing cheques gives me the whole panorama of what is happening in three hours a week. I am not involved in most of the daily aspects, but I make sure I sign the cheques.

Where the women were the sole or majority owners they had no need to justify their exclusive right of signature; but where they were in partnership with their husbands they needed to explain this unusual practice in which the wife and not the husband held the financial control. Nina Dean (annual sales £9 million): 'My husband never signed a cheque in his life.' And Jay Simpson (annual sales £4 million): 'My husband runs the factory and I run the office. He doesn't even know how much money we make.'

In most of the wife and husband teams the husbands were only too glad to let their wives take over the financial control and leave them to devote themselves to more inspiring pursuits. In a small business it is customary for the owner to have the only authority to sign cheques. But in large businesses where owners are constantly required to attend to major decisions, the signature rights for small amounts, in the region of $5,000 to $10,000, are usually delegated to directors. For the owner of a $32 million goods chain, employing 275 persons, to sign every cheque over $100 herself is typical of the methodical way the women in the survey run their businesses. Doreen Hartman explains: 'Over $100 I sign. My dad thinks I am stupid. But it is important for me to know where the money goes. Ours is a very low margin business.' In matters of finance the women were cautious leaders. Despite their wealth, extravagance and unlimited expense accounts were not their style. Owners of $100 million and $80 million businesses prided themselves on being cost conscious. A typical comment was: 'I run the business the way I run my home. No waste and no extravagance.'

Outsiders from the Business Community

For those business owners whose appetite for leadership exceeds the scope of their own business, and for those who need to relieve the loneliness of leadership, the business community has created thousands of different trade and business associations, to accommodate all occupations and managerial ranks.

In the USA there exist some 3,500 such trade associations, and in the UK about 3,000. There exist a Buttonmakers' Association and a Lacemakers' Association, an Association of Leisure Goods Manufacturers and an Association of Handicraft Manufacturers, an Association of Stationers and an Association of Chemical and Allied Trades. The travel agents have their own organisation and the toy makers theirs. Advertising agencies have their own society which is independent from that of the market researchers, who are themselves separate from the association of the public relations firms. In addition to the trade associations that cater for each sub-section of the economy, there exist also business organisations which aim to bring together businesses of similar size or function, or business persons of similar ranks. Thus big businesses have their associations and small businesses theirs. Directors are separated from managers, and exporters from bankers.

Not dissimilar to the guilds of the Middle Ages, but with less authority and power, these associations aim to promote their members' interests by providing technical and managerial know-how and training, and making representations to government bodies. Although membership is not compulsory, it is customary for a business to join one or several associations. On the whole, as in most organisations of such a nature, few of the members are active and the majority are content just to pay their dues.

For a business person who wants to expand the territory of her leadership and elevate her social status, activity within these associations offers great scope, as each has to nominate a president, a vice-president, a treasurer, secretaries, and directors, as well as members of its umpteen committees. Cynics and single-minded business persons do not set much store by these titles, as there is no proven link between them and business advantages. But for those who aspire to establish a public career or who enjoy being in the public eye, these posts may offer a stepping stone to higher public appointments.

For the purpose of promoting women it is important that women should be seen to hold such posts, particularly as, to the uninitiated, they seem grander than they actually are. When a woman becomes the elected president of the Toy Manufacturers' Association, or the vice-president of the Kitchen Furniture Manufacturers, other women feel that the barriers which prevent their advancement are beginning to crumble. In view of this it is regrettable that only 33 per cent of the millionairesses have bothered to get involved with their trade and professional associations, beyond the fee-paying stage. Although in percentage terms more businesswomen than businessmen are active in trade associations, because there are so few of them they are hardly noticeable.

The main reason the women abstained from activities in their trade associations was lack of time. 'If you did not need to work,' Jane

Auerbach, fashions magnate, explains, 'you could go from one meeting to another and from one conference to another. I shall do it when I retire. But meanwhile work and family take all my time.'

The excuse of 'no time' seemed to be a cover for a more genuine reason: lack of interest. If these capable women had been interested they would have found the time. But, being the individualists they were, they found that joining and committee work, the two essential ingredients of public activity, were not in their line. Niki Summers (in cosmetics for black women) says:

> I am not much of a joiner. Mainly because I can't stand seeing things analysed to death. I am an action person, and I believe that you have to know the facts, and I hate paralysis by analysis.

Market researcher Daphne Glover expresses herself still more strongly:

> I found that I'm not a committee person. They drive me mad. You sit there and you think, 'My God, why don't they do something about it?' You can decide on something right from the start and then you have to go through all these committees. It has to go through the subcommittee for this and the subcommittee for that, and two years later it still hasn't been done.

In their preference for action over discussion, for solitary decision-making over communal agreements, the businesswomen were similar to most business owners who, unless fired by greater ambition, preferred the private world of their businesses to the public one of the trade associations.

9 | Discrimination: Yes or No

Women are still discriminated against in many areas: that is a fact of life, although since the introduction of anti-discriminatory legislation in the USA and Britain, blatant discrimination has disappeared to be replaced by a subtler strain which is difficult to detect and eliminate. There are those who choose to believe that high achievers like Margaret Thatcher, Indira Gandhi and the business Amazons prove that it has vanished altogether. However, those who are convinced that women continue to be discriminated against claim that these high women achievers succeeded despite discrimination and not because it no longer exists.

Business ownership has always offered a sanctuary to socially marginal groups such as Jews or Armenians, or plain nonconforming individuals, a sanctuary where they could prove their worth regardless of their race or creed. Recently it has extended this protection from discrimination also to women, who even in the large corporations are not treated as equals. By the nature of business ownership it is the owner who dictates the rules; and she cannot therefore be discriminated against in her own workplace.

The human face of business is that it judges the product and not the producer. As long as a product or a service is required, the race and sex of the supplier are irrelevant. But when the market becomes a buyer's market, or when the services the owner requires to activate her business are in scarce supply, then the business owner is no longer exempt.

It is interesting to find that in spite of the relative freedom from discrimination, 60 per cent of the business Amazons were convinced that in order to succeed in business a woman had to be better than a man while the remaining 40 per cent claimed that far from being discriminated against, being women gave them a positive advantage over men.

To Succeed a Woman Has to Be Better than a Man

The three areas in which it was argued that a woman needs to be better than a man are summarised below.

A better business person

What legislation has done for women is to give them the chance to enter male territories. What it cannot do for them is convince men that they deserve to be there. Thus women like Nancy Gardner, the owner of an $80 million food business with a twenty-year track record, still have the problem of not being taken seriously. 'I have to establish my credentials time and again.'

It is inconceivable that a man in this position would not be taken seriously but when a woman is head of an organisation even her employees feel entitled to question her merits. As for younger women with less well-established businesses, they have a harder time still. After seven years in the fast food business, thirty-one-year-old Claire Smith is still being taken for a secretary: 'A supplier or shopfitter would ask for the boss, and when my secretary directs them to me, they say: "Not her – we want to see the real boss." '

This is a classic anecdote and illustrates a central dilemma concerning status: if she dismisses the wrong identification lightly, this is taken as a sign of weakness, and if she dares to get angry – a perfectly normal reaction to being constantly taken for one's own secretary – she is labelled as aggressive and unfeminine. What enrages businesswomen is that they have to re-establish their credibility time and again and since the only way to do this is to excel in all the aspects of business – whether production, finance or marketing – they carry a heavy burden. Fiona Devlin sets out the problem:

There is no doubt that women have a credibility problem. I would be kidding myself if I believed otherwise. In the line of work that I am in I have an enormous problem because I deal principally with tax legislation, and where a man can make a statement like "One per cent of the investment tax provides x million dollars' worth of revenue," I would have to have all the facts and have them exactly right – because they don't expect a woman to know tax policy, and are always waiting to catch you out.

More confident

To succeed in business women have to be *more* confident than a man. First, they have to overcome the handicap of their non-assertive feminine upbringing and then they have to convince everyone that business is a suitable occupation. Daphne Glover expands on this:

Women in business are up against a lot of problems, like justifying why they are in business in the first place. As if they are constantly trespassing on someone else's property. Then if they are single like myself they may have parents who, instead of supporting them, nag and warn about the perils of business and its unsuitability for women. What they actually mean and don't say is that they are worried lest the businesswoman's image will be a hindrance in finding a husband.

Better at absorbing stress

Even without the additional problems of family and children, business is a stressful occupation. *With* them, it is amazing that these women survive. The stress factors, especially for mothers, are constant and inescapable. One example can stand for all.

Zelda Main arrived home one evening after a day's work that had started at six in the morning. She had taken a flight to Germany where she spent the entire day in court, not returning to London until nine o'clock that evening. No sooner did she get in the house than her thirteen-year-old son asked her to help him with his Latin homework. 'I remember saying: "Bernard darling, I am busy, I will look at it after dinner" – when my mother, who happened to be in the house, turned around and said: "Zelda, if you haven't got the time to help Bernard with his homework, it's really time for you to give up work." What mother would suggest that a son who headed a £6 million cosmetics empire should give up work because he was too tired to help his son with his Latin homework. He would probably have been scolded for daring to bother his father, who had more important things on his mind.'

Being a Woman Makes it Easier

Not all the businesswomen agreed they find the going tougher than men. A good 40 per cent claimed that being women made it easier for them to succeed in business: 'The women's lib movement are going to be very unhappy with this statement,' said travel agent Ellie Leonard, 'but I maintain that a woman in today's market has a better chance of going to the top than a man has.'

The case for the advantage of being a woman is based on three arguments. The first is that sectors such as fashion, retail, and services are becoming established as female territories. The second is that as the weaker sex, women are not always considered 'competition' and sometimes even get help from male colleagues. The third is that the novelty of women in business gives them greater visibility and so improves their chances of attracting business. From the wealth of testimony, here speak a political lobbyist and a young English 'keep fit' tycoon who floated her company on the stock market after four years of business:

> You don't have to give up being a woman. I love being a woman and I don't see a conflict between it and being a business owner. On the contrary, I work in a 100 per cent male world and I found that stressing my femininity, by wearing my violet crepe dress for example, makes men treat me slightly less harshly than they would treat other men.

And:

> Because I was a young woman, my going public excited the media and gave me such press and TV exposure that the shares just zoomed up. Had I been a middle-aged businessman it would not have had the same impact. So being a woman was a great asset.

These are the realists who do not delude themselves about the possibility of eliminating sexual advantages or disadvantages altogether.

Discrimination by Financial Institutions

Entry into the business fraternity is open to anyone who subscribes to the aim of making money. It seems that for this purpose all were created equal. History is full of examples where the prospects of an advantageous deal led to barriers of religious hatred and political animosity being tacitly dropped. Recent news is full of similar tales. The communist regimes of the USSR and the People's Republic of China trade with capitalist countries. The Iranians buy arms from the Israelis, and the black leaders of Zimbabwe trade with South Africa. The list is long. In comparison, it is a trivial affair for men to trade with women.

One of the reasons why minorities are attracted to business ownership in preference to employment is that the business community is relatively tolerant of newcomers. It can afford to be tolerant because the interaction between members of the business community is usually limited to the business transaction itself. As long as the newcomers adhere to the group's self-regulatory conditions, which are usually satisfied by fair trading, the fact that they are new or different can be overlooked.

Obviously, as in any situation where one is trying to gain acceptance, the less one demands and the more one contributes, the easier and quicker one becomes integrated. In business terms, this means that the more the established members manage to profit from the newcomer and the less the newcomer manages to profit from the established members, the easier it becomes for the newcomer to strike deals. In money terms, the more value the seller offers to the purchaser and the less he profits himself, the more customers he is bound to attract. The same formula applies to businesswomen. As long as they offer well-priced products or services for which there is a market demand, there can be no valid reason for discrimination or bias against them. The buyer is interested in only one thing, a well-made and competitively priced product or service. When businesswomen change their role from sellers to purchasers the same rules apply, but in reverse. As long as they are ready to allow the seller a decent profit they should not encounter any bias. The scene changes, however, when the newcomers start demanding a bigger slice of the cake; in other words, when they stop selling cheap and buying expensive and become no different from other suppliers or purchasers. That is when bias and the consequent discrimination set in. It is then that the Jew becomes the 'greedy and dishonest Jew' and the woman an 'aggressive and stupid bitch'. The test of whether women are discriminated against in the business world has to be carried out in a neutral setting where the woman is just another business person competing for the same market with a similar product.

Banks are therefore an ideal testing ground. Bank loans are usually in short supply and competition is fierce, yet 57 per cent of the business Amazons claimed that they did not encounter discrimination by banks. Still, the fact is that the majority of these did not deal with the banks themselves but used husbands or male partners for this, and a further 12 per cent had minimal loan requirements.

Hiding behind a male partner is obviously one way to avoid discrimination; not asking for loans is another. But to claim that only businesswomen who fell into these categories were not discriminated against would be incorrect, because others beside these claim to have been treated fairly. Among the reasons they offered for their good relations with the banks were their knowledge of the facts and figures and their femininity.

The claim that it was knowing their facts and figures that got them facilities from the bank is reasonable but the claim that femininity played a part is suspect, for when these claims were investigated in detail, it emerged that the business proposal and the collateral as well were extremely sound. The fact that the applicants were women seems to have had little effect on the banks' co-operation. Tricia Williams, in property, reckons: 'Knowing banks, I do not think that they actually lend money because they like someone; they have to like the project, and not the person. I don't think that they have a bias against or for businesswomen. They have a bias against people generally.'

The greater bias of American banks

Surprisingly, it was American banks that were more biased than British banks. Fifty-six per cent of the American businesswomen in this study encountered discrimination as against only 28 per cent of their British counterparts. There is no obvious explanation for this variance as both countries enacted protective legislation at the same time. In Britain the Sex Discrimination Act of 1975 made it illegal to withhold credit facilities from any person because of his or her sex, and in the USA the

Equal Credit Opportunity Act did the same thing though in greater detail. Before 1975 a bank manager was within his legal rights in turning down a woman's loan request for the reason that he did not believe women were a good risk; and a credit card company or a store offering charge account facilities could insist on the husband's signature to authorise his wife's spending even if the wife worked and had an income of her own.

Given the present equality in law there are two possible explanations. The first is that the American women, who on the whole owned bigger businesses than their British counterparts, sought larger loans for faster expansion. The second, which might reflect the situation more accurately, is that the British businesswomen were and are apathetic towards the issue of women's rights.

In business it is not difficult to avoid issues. Every business person learns very quickly that there are a hundred and one ways to avoid confrontations without sacrificing the goals. A bank's reluctance to lend to women can be circumvented by nominating male 'straw men' as directors. The 'straw man' can be a relative or an outsider, usually an accountant. Although this procedure is cumbersome and time-wasting, it is a perfectly legitimate course of action.

Obstacles can be overcome in two ways. Either one takes a detour which, although it may be lengthy and costly always gets one there in the end or one stops to remove the obstacle. This can turn out as expensive and protracted as the detour, and there is no guarantee of success.

The British women tycoons are like the drivers who, encountering a fallen tree in the road, take a detour and reach their destination more quickly than the drivers who stop their cars to remove the obstacle. But the second drivers clear the way not only for themselves but also for all those behind. Not being as concerned with women's achievements and less oriented towards success than their American counterparts, the British businesswomen did not attempt to meet the banks head on. What would happen if they did remains a question.

Other biases

Since the introduction of sex equality legislation, no bank manager is going to be so stupid as to tell a businesswoman that he is refusing her a loan because she is a woman although market researcher Daphne Glover found her London bank manager did not beat about the bush but asked her, 'What would happen if you got pregnant?' In any case there is no need for a bank manager to resort to illegal bias, when he has at his disposal many legal ways in which to discriminate against women. Because of their great discriminatory powers bank managers can decide from whom to ask for collateral and from whom not; and whose loan to call in before its maturity and whose loan to renew. With such legitimate powers of discrimination it would be difficult to prove that a bank was biased against the owner because she was a woman rather than because her business was not viable. Although concrete evidence of discrimination may be lacking, there exists sufficient circumstantial evidence to make one doubt their fair treatment of businesswomen. When a bank manager dares to suggest to someone who heads an $80 million business, that she should consult her husband who has no equity in the business, it is difficult to believe that he applies the same criteria to her loan application as he would to a man's.

Each businesswoman is prey to her own bank manager's particular image of women. Lena Gouldwin's does not tell her to consult her husband. He has his own method of reminding her that he does not take her seriously. He calls Lena, the owner of a $50 million construction conglomerate, 'Honey'.

It is such small, insidious incidents that reveal the true state of affairs. And the women let them pass because they do not want to seem paranoid about their femininity. Lena admits: 'It grates on my nerves but it's not important enough to make an issue. And I never make issues unless it is important.'

A way out

One way to improve relations between bankers and businesswomen is to have more women on the inside of banking. In the USA banks have started to nominate female directors to their boards; in Britain only two women have managed to scale the heights (and unfortunately as successors to the same seat). At present the appointment of women directors is more an exercise in public relations than a sincere effort to redress the imbalance of decision-making power; but it is a welcome step that might lead to more permanent changes in banks' attitudes to women.

An insider's view of how banks regard businesswomen has been provided by two of the Americans, Barbara Carpenter and Pamela

Carter, who have both been non-executive directors of large banks. Both became businesswomen as a result of widowhood and both stepped into established family engineering businesses, which meant that they did not have to face the usual struggle that the self-made businesswoman has with banking authorities, and therefore did not feel as bitter about them as the self-made woman does. As a result they were also more objective and could see both points of view, the bank's and the businesswomen's. Barbara comments:

> To start with bankers are super-conservative, and this attitude is not exclusive to money but is carried through to any innovation, including women in business. Then you have to realise that those who are giving out loans are mostly men. They are still biased. Not that they really want to be. But it is a cultural thing that is still there.

Pamela's view is:

> I don't kid myself that I was appointed because of my great financial expertise. They wanted a woman on the board because it is fashionable and makes them look progressive. It also placates women customers, but they don't want a woman who is going to come and upset the structure and turn those men upside down. Had I started to throw my weight around they would have fired me. They are not ready yet for aggressive women. It might come in time – but the time has not come yet. Meanwhile I hope that my being on the board is helping other women, because they do look a little bit more carefully at the balance sheets when women own businesses. The more they get used to seeing women in key positions the easier these conservative men will feel with them and the more beneficial it will be for women.

Claire Whitman who is in finance herself sees the male-female conflict between bank managers and businesswomen as part of an overall pattern, which cannot be construed as conscious discrimination against women but reflects men's inability to split the feminine image into two: a woman and a person. The businesswomen wanted to be treated just like any other person; but for most bank managers 'any other person' means a man.

10 | Are They Feminists?

Ninety per cent of the business Amazons dissociated themselves from the title of 'feminist'. But what people say and what they do can be different. There are many once vociferous advocates of the women's movement who settled happily into the subordinate role of the traditional wife at the first serious offer of marriage. On the other hand, there are women who seem to have accepted their biological role and status but are, in effect, a fifth column, steadily and stealthily acting to undermine male supremacy. The women in this survey are to be counted among these.

Judged by their deeds and not their words, they must surely be considered as arch-feminists. What else can a woman be who has liberated herself so successfully from male domination? The answer to whether the businesswomen are or are not feminists has been sought here by examining the degree of their solidarity with other women:

a whether they preferred working with other women;
b whether they promoted other women in their organisations;
c whether they encouraged other women to start their own business;
d whether they joined exclusively female business associations.

Do They Prefer Working with Women?

Sixty-one per cent of the business Amazons denied preferring to work with one sex or another. The remaining 39 per cent, who had a distinct preference for working with one sex or the other, seemed to be almost equally divided, with 20 per cent preferring to work with men and 19 per cent with women.

Men are easier than women

The 20 per cent who preferred working with men had many complaints about their female employees. These are the ones that recurred most often:
Women:

> are petty
> are bitchy
> are difficult
> take things too personally
> lack confidence
> are not career minded
> are unreliable
> lack qualifications
> resent women bosses.

What the women employers liked in their male employees was their greater reliability, confidence and career mindedness, their generally better qualifications and the fact that they tended to be 'more interesting as people'. But what they liked above all was that they were easily manoeuverable. This was because they were less realistic than women and had oversize egos that responded to flattery. Trivial rewards such as titles and status symbols went much further with men than with women.

'I like men,' says engineer magnate Pamela Carter. 'I like them better than women. I find them more interesting and I appreciate the male ego. I had a husband who had a big ego. A man who doesn't have an ego is a mouse.'

As for men being manoeuverable, Rachel Black provides a classic example: 'It is so easy to handle men. All you have to do is get to their ego. For instance, we had a manager with whom we were not very satisfied so we promoted him to be the export manager. This was a job with a title and no content. I could not have done that to a woman. A woman would have said: "Mrs Black, what is the big deal and commotion? Where I was before I was in charge of ten people, and now I am only in charge of myself. That is not a promotion." To him I said: "You are now the export manager, and here is your new visiting card in three languages, German, French, and English." This was enough for him.'

Women are easier than men

Nineteen per cent of the women business owners preferred to work with women because they found men's inflated egos and their almost universal resentment of women bosses a strain. All the business Amazons, including those who preferred working with men, agreed that men were vain and have ridiculously inflated egos. And although in less senior positions this could be an advantage as we have just seen, when they held senior positions they had to be humoured and this ego-caressing could soon become tiresome. Julie Kitson complains:

> As I work with men who are experts in their field [aviation], I have to flatter their ego if I want to get results. Instead of telling them what to do, I have got to ask for their views before I formulate an opinion. I manage, but it is a constant strain.

And Denise Philips who should know as her business is employment:

> Men need titles. They are very status minded. Women don't mind what they are called. They want to do an honest day's work for a good salary and get the respect that goes with it, but men are hung up on titles. I am not against titles, but I am against people for whom the title means more than the job.

Among the women in the survey it was a common finding that men resent women bosses. Hitherto, any man was held to be superior to any woman. Nowadays some men are ready to admit that women like Golda Meir and Margaret Thatcher were and are superior to most men. After this it could be expected that they would at least concede that all women were potentially equal to all men. Nothing of the kind: on the contrary, they claim that these unusual women are exceptions and the majority are in every way inferior to themselves.

It follows that to work under a female boss is a comedown for a man. Some even give up their jobs rather than work for a woman. Susan Taylor reports: 'When we took over the public relations business, several men actually left because they would not work under women.' Amelia Jaeger's problem of permanently disgruntled male employees (she is also in public relations) is more common:

One of my directors disliked all women. I know how he treated his wife, which was like a piece of dirt with the occasional beating up. Naturally he could not and would never ask advice and would not take any from me.

What should a woman boss do with the male who stays put but resents her leadership? Should she allow such a fifth column to exist within her organisation? Or should she try to win him over? Being businesswomen rather than revolutionaries or reformers, the women treated their insubordinate male subordinates according to how much they needed them. Where they were dispensable they ignored them. Elaine Johnson who is in the car business puts this bluntly: 'I take no notice. It's their problem, not mine. They have a choice. Either they get on with the job or they go.' Where they needed them, they had to tread more carefully and collude to some extent.

But what made the 19 per cent prefer working with women was not only the inadequacies of men but the positive qualities of women. Contrary to popular belief, they found female employees intelligent, hard working, and trusting. Women are more intelligent, says hotelier Tricia Bishop: 'I find that in the same category of work, women are twice as intelligent as men. I think that they are more quick-witted. Men carry an air of knowing and being more in charge but basically they know less than women.' Hilda Bergdorf agrees: 'I'll take a good intelligent woman any time – you can keep all the men. An intelligent woman is a pleasure to work with; an intelligent man has to be revived with flattery a few times a week.'

'Women work harder,' asserts Sara Holt, a cosmetics specialist. Construction boss Nancy Lennon agrees: 'Women employees are usually so much better than men in so many ways, primarily because they work harder.'

'Women are more trusting,' claims lingerie magnate Linda Bailie: 'They are not out to prove you wrong and catch you out. They are less into the game that men have been trained to play.'

Of the four tests designed to establish whether the business Amazons were feminists or not, the first test, their preference for working with other women, resulted in a draw.

Do They Promote Women?

The reason for the promotion of women by women being an indicator of feminism is that feminists subscribe to the promotion of women's interests. Evidence that the businesswomen in the survey promoted women would establish them as feminists. Alas, according to the results of this second test, the business Amazons were no feminists. Only 16 per cent of them would have considered female applicants more favourably, while the rest espoused only one criterion: 'The best person for the job.'

Against positive discrimination

There is no denying that the business Amazons' prevailing disregard of sex as a factor in promotion is the fairest attitude; but it is not beneficial to women. Before the emergence of women bosses, women employees hoped female employers would grant them the same preference that male bosses gave to male employees. However, the businesswomen in the survey did not feel it was up to them to redress old wrongs. Their single-minded aim was to run an efficient and profitable business. In their choice of employees, therefore, they had only one consideration: ability to contribute to their success. Here are some typical responses: 'Women should only be promoted if they are good. They should not be promoted because they are women.' 'Women should be promoted only if they are qualified. As to "encourage" I think we should encourage anyone whether they are pink, blue, green, or purple.' 'I am not going to promote them over a man just because they are women.'

It seemed that positive discrimination was not something they subscribed to. As to whom they would select when faced with two equally good candidates, one of each sex, many were at a loss: 'There hasn't been a situation like that. I don't know what I would do . . .' or considered it a hypothetical question and avoided a direct answer.

Only Sonia Kaplan, the mail order tycoon, was ready to speculate on whom out of two equals these women would promote. When it came to the crunch, she forecast women would desert women: 'If a woman boss was faced by two identical candidates, one male and one female, she would probably promote the man as she would not want to be accused of promoting a woman because of her sex. Women are harder on women than they should be.'

Why should high achieving women be so hard on other women? Why have the women prime ministers of recent years not promoted other women? Were they simply worried about competition? The business Amazons offered three explanations as to why they did not go out of their way to help other women.

Firstly, most women are not ambitious enough. Secondly, business-women ought to put the interests of their firm first, and thirdly they do not forget that they themselves made it without help. Machinery industrialist Pamela Carter states this very plainly: 'I am not a feminist, I am a traditional woman. I think women should get everything they deserve the same as men should, but they should not get it only because they are women. I have been denied special treatment and I have managed. But some women don't feel that way. They feel that they should be treated more leniently.'

These three reasons, and in particular the last, in which the business Amazons claimed that other women could match their own achievements if only they made the effort, sum up the feelings of 84 per cent.

For positive discrimination

For the small minority of 16 per cent who take the opposite view, even asserting that many of the businesswomen had had more help than they cared to admit, let Dorothy Simmonds, who is an oil equipment dealer, be the spokesperson:

Women in a position of power ought to promote other women. I don't have much sympathy for women who have been successful in their careers and believe that they have some magical, exceptional qualities that put them where they are. There are millions of us out there and I'm not exceptional. There are a whole bunch of women scrubbing their kitchen floors right now who are talented and more intelligent than I am. What are they doing wasting their productivity scrubbing a stupid kitchen floor, when we need their brain power making this world work? A highly placed woman who denies that she has had a lot of help to reach where she is is simply dishonest with herself. Every woman who has reached a high position has been helped by thousands of men and women whom she might not even know: the ones who campaigned and marched in Washington to change the laws that discriminated against women. By promoting other women they can repay their debt to them.

Dorothy is right. Much as the women owners would like to believe that they have made it on their own, the truth is that they have not. Fights that have changed laws and rebellious women who have changed attitudes have prepared the path for their success. But this the business Amazons, like most successful people, prefer to forget.

The results of the second test are clear. The business Amazons are no feminists on this issue. Their sole concern is the success of their business, and the promotion of other women is not part of it.

Do They Encourage Other Women to Become Successful?

Women prime ministers are no feminists because they realise that being unique is a part of their success. Would Margaret Thatcher or Indira Gandhi have seemed as remarkable if their foreign ministers had also been women? The businesswomen are in a somewhat similar position. Having reached the top, they enjoy unique status and privileges. Their readiness or reluctance to forsake their uniqueness and see more women enjoy similar privileges is a sign of the extent to which they are or are not feminists. Having conquered the route to success, are they ready to let others tread it, or do they see themselves as an exclusive sect with strict entrance requirements?

To encourage women to become business leaders means making it clear to them that they have a better chance to succeed if they build up their own businesses than if they join corporations. It also means awakening them to the fact that some forty years after the Second World War, when the big rush of women into the corporations took place, female executives are still a rarity in boardrooms; and that, particularly during periods of economic recession and job scarcity, it has been the female executives who have fared the worst.

—

The wish to open up their ranks to more women was shared by 65 per cent of the women studied, who believed that women should be positively encouraged to become business owners. In the USA the percentage was higher (78 per cent) than in Britain (52 per cent) on account of its higher social status. In Britain, as hotelier Tricia Bishop points out, 'Business is somehow still a dirty word and therefore it's difficult to encourage women to become businesswomen.'

Encouragement

The reasons the majority of those in the survey wanted to see more female business owners were:

a because women made excellent business owners;
b because women encountered promotion difficulties in the corporate structure;
c because business owners could combine motherhood and a career with the minimum of trauma; and
d because businesswomen, being above office rivalries, were nicer people than women executives.

Discouragement

Just as convinced as the majority who believed in the need to encourage women to become owners, the minority clung to the opposite view. Their reasons were as follows:

a that business was a natural talent, and could not be brought out by encouragement;
b that business *was* an exclusive club, and wholesale encouragement might attract the wrong people; and
c that as most women were happy to be housewives, they should not be lured away from the home.

Pragmatists rather than crusaders, many of the business Amazons felt that trying to change the world was too big a task for them. Even so, in this third test, the majority turned out to be true feminists. They genuinely wanted to see more successful businesswomen and believed that they should be encouraged.

Do They Join Women's Business Associations?

Organisations flourish because groups are more powerful than individuals, and can therefore promote their interests with greater success. The reason for the proliferation of organisations is not only that people's interests vary and that each organisation represents the interests of one group, but also that the same person can have different interests which are served by different organisations.

Knowing whether the business Amazons are for or against joining women's business organisations will indicate whether they are feminists, because it will demonstrate whether they believe that their salvation will come through joining forces with their own sex or through assimilation.

Fifty-two per cent of them believed that the interests of businesswomen would be better served by exclusive women's associations than by those where businessmen were always going to be in the majority. By declaring themselves in favour of segregated associations, a narrow majority thus declared themselves feminists.

The main reason why the 48 per cent minority thought segregating businesswomen from the mainstream and herding them into self-governing ghettos, was a bad idea was because it lulled them into a false sense of power which would not stand up to the tests of the real world.

Women's business associations are unnecessary

The minority's objections to exclusive businesswomen's associations were on the following grounds:

a that women's insulation and isolation were wrong;
b that they gained no business advantage;
c that women's organisations were a bore; and
d that on principle they were non-joiners.

Various views were expressed to support the theory that women's insulation and isolation are wrong. 'I don't think that there should be a female network. The most important thing for us is to get into and stay in the mainstream.' 'I think women should join organisations that cut across the sex line. In other words, a professional organisation. There is also no reason why we should not network with men as well as with women.' 'A woman should be in a man's world and men should learn how to deal with us as colleagues. By getting out and mixing in the men's world, keeping their ears open and keeping their mouths shut, women will learn more about business than by sitting together with other women on committees.'

As to there being no business advantages in segregated organisations: 'Women's organisations consist of such a variety of professions that for me it has no use. I need help from somebody in the industry.' 'Exclusive women's business associations are a good idea for social interaction but not for business.' 'Membership of women's business associations is useful for businesswomen who cater for women, like the president of the Women's Bank in New York or the owner of a health spa, for whom interacting with other businesswomen means acquiring new customers.'

Several simply felt that women's organisations are a bore. 'I have joined them off and on and I can't stand them.' 'I work with women all day long and quite honestly I can live without them in the evening.' 'I instinctively think: another extremist feminist group.' Or, more graphically still: 'In the States there was the Quata Club. It is similar to the Rotary Club for men. Frankly I couldn't stand it. In a small town a club like that is pathetic, because it deals with trivialities. Arranging banquets, who is going to prepare the tablecloths and the teas, and things like that.'

And some women were just non-joiners. 'One of the reasons I started my business was that I couldn't work for anybody and had difficulties at getting along with people. Even today I am not a committee person, I hate discussing things with people. So I don't join any organisations where they talk a lot.'

Women's organisations are a must

The 52 per cent majority of the business Amazons who favoured exclusive businesswomen's organisations hoped that by 'networking' they would:

a promote understanding between successful businesswomen and other women;
b introduce successful businesswomen to each other;

c enhance the visibility of successful businesswomen; and
d encourage other women to enter business.

The reason for hoping that the organisation would promote understanding between successful businesswomen and other women was that successful women find themselves in an untenable situation. Cornered between males who ignore their success and females who resent it, they are denied the support of either. The degree of alienation from other women is vividly described here by Lena Gouldwin:

> A man will help me sooner than a woman. Women just hate successful women. When I call up a government agency for information and pretend that I am a secretary, I will get a tremendous amount of help from the secretary on the other side. But if I call up as the president of a corporation, I could chew nails and no woman in the government service will help me in any way. They will throw every single possible boulder in the way. Women just do not seem to have the capacity to understand that when they help successful women they help themselves as well. Jealousy gets in their way. As long as the other woman is also the underdog then it is one underdog helping the other. But when she is successful she becomes the enemy.

Another hope was that the associations would introduce businesswomen to each other. Unlike female executives, women business owners have few opportunities to meet women with similar business interests; and when they join the general business associations they find that businessmen are uncomfortable in their company. Lena Gouldwin describes what joining the exclusive Committee of 200 meant for her:

> Someone who is not in business may not understand that you can have $10 million and yet not have enough to meet the payroll. It is very difficult to explain to them the cash flow and the business, the constant hassling. With the Committee of 200 it is different. These are successful women who are in the same spectrum that I am in and have to deal with similar problems to mine: problems with husbands and children and corporate executives and cash flow. I loved the meetings we have had and I go to them religiously. It has been a super outlet for me. I can now talk to people with whom I can relate.

Another advantage was that the associations would enhance the visibility of successful businesswomen who, like successful businessmen, reach a stage where they hanker after the respectability and public acknowledgement that tend to elude business people. Women's business organisations enable them to achieve it by providing them with a platform from which to voice their opinions and demonstrate their civic generosity, and since they cannot become role models for male entrepreneurs, it is a female audience that they seek to influence and guide.

The advantage gained from sharing experiences and increasing one's visibility was not the only reason why the businesswomen joined women's business associations; there was also an altruistic motive, that of encouraging other women to enter business. They believed that the visibility of their success would encourage more women to join the ranks and make the grade. In contrast to militant feminists, they believed that women's equality would not be won on the barricades or by alienating men, but by increasing the numbers of successful women. The more women became successful in their respective fields, the more equal their unsuccessful sisters would become. Numbers were what counted. If women were to prove to themselves as well as to men that they were equal, they required battalions of successful women, and not just a sprinkling of celebrities: 'Success is power. Power is equality. The more successful businesswomen there are – the more equal women will become.'

Beyond Feminism

So what is the final score? One 'for', one 'against', and two near draws. It has to be concluded that although not dyed-in-the-wool feminists, the business Amazons inclined a little in that direction. So what prevented more of them from identifying themselves publicly with the women's movement? Why did 91 per cent of them state they were not feminists? Was it the typical caution of business people in refraining from support of unpopular causes? Or was it the typical stand-offishness of those newly successful from those still engaged in the struggle?

The fundamental reasons why, despite their sensational championship of women's rights, the business Amazons dissociated themselves from organised feminism were that the women's movement had no place for them and that women's liberation was felt to have outlived its purpose. Over the years the women's movement has become associated socially with the underdogs and politically with the left of centre. Hardly underdogs or socialists, the business Amazons felt that they could not associate themselves with organised feminism. Here is the view of Mary Mead, the keep fit organiser:

> The feminist movement has not allocated space for successful women like me. They criticise me for having a housekeeper, whom I cherish, and whom I consider my most valuable employee because she enables me to be a career woman. According to them no woman should employ another woman in demeaning jobs.

Independently of any personal grievance against the women's movement, the women in this survey also felt that the wider population of women had little to gain from the movement's continuance. Rose Kraus, owner of radio station, expresses the widely held view that the movement has outlived its usefulness:

> The younger generation do not have the inequality problems we had. I see young married couples sharing the housework, the cooking, and the looking after the children. As far as education is concerned people don't differentiate between sons and daughters the way they used to. Girls get equal education to boys.

And Zelda Main, in cosmetics, says simply: 'I feel that we are equal and therefore we don't need more pressure to make us more equal.'

Having achieved equality and reached beyond it, according to their own brand of feminism, these women were no longer in the market for philosophies of the women's movement. Yet, unlike Phyllis Schlafly's Feminine Movement in America, they did not oppose it outright. Their position is accurately summarised by garment manufacturer Golda Harris: 'So I'm in the middle, not with the women's movement and not against it. I don't ask for privileges, just equality. I do not need positive discrimination, but not negative discrimination either.'

Their brand of feminism postulated the division of women's life into work and after-work zones, and the practice of two different orders: the new one, where women were equal to men, which they practised at work; and the old one, where men made the decisions and women executed them, which they reserved for after work. Work was where these women exercised their power, and here they did not ask for privileges or concessions. The only thing they asked for was equality.

But after work they reverted to their feminine role. In the words of talent agent Genevieve Rouche:

> Most businesswomen who are over forty, not the heavy ones from the national women's organisations, don't like to carry out their role of chief commanders twenty-four hours a day. I don't want to make the decisions about where to go for dinner, or which play; I want the men to do that. Probably that is why I have always chosen the men I have chosen. People who know me are very surprised at the kind of men I go out with, because they dictate to me.

Having managed to combine the best of both worlds, it was no wonder that these women were immune to the appeal of the women's movement, with its proclaimed aim of escalating the fight for equality and spreading it into the home. They were so confident in their equality and success that letting a lover or a husband decide to which restaurant they should go or which dress they should wear was a gesture of magnanimity and not of weakness; they could not subscribe to the teachings of those for whom the only place to establish their equality was the company of their loved ones.

11 | **The Successful Talk about their Success**

To be considered successful by others is often an easier achievement than to consider oneself a success. The fact that 81 per cent of the business Amazons considered themselves successful is an indication of their high self-esteem, a trait rarely associated with women. Only 2 per cent did not consider themselves successful, and a further 17 per cent wished they were more successful.

What made most of them feel successful or unsuccessful was not the size of their business or its profitability. Sonia Kaplan considered herself 'enormously successful' with a $100 million mail order business, while Lisa Collier felt the same with a keep fit business one twentieth the size of Sonia's. 'From the day I opened my toy business [now worth $10 million] I knew it was going to be a successful international organisation,' Delia Lewenthal recalls, 'although I had never been in business before and have never aspired to be a business-woman.' Feeling successful, it seems, is an attitude of mind.

Although this seems to indicate that self-confidence is imperative for success, this is not so: not all the women were as confident about their prospects as Delia. Some like Genevieve Rouche, could not believe their success, even after twenty-one years in the employment business: 'When I read an article about myself, or see myself on television, I'm stunned, I can't believe that it's all about me.' And Denise Philips, in the same field but British, was actually scared to admit her success lest she tempted her luck. 'I would be terrified if I thought I was successful. The day I think I had got there I would think, "I shall lose it all." '

Just as success means different things to different people, so lack of success has different interpretations. One person feels unsuccessful because she aspires to be more successful, another because she realises she is not going to be more successful, another because she does not believe she deserved it. Julie Kitson belonged to the first group. She was not content with her present achievements in aviation technology and constantly assigned herself new challenges: 'I am not successful enough yet. I have this massive challenge in the new division of the business. When this is off the ground I shall consider myself successful.'

Barbara Chandler belonged to the second type. At fifty-nine she reconciled herself regretfully to the fact that her specialist car business would never be as big as she hoped it would: 'I have always felt that I would like to be more successful than I am. I have always felt that it would suit me to be the chairman of a great big company. But regrettably in our type of business it would be difficult for us to get bigger than we are.'

Janet Draper typified the third category. Despite a $40 million engineering business she still did not consider herself successful, because she believed she did not deserve it:

> I consider myself lucky – not successful, because I have seen a lot of people that deserve it a lot more than me and are not successful. A lot of success is luck. There are a lot of people who if they had my luck would probably be further along the line than I am. I see them every day of my life. I see women with the sole responsibility for their children, not knowing where their husbands are. I see them take care of those kids, guide them, work, do everything that I have done and do it better, but they just have not had the breaks I have had.

Whatever it was that took Janet to the top, luck or her own efforts, what counted was that it was she who was sitting there at the top and not someone else. The claim that women only attribute their success to luck because they lack self-esteem is nonsense. Not only is this attitude not exclusive to women but it has its roots in our culture. The other day Margaret Thatcher, whom no one could accuse of lacking self-esteem, attributed her success to being lucky that her husband's job was in London, so making it possible for her to combine motherhood and politics. Luck, moreover, does not have to imply helplessness. Luck helps those who help themselves.

Successful women are as much a novelty to themselves as they are to society, particularly when they are not the 'token women' whom men have allowed to escape from the herd, but a whole tribe whose success has been independent from male benefactors or mentors. What success did for them, how they exploited it, and whether they thought it was worth the effort, is therefore of the utmost importance to us all.

Is it Important to Appear Successful?

Sixty-two per cent of the business Amazons believed that, regardless of their personal preference in the matter, being businesswomen they had to appear successful because in business impressions counted. This was as true in Britain, from which all the following remarks came, as it was in the USA, despite the traditional British fear of appearing ostentatious. For example, caterer Sue Heathcote says:

> It is terribly important that people should know about my business success. The public relations element of success is important. I am not going to tell people that the recession has hit us. I would fib about it. If I meet one of my customers and they say, 'I was in your restaurant last night. It was absolutely packed, you must be doing tremendously well,' I would never say, 'Well, actually we are 20 per cent down from two years ago.' A bit of bluff is necessary.

Lucy Curtis:

> In publishing it certainly helps to be seen to be successful, because I have to persuade people to do books for me. I have to talk about myself as being successful, even if I'm not. If someone asks me how I'm doing, I can't really afford to say 'Not good.' I have to say 'Marvellous.'

The stories about what the right image can do for a laggard business are legion. It is a common practice to 'dress up' the financial standing of a business in order to gain customers' or employees' cooperation. Denise Philips:

> It is dreadfully important to be seen to be successful, particularly when you are not. It is amazing. We had two insolvent companies, we bought an expensive new car and never looked back. It's crazy.

Clients want to deal with a successful business and, as they have no easy access to the company's balance sheet or its bank accounts, often their only means of appraising its success are the company's premises and the owner's lavishness. Bridget Hutchinson, employment agent, explains:

When we started we bought these premises although we could not afford it, because I thought that we must appear to be successful immediately. From a client's point of view this is important. So I started with full staff rather than just me at the telephone.

Nina Dean had the same experience:

Whenever we attended functions with our clients I would buy the best clothes I could afford, and my husband used to say, 'Don't you think they would think that we are doing too well out of them?' I said, 'No, they want to go with a successful company, and therefore I shall look good. They don't want to go with a down and out firm.'

It is not only clients who want to know that they deal with a successful company; employees feel an equal need and 'You don't attract the best staff into your company unless you are seen to be successful,' was a common sentiment. The extent to which employees like to work for a successful boss was discovered by hotel owner Frieda Marks when she indulged herself and crossed the Atlantic by Concorde. 'The extraordinary snob aspect that this had on everybody else was incredible. I found that the staff were saying, "Frieda has just been on one of her Concorde trips," and customers used to say to me, "You have been on Concorde?" And I thought what snobs people are. But images in business are important.'

In the USA, where people are not ashamed of success it is taken for granted that it is important to be seen to be successful. But in the UK, where to succeed in one's own right is still considered vulgar, the fact that employees actually liked their boss to appear successful surprised the British business Amazons. Jennifer Durham who owns a printing works recalls:

Last year I went off to the West Indies for a holiday. I didn't want to say where I was going because I thought that the staff would think I was being extravagant. But I have actually discovered that they were all proud of me going there. This was not my style of leadership, but I learned that it is important to the staff that I am seen to be successful. The other day I was invited to a reception that Mrs Thatcher gave at 10 Downing Street for heads of industry. The press wrote about it and I was interviewed on television. That was very good for the staff. They were very proud and very pleased.

This need to act the successful boss, to fly Concorde, take holidays in faraway places, and shake hands with prime ministers might not seem an ordeal that calls for sympathy. But for married women especially public success could be a handicap in their private life. Debra Manham, who is in the fashion business, found it difficult to cope with the dual roles of successful businesswoman and humble wife:

> As my husband is not interested in success one bit, and my marriage means a lot to me, when I am at home I underplay my success. So although I could afford it, I do not have flash cars and I do not dress up immensely. But as a boss I have to act like a boss and I found that employees would much prefer me to dress better and have a flash car, so that they could say: 'Oh, look at that, I work for her.' So I found this a difficult area and I am really torn.

And finally, as Elizabeth Lyon makes clear, it helps the cause of women's advancement: 'Only by publicising our achievements will we stop being the "token woman". The more our achievements are publicised, the easier we make it for younger women to be accepted on their face value. As a woman I think it is important to be seen to be successful because we are judged by what we are seen to have achieved.'

Keeping a low profile

Although 62 per cent of the business Amazons were convinced that keeping up appearances was important, the 38 per cent who chose to keep a low profile were not handicapped by doing so. This was true even in the USA where travel magnate Lydia Eastern reported: 'It is not important to be seen to be successful. A lot of people never heard of us until we went public. The results count, not appearances.'

The main and often contradictory reasons offered for the low-key approach were:

a not to antagonise employees;
b not to alienate family and friends;
c the depressed state of the economy; and
d personal preference.

Among those who felt it imperative not to antagonise employees was British fast food tycoon Claire Smith: 'To be seen to be successful is a disadvantage because of the comments that people make. You can't tell the staff that the profits are not very good this month and walk out and step into your Rolls-Royce. They are not going to believe you.' Jay Simpson, the food additives millionaire, has her Rolls-Royce story too: 'For twenty years we ploughed everything back into the business, so there was not any spare money to flash around. But then in the mid-sixties we were tempted and bought a Rolls-Royce, but we could not and dared not use it to go to the factory. Twenty years later it is still in our garage with only 6,000 miles on the clock.'

Those who wished not to alienate family and friends included Marlene Jacobs, the dance promotion entrepreneuse who expresses a similar view: 'I consciously try not to look successful or talk too much about my success, because the people you grow up with don't really like you to be too successful. For me friends are important. My closest friends are still my art school friends, even if they are not as successful as me at the moment, which is a shame.'

The depressed state of the economy was cited by both British and Americans. 'Today, especially with unemployment being so high, I don't want to be out on the road and identified with the successful,' was one – and a typical comment.

As for personal preference in the UK, Tricia Williams, in property, says: 'I have never been a particularly high liver, and anyhow we were always brought up not to spend any money. I still have a great sort of problem in spending money. I feel rather humble about my wealth – which is a little bit of false pride, really.' Jenny Cox, a retailer and also British, comments: 'I do not have an image thing. I drive an eight-year-old battered car. I wear jeans and sweatshirts quite a bit to work too. In fact I am always suspicious of people who are driving flashy cars and I think: "How well is their business really doing? Is that where the profits of their company are going?" '

The great thing about business ownership is that it can accommodate a multitude of characters and attitudes. Extroverts and introverts, publicity seekers and lovers of anonymity seem to achieve the same degree of success.

Material Status Symbols

The trappings of success long associated with the successful businessman are expensive cars, fashionable restaurants, luxurious holidays, exclusive clubs – anything that is both expensive and visible, often including a beautiful wife. But what about those newcomers, the business Amazons? What are their success symbols? Surely they haven't followed in the footsteps of the men.

Expensive cars have always been the most popular male success symbols, not so much for their speed and power but because they are the largest visible item a person can take most places with him. The business Amazons' choice of cars therefore should indicate whether they have adopted the businessmen's status symbols or whether they have developed their own. Between them the women in the survey owned twenty-two Mercedes, including a rare 1967 convertible model of which only five hundred were ever produced, and whose market price is around $50,000; nineteen Cadillacs of various models; eight Rolls-Royces and two Bentleys; ten Jaguar XJs and an elderly but classic XKE; a solitary Aston Martin; and three chauffeur-driven limousines of other makes: in total a fleet of sixty-nine visible mobile symbols of success.

Had they not denied their vulnerability to the trappings of success, and had they not insisted that the Mercedes, the Cadillacs, and the Rolls-Royces were merely means of transportation, their luxurious cars could have misled innocent observers into believing that the business-women were carbon copies of their male counterparts. For someone acquainted with the enjoyment men derive from the ownership of such mobile palaces, it would indeed be difficult to reconcile such statements as 'Any four-wheeler will do for me' with the ownership of a Rolls-Royce. But for these women this apparent contradiction is not too difficult to explain. Some felt they had to have one because it was expected of them, or for the sake of the business. Others were simply looking for comfort. There genuinely seems to have been very little mere status seeking.

Those few who had not been able to resist the temptation to parade their success found the pleasure shortlived. Hilda Bergdorf the babywear manufacturer confesses: 'Having started from nothing, I had this stupid dream of one day driving in a white Rolls-Royce. So now I have it, and for a time it made me feel double my size. But I plan to sell it because it is not really me.' Like Hilda, travel tycoon Lesley Trance lost interest in her Bentley once she had acquired it; she realised that with or without the Bentley she was the same Lesley.

It is an age thing. From thirty-five to forty-five one is very conscious to show what one can achieve, and have. Four years ago I went out and bought a Bentley, and I have done six

212

thousand miles on it and it has always got a flat battery. I just cannot be bothered to take it out. My normal car is a Rover [a respectable but not ostentatious make].

The more sophisticated of these women, who could not admit to such a weakness, found it simpler to reconcile the contradiction of an expensive car with their indifference to status symbols by claiming it to be a business imposition. Investment broker Elizabeth James explains: 'I could not go on taking clients in an old Volkswagen and talking about a $20 million deal. It started looking too eccentric, which was not good for the business. So I went and bought a Cadillac. It makes me look more solid.' As for those whose businesses did not involve taking clients in their cars, their reason was the need for comfort. Marketing expert Joan Sheldon was among them: 'I can't deny that being chauffeur-driven is more comfortable than driving for one hour each way. I come to work fresh and can start the day immediately. But as far as visibility is concerned I don't need it.'

Whatever the business Amazons' reasons were for driving expensive cars, the fact was that like their male counterparts they owned them, drove them, and were seen around in them. Thus it would seem that the only difference between the two groups – if there really was a difference – was in their motivation.

Flashy cars were not the only trappings of success to which these women were generally indifferent. Even the typically feminine ones of furs and jewellery had little appeal. Lesley Trance says off-handedly, 'Oh yes, there was a period when I went into fur and a lot of jewellery. I never wear any of it, it all sits in the bank now because I just cannot be bothered.'

Personal success indicators

If, as the business Amazons claimed, expensive cars, furs and jewellery did not give them a thrill, what did? Were they so humble that they required no external acknowledgement of their achievements, or did they look for reward in a different currency?

It transpired that they were not that humble; what they sought was the recognition of their talents and abilities rather than of their wealth. All the status symbols they aspired to revolved around their standing and capabilities as businesswomen. Harriet Hartfield, with her building construction business, says, 'For me success is to have my work published in architectural magazines, and have the editors of the trade magazines ask me to contribute an article.' Julie Karr, in filming: 'For me a symbol of success means to get awards.' Ulrike Jameson, owner of a pharmaceuticals firm: 'For me success manifests itself in our full order books. Customers are ready to wait seven to eight months for our products. We are highly thought of.' Sue Heathcote, restaurateur: 'I get a lot of press and media coverage. I mean the fact that I am quite well known is the symbol of success, more than a Rolls-Royce or anything else.' Sara Holt, with her cosmetics firm: 'Yes, I like my name in lights. I had an article about me in the *Daily Express*. I like success. It is not power, but it is success.' And Lisa Collier, health farm owner: 'I've had many television appearances on chat shows and health and fitness topics. I consider this a sign of success.'

In essence, social acceptability was the reward for success that the business Amazons coveted. One of their greatest ambitions was to become recognised role models whom younger women would respect and consult. Another was to gain office within the male bastions of government and finance. Niki Summers, cosmetics pioneer, says:

> It is important that we be asked to join boards of local and national companies. Not just the odd woman, like your Margaret Thatcher, the token woman whom it is not easy to admire because she is no threat to the existing pattern of society, where women are invisible. What we need is a large representation of women in the financial institutions and in the business board-rooms.

Alas, Niki Summers' is still a voice in the wilderness. Very few of the businesswomen have been invited to sit on the boards of public corporations. In the USA only four of them have been offered such posts, and in the UK none. Despite repeated noises about the need to involve women in boardroom-level decision-making, particularly from corporations catering for female consumers, little progress has actually been made. For the women in the survey such appointments have no financial incentive. On the contrary, they consume time and effort which they could more profitably devote to their own business ventures. But it was the wish to participate in a wider and more influential decision-making process that drove them to seek these appointments.

If a place on the board of a large public corporation was a sought-after sign of success, sitting on a governmental committee or task force was the crowning glory. Janet Draper discloses: 'Yesterday I received a cable from the White House asking me to come up to Washington. I don't know what it's for. I might be offered a typist's job, or I might not be offered anything at all. But if I were I would take it. It will be a great honour for me to serve my country.' It seems a pity that so little notice is taken of all this willingness to serve. Only 7 per cent of the business Amazons have ever served on a governmental committee, board, or task force. What a waste of resources!

12 | **Warriors – Worriers**

The ability to make decisions and take action without worrying is what distinguishes a warrior from a worrier. Not that warriors have fewer problems than worriers, but they are more capable of solving them; and when they cannot, they adapt.

Excessive worry is recognised as one of the biggest health hazards afflicting business people. However, when it relates to men it is given the grandiose name of 'pressure', which sounds more rational and masculine than 'worry'. Thus men tend to suffer from work pressure, family pressure, and decision-making pressure, all of which sound mighty important, while women just seem to worry about children, husbands, unpaid debts, and similar mundane topics. In fact, one is in no way preferable to the other. Both have the same results: bad health, wrong decisions, and a troubled private life.

At a time when the symptoms of worry – ulcers, high blood-pressure, and coronaries – have become the hallmark of the business community, it is incredible that as many as 95 per cent of the business Amazons declared themselves to be in good health. And since their lives cannot possibly be free of worry, their good health has to be attributed to an ability to tackle life rationally; an ability rarely associated with women.

Sleepless Nights

Being rational means being able to detach oneself from one's problems and see them in perspective. It also means knowing when and how to

---

switch off. This ability to detach oneself, or switch off, is a great asset; the fortunate are born with it, the less fortunate have to learn to master it. One way or another, through nature or nurture, the business Amazons possessed this rare and precious gift.

A manifestation of it was their capacity to sleep well whatever the day's events. With the reliability of a pre-set timer they fell asleep at the end of the day and arose fresh the next morning ready to take up where they had left off the night before. 'Never had a sleepless night. I am terribly lucky. I can put my head on the pillow and I am out.' 'Once I go to bed I read and I drop off to sleep.' And, disarmingly: 'I am pretty good at getting to sleep. I don't think about the business. If I cannot get to sleep I think it is because I have overeaten. I am a good eater. But not ever the business, never.'

Of course this ability to sleep even when the going gets rough has everything to do with their astonishing ability not to worry. 'No, I don't have worries. I don't understand why the business does not give me worries, but it never has.' 'I just refuse to worry over the business. My husband does the worrying. He is the one that can be up all night. I am more likely to be worried about somebody who is ill. I feel there are more important things in life.'

The ease with which the business Amazons have eliminated the word 'worry' from their vocabulary seems almost superhuman till one remembers what a futile activity worrying is – wholly unsuited to the temperament of these particular women who thrive on action. 'I don't sit and worry,' says cosmetics expert Rachel Shapiro. 'If there is a problem I would say, "Let's see how we can solve it." I'd rather work on solving problems than just worry. I try to be a positive person.' And Jane Auerbach, in fashion: 'I have no time for worries, I am a doer. If something is wrong, instead of worrying about it I decide to find out what I have to do.'

The advertised product is superb, a clan of female warriors who have conquered worry. But not all of them started that way and one of the few situations that caused real anxiety was when the actual existence of their businesses was threatened by shortage of money, or a labour dispute. Fast food specialist Claire Smith recalls:

There were occasionally low patches where you thought there was no light at the end of the tunnel. The overdraft was not coming down, the franchise was not taking off and there was no money coming in, but there was money going out. I remember that I had some sleepless nights then, but not since.

217

And supermarkets owner Doreen Hartman:

> The only time when I literally had sleepless nights was during our last union negotiations, which was about two years ago. We avoided a strike. Costs are so sensitive in our industry that had the union persisted in asking for a higher wage increase than we could afford we would have been wiped out.

But experience, and with it the realisation that business is based on a repetitive pattern, have taught the business Amazons how to take life more philosophically. Deirdre Bovis says: 'I was a real worrier, but when you grow you have got to learn to cope with it. I always say it is not the end of the world. Now my son is the worrier and I tell him: "As long as you are in this job something will always go wrong – so better get used to it." '

A philosophical attitude coupled with financial success has stopped the businesswomen from worrying over money and general business problems. Rebecca Kemmis explains: 'I do not worry any more because I have many properties and I know that if the business is squeezed, I could always unload one of them.' But it has not stopped them from worrying over people. It is amazing that although they are businesswomen, and business is after all about money, when these women worry it is not over money but over people. For example, Jay Simpson: 'Funnily enough I never worried over money. It could have been anxiety over employees or it could have been anxiety over a customer. It was people problems, not money problems. Never money.'

People were the only area where the business Amazons' self-control and ability to switch off malfunctioned. Professional and tough as they might be, they could not ignore the people they worked with. And when in their efforts to run a good show they inadvertently hurt them, they paid the penalty of sleepless nights. Radio stations owner Rose Kraus admits: 'People's problems give me sleepless nights. For instance if you decided not to give someone a raise or if you fire someone I worry about how I am going to do it. Anyone who pretends that firing is fun or anyone who gets used to firing is ridiculous and should not be there. When I have to do it it gives me sleepless nights.'

Coping with Disaster

It is often said of successful women that they must have been lucky or they would never have made it. Is this true of the women in the survey? Was life kind to them? Were they spared the traumas most of us experience?

The facts do not support such assumptions. On the contrary, it would seem that the business Amazons have had more than their fair share of adversity. What greater disaster can befall a mother than the untimely death of her child? Yet 7 per cent of these women endured just this. Sickness took the lives of four of their children and accidents the lives of another three. Two of the deaths occurred before they started in business and the other five during it. The ages of the deceased varied: four were under the age of ten, two were in their teens, and one was already a mother.

A misfortune of such magnitude is not less painful when suffered by a warrior. The difference is that a warrior does not allow it to paralyse her for long. On the contrary, the death of Lisa Collier's three-year-old son because of inadequate medical emergency facilities in their home town spurred her into a campaign to improve the local hospital. The death of Denise Philips's four-year-old daughter made Denise realise that she had more in her than she had ever known.

Accepting what cannot be changed, and salvaging whatever is left was the practical philosophy that supported these women through their individual tragedies. When Barbara Carpenter's fourteen-year-old son was killed in a car accident, it was the second loss she had suffered that year. Eleven months before she had been widowed. 'That was terrible. A husband, you can say, "Lord, I had him for twenty years, thank you." But a young boy, who will never become a man . . .' Yet despite the loss of both husband and son Barbara did not indulge in self-pity. She immersed herself in her late husband's business and considered herself luckier than others in her position. 'I am very thankful for what the Lord has given me. Children, a good husband, and now a new career opportunity. How many people in their mid-fifties have had the opportunity of a complete new career? Not many.'

In their efforts to overcome such crushing blows, those business Amazons who were already in business were helped tremendously by the fact that they were needed. That was what took Barbara's mind off her loss, and it was what saved Nina Dean from going to pieces when her thirteen-year-old son died from a brain tumour. 'Having the business helped me to overcome the shock. It was terrible. One day you have a healthy child, the next he has a tumour, and a month later he dies. But the business forced me to pull myself together.' And it was also business that kept Deirdre Bovis from going out of her mind when her forty-year-old daughter died in a fall that broke her skull. The fact that not only one, but sixty families depended on her ability to hold on forced her to superhuman efforts. 'It has been the biggest tragedy of my life. We were very close. She would ring me three times a day. You see, having been a widow for so long, we were much closer than normal mothers and daughters.'

In the scale of personal tragedy the death of a child is almost equalled by its being maimed or disabled. These women did not escape such miseries. Two of their sons lost an eye, one in a shooting accident, and one in a car accident. Two of their children were retarded. One, a girl, was still a child and at home and the other, a son in his mid-twenties, had had to be put in an institution.

Fate struck not only their children, but also their husbands: 25 per cent were widowed, two of them twice. In the USA 44 per cent of their husbands' deaths were in airplane crashes, and in the UK 44 per cent of the husbands died from heart attacks.

In fact the women's history of misfortune started long before their adulthood: 21 per cent of them had had some traumatic experience with one or both of their parents during their early life. Two of their mothers died at birth, leaving their daughters to be brought up by fathers who never remarried. One had no known father and was brought up by her grandmother. One had no known mother or father and was given for adoption. One mother committed suicide. Three fathers died when the daughters were young. Two fathers died when the daughters were in college. Two mothers died during their daughter's teens. Two lost both parents when in their early teens. Two fathers left home never to be seen again. Five had parents with multiple divorces and marriages; one mother had five different husbands.

The business Amazons are not the only ones to have lost loved ones. It happens to everyone. The aim of these revelations is not to generate compassion for these remarkable women but to scale them down to real life proportions. They are not invincible. They are not larger than life. They hurt like the rest of us. Theirs was not an easy life. They were

---

not less or more lucky than hundreds of other women. They had their fair share of catastrophe, sometimes more than their fair share. But what sets them apart from the rest is that they did not allow their misfortunes permanently to extinguish their zest for life.

13 | Health and Beauty

In a society obsessed with success, the unsuccessful watch out avidly for flaws in those who have made it – if not out of pure malice, then in order to justify their own lack of success by being able to claim that the price paid is not worth the results. Their line on the business Amazons would be: 'So they are intelligent and successful, but what about their health and their looks . . . ?'

The Amazonian Look, Then and Now

Sexual affiliation is the most important determinant of good looks, more important than history or geography. Regardless of time or place, in order to qualify as good-looking one has to conform to the norm for one's sex. An effeminate male or a mannish female would not be considered presentable, however highly he or she might rate in the 'wrong' category.

The word 'Amazon' conjures up an image of a hermaphrodite, or at least a woman whose femininity is questionable, because although she might look like a woman, she behaves like a man. But times have changed, and brains have replaced muscle as the requirement for women wishing to assume roles hitherto reserved only for men. Outwardly the modern Amazons are no longer distinguishable from their more conventional sisters the homemakers. Even their looks do not seem to have been affected by operating in men's territory, for as a group the business Amazons were striking in their overall good looks. The stereotypical businessman's big paunch and general air of overindulgence does not apparently have a female equivalent. Indeed, it would seem that the more successful the business Amazons became, the greater their efforts over their appearance. Of the two national groups, it was the American business Amazons who were better groomed. Their hair was more coiffed, their faces less wrinkled, their heels higher, and their nails longer and redder.

Women pay a great deal of attention to their appearance because for millennia it has been their greatest asset and such ingrained behaviour cannot be eradicated in one generation. Lacking any other significant heritage, and not yet confident of their new role in society, women are forced to cling to the only marketable asset they have. Even such pioneering women as those in this survey had not made the break with that particular tradition.

Dressed for Success

There is no disputing that appearances count. Nor can it be denied that in business one stands a better chance of inspiring confidence if one looks prosperous. The business Amazons, like most women, were prepared to put a lot of time and trouble into getting their 'packaging' right. One of their chief concerns was that they should be recognised for what they were, and not be mistaken for the housewives or the secretaries most women were expected to be. Fashion designer Debra Manham asserts: 'A businesswoman has to dress well, so that she looks like a businesswoman, and not like a woman who is going shopping. She has also got to dress in such a way that she cannot be mistaken for the secretary.'

This preoccupation with looking the part was more prevalent among the American businesswomen than among the British ones. In the USA the way a businesswoman ought to dress is a whole science. Complete books have been written about the subject, and lectures dealing with the correct dress code for career women are constantly being delivered to women's groups. One of the classic hints to the aspiring executive is that she should never wear slacks: 'Secretaries wear slacks, executives wear suits.' This anxiety about the right appearance has been explained by some of the businesswomen as a result of women's slight physique. Debra Manham says: 'We have to take great care of our appearance because we are usually physically small and as a result insignificant looking.' A small, insignificant-looking businessman enhances his visibility with a large car and a large cigar. A small woman resorts to clothes in order to achieve the same effect. Thus it would seem that women's preoccupation with their appearance is not only a compensation for their lack of confidence but also a compensation for their size.

Only 5 per cent of the women did not attribute much importance to the way they dressed at work and, instead of following the accepted dress code for businesswomen, felt confident enough to wear what they liked. An additional 6 per cent, although critical of the obsession businesswomen had about their appearance, did not have the courage to rebel. Statements such as finance broker Adele Benn's 'The way a woman dresses for work should not be important, but it is' are heard only too often from those who do not have the courage to follow their convictions.

The need to be identified as a businesswoman, rather than just any woman, was so great that even a highly educated woman like Nancy Gardner was in its thrall. She admits: 'I am reluctant to say that it is important that I wear a business suit, because like a child's messy room does not mean a messy mind, the clothes one wears are not an indication of one's abilities.' And she has never worn anything but a business suit to work. In twenty-one years she has built an empire and commanded hundreds of people and millions of dollars, but has never worn a dress or pants to work.

Like businessmen who wear only suits to work, so the American businesswomen accepted the fact that a uniform was an inseparable part of their role. Their conformity was surprising, because one might have expected that as their own bosses they would have taken advantage of their supreme position and dressed in the way they wanted; but alas, they did not. Valerie Reynolds, with a $7 million electronics firm, complains: 'Women in corporations have to live with that, but entrepreneurs have a little bit more freedom of expression, yet they do not seem to take advantage of it.' Nevertheless, a few did and their businesses prospered despite their nonconforming attire. Sixty-one-year-old Laurie Richards was one of them. Not only did she not dress like a tycoon, she also did not dress like most women of sixty-one. Yet her marketing empire did not collapse. She says with some pride:

> My son comes in and says, 'Oh my God, we have got these people
> coming today and you have gotten on this velvet jumpsuit with

the baggy pants, and your horrible jewellery.' He always asks, 'Why do you wear all the junk jewellery?' My son is a total conformist. I am unlike most businesswomen, who dress very conservatively and are afraid to stand out.

The business Amazons' reluctance to exercise their boss's prerogative and dress individually stemmed from their concern that unless they dressed severely, they would not be taken seriously. Even a free soul like Janet Draper, who dashes around her 400,000 sq ft engineering plant in blue jeans and sneakers, hurries to dress properly when outsiders arrive. She justifies herself: 'I'm not trying to impress the staff. My authority with them doesn't stem from my clothes, but from my know-how. But it is customers and visitors, whom I don't have time to impress with my ability, that I have to dress properly for.'

Despite the constant reference to the proper way in which businesswomen should dress, it seemed that the magical style that kept them covered, gave them confidence, and bolstered their egos was not universal, and the tastes of the British and the American businesswomen differed considerably. While the British Amazons dressed more individually, the majority of the Americans subscribed to a uniform, the mannish tailored suit, which was last worn by European women in any number before the Second World War. Although every few years elegant female trendsetters adopt the mannish suit for a few months, it has not become a permanent feature in European women's fashion as such, and is definitely not identified there as a businesswoman's attire.

American businesswomen try to emulate men's clothes because they feel that they are trespassing on male territory, where the best way to avoid detection is camouflage. Confectioner Nancy Gardner discloses: 'The women who come out of Harvard Business School are advised by the consultants to wear black and navy suits, as the safest and least obtrusive attire.'

The American businesswomen have interpreted the advice that they should dress similarly to men literally. The majority of them wear dark tailored suits with white starched shirts and ties. The more adventurous replace the white shirts and ties with a silk blouse and feel that they have made their gesture against convention. And the 'real' rebels cast away the tailored suit for the more feminine Chanel type, but a suit it still is. The wish to merge into the background is pathetic, not because it is undignified but because it does not work. Since there is no mistaking a woman for a man, not even one in a tailored suit, why enter the straitjacket to start with?

The fashion leaders among these women comfort themselves that with time businesswomen will feel confident enough to drop this uniform of mannish suits; but until they develop their own dress style they feel that the 'uniform' is preferable to an unprofessional look. Marion Little, conferences promoter, states: 'You see a man, the lowest stock clerk, and he will have on a jacket, and you see a woman in a clerical position and she looks as if she is dressed to take out the garbage or the laundry. She doesn't look professional.' Stevie Frederick who distributes electronics components believes that, with the increased number of women turning to business careers, their need to camouflage themselves in men's attire will eventually disappear.

The younger businesswomen feel schizophrenic about the whole situation. They hate this uniform, yet they are afraid to discard it for fear of being considered too feminine to be taken seriously. Marion Little admits: 'I wear suits, but I hate it. Yes, it is a uniform which we wear because we don't have the confidence to wear what we would like to wear. I have a thing against these damn ties. When I walk to work in the morning I count how many women look like men in business suits.'

For most of the women business owners the clothes they wear at work are costumes that go with the role they play. Eva Helsing is one of the most elegant women around. Hers are the pale pastel-coloured suits that only the rich, who are not bothered about dry cleaning bills, can afford to wear. Her platinum-toned hair, suit, and shoes are set off by her platinum jewellery. She looks as if she had just walked out of a mix and match parade, radiating the effortless perfection normally restricted to *Vogue* models. It is unbelievable that this symbol of perfection at work is a chronic slob at home. But so she is, in her own words: 'At home I am a slob. I have very bad feet so after a day in elegant shoes I enjoy wearing old yukky shoes and yukky clothes. It's so much more comfortable. I don't really care much about clothes, but when I'm out in public I dress up. I have to look prosperous. I'm in the money business.'

At home, where their role playing stops, these women relax from their business image and dress in the way they want. The uniform that distinguishes them at work is discarded, whether in favour of jeans and T-shirts, or of long, soft, frilly gowns. But some do not find the strength to switch into a new role. After sixteen hours at work Dorothy Simmonds (oil equipment dealer) could not be bothered with selecting a different outfit to wear. She had only one change of costume: 'You are kidding, who can think about what to wear after a day's work? I have only two outfits – my suits and my pyjamas.'

Despite what would seem an additional burden on businesswomen to dress in conformity with others' expectations, 66 per cent of the women tycoons did not feel that theirs was a greater burden than that of businessmen, who were expected to conform to a specific dress code. But the 34 per cent minority that thought otherwise felt that business-women had to pay much more attention to their appearance than men. Linda Bailie, lingerie magnate, expostulates: 'We are expected to be good businesswomen, good wives, good mothers, and also good-looking and well groomed. No one expects so much from a man. He can get away by being a good earner. We can't.' They resent not having been allowed to unburden themselves of the classic feminine obliga-tions – of which a good appearance is only one, but one too many for them. They feel cheated, because they had thought that once they had proven themselves in a man's world they would have been absolved at least from some of the obligations imposed on women. But they have found out not only that they have not been let off any of women's duties, but also that they have accumulated some of the men's obligations. An example of this double bind is keeping one's body in good shape, something that many businessmen do not bother with. Genevieve Rouche, the talent scout and an elegantly thin person herself, comments:

> A woman has a real disadvantage. It is too bad that women have to age like men, because we are treated equally. You have fat, sloppy men but they get away with it. They are millionaires and everyone treats them with respect. When a millionairess happens to be fat and sloppy no one remembers that she is a self-made, capable person. What they do remember is that she is fat and sloppy.

The difficulty experienced by the business Amazons was not only that they had to dress well and look beautiful, but that they were supposed to achieve it without looking too feminine. When they dressed as if they belonged in the boardroom and not in the kitchen, they were accused of being unfeminine; and when they looked as if they should be in the bedroom and not in the boardroom they were accused of being unbusinesslike. The question to be asked therefore is: why, if it required so much thought and planning, did the businesswomen bother to conform? After all, no one put a loaded revolver to their temples. The answer is simple. Although they were not forced to dress or look one way or another, experience has taught them that if they wanted to integrate into a man's world they had to underplay their femininity without looking masculine. 'If you want to be a pal, you should not remind them of their wives or mothers, whom they might love dearly, but whose business acumen they do not hold in high esteem' was the advice often given to businesswomen who wanted to get on in business. Such advice was probably sound, but regrettably so. Businesswomen are not taken at face value as capable persons, but have constantly to walk the tightrope of being not too much of the one and not too little of the other.

Despite the minority's sharp grievance about the burden of 'looking good' the majority did not feel that businesswomen had a harder time here than businessmen. Public relations millionairess Amelia Jaeger remarks: 'Men have also got to put a crease in their trousers, polish their shoes, and wear a clean shirt.' Nor did they feel that they were viewed differently. Film maker Alice Whitmarsh comments: 'The bank manager does not only look for a laddered stocking [that is, with a run], but also for a frayed shirt.'

Among the British women asked, the issue of how a business owner ought to look and dress was virtually non-existent. Within the constraints of their particular occupation, they dressed according to their tastes. A garage owner who had no dealings with the wider public paid less attention to her appearance than the cosmetics tycoon, who used herself as an advertisement for the effectiveness of her products.

The greater readiness of the American businesswomen to conform to a dictated dress code stemmed from two cultural differences. First, the social phenomenon of 'joining in' is more pronounced in the USA than in Britain; and second, in contrast with Britain, a demonstrative eagerness to succeed is accepted normal behaviour in the USA. As a result the loss of their individuality of appearance was hardly a sacrifice for the American women, for whom the result of success justified the means.

Lest it be concluded that because the British women dressed more individually than the American ones, they were wild dressers or that they approved of such taste in their female employees, it should be pointed out that they too believed in a low-key dress code. The essence of that code was that the corporation's interests stood above the individual's need to express her personality. A top secretary with bells on her ankles had to take them off because customers and colleagues alike were distracted, and a bright personal assistant had to be told to wear a bra for similar reasons. On the whole, the consensus among the female bosses was that their female employees should be neat and tidy and, above all, not provocative in appearance. The British property dealer Tricia Williams recalls an incident: 'I told her that her flamboyant clothes were inappropriate for a business meeting. Although she is very clever and efficient she looks frail and young and could look a bit frivolous or silly in such clothes. It is a quicker way of getting business if you do not confuse people with your appearance.'

The requirement that their female employees should subdue their femininity, and project themselves as persons and not as women, was the essence of the British business millionairesses' own dress code. But although it might be more practical and less complicated for women to dress unobtrusively in business, it was reassuring to encounter a handful of flashy dressers. It proved that submerging one's feminine appearance was not a prerequisite for success in business, and that with the right flair one could look and dress as one wanted. British employment agent Sally Harper says:

> I tend to be a little bit flamboyant in and out of work. I don't dress conventionally. I buy things that other people would not buy; I put clothes together differently. I would wear, if I fancied, a jacket with gold on it in the day. The older I get the more outrageously I dress. Now I wear a hat when I go shopping with a feather in it, and a bright yellow coat, and I feel quite happy in it, whereas maybe ten years ago I would have thought I'd better not wear yellow. It is the confidence of being successful that enables me to disregard convention.

Health

Non-achievers comfort themselves with the thought that one cannot achieve wealth or fame without the loss of health or privacy. So they see the ulcers and coronaries of top businessmen as a just penalty for their success. But if they expect top businesswomen to fit the same pattern, they are in for a surprise. For it seems that the long working hours, and the continuous fight to stay at the top have not taken a similar toll on the business Amazons.

Ninety-five per cent of them rated their health as 'excellent', 'very good', or 'good'. Debra Manham, aged forty-seven: 'I am just never ill.' Ellie Leonard, sixty-seven: 'I probably go to the doctor every five years when he drags me in for a medical.' Niki Summers, fifty-three: 'So far so good. I have a high energy level. I can go for long hours on that same peak without crashing.'

Even the additional duties of homemaking and motherhood did not seem to have affected their health. Laurie Richards, sixty-one: 'I have just had a complete physical and the doctor said, "For somebody who lives your kind of life, leading your kind of pace, you are unbelievably fit." ' Genevieve Rouche, fifty-one: 'I am in such good health that my doctor does not believe it. He said, "You have no right to be in such good health." ' And at the age of seventy-two, after forty-two years in business, the only complaint Sadie Fairweather had about her health was that she was sometimes 'a little bit short of breath when I run.' But it went even further than this. Many of the women claimed that their health had actually improved. Here are a few examples: 'Before I started in business my health was not so good. I used to get ill quite often.' 'Before I started in business I used to suffer with my back and digestion.' 'I have not seen a doctor since I started in business.'

What could be the explanation of their robust constitution? What was the secret of their good health? As we know, theirs was not a pampered existence and they were no youngsters either. Only 2 per cent were under thirty, which in medical terms means that 98 per cent had passed the peak of physical fitness.

There are only two possible explanations. Either they were startling examples of natural selection or 'the survival of the fittest'; or it was a matter of mind over body – a refusal to succumb to the weakness of the flesh. There was no evidence to support the first explanation. There was plenty to support the latter. 'I do not have time to be ill,' was a typical response. So too: 'The whole thing about women being ill was a Victorian thing, which fitted the image of women on chaises longues who had nothing but their health to think about.' And the clincher: 'If you have something exciting to look forward to, you are not ill. I have never known a woman to be ill on her wedding day.'

Further proof that it was the purposefulness and excitement of their lives that accounted for their good health, was the fact that the business Amazons' medical histories did not always correspond to their optimistic descriptions of their health – a fact which demonstrated their mental resistance to giving in to illness.

	Subjective view	*Facts*
Jane Auerbach	'good'	thyroid operation hysterectomy
Tricia Bishop	'100 per cent'	high blood pressure obesity
Rachel Black	'excellent'	several near nervous breakdowns
Nina Dean	'very good health'	gallstone operation burst appendix operation various gynaecological problems
Janet Draper	'good'	polio when a teenager tuberculosis in mid-thirties cancer of the reproductive organs nine years ago
Renée Ellis	'terrific'	mastectomy two years ago
Sally Harper	'strong, fit'	gall bladder removed stomach ulcers Caesarean with first child miscarriages high blood pressure obesity
Golda Harris	'I am not a sickly person'	hepatitis with jaundice gallstone operation two other operations
Elizabeth Lyon	'wonderful'	cancer of the womb – complete hysterectomy six months ago
Denise Philips	'strong and healthy'	debilitating migraines
Jay Simpson	'exceptionally good'	varicose veins operation suspected breast cancer
Lesley Trance	'good'	nervous breakdown lasted two years various gynaecological problems
Susan Willards	'good'	arthritis in hips, slight limp

Health and Beauty

From their medical histories it would appear that the business Amazons are as prone to illness as the rest of us. What distinguished them was their refusal to go under. Renée Ellis had just embarked on an entrepreneurial career in catering when she discovered that she had breast cancer. Two years after a mastectomy, and with a flourishing restaurant business, she talked about her 'terrific health'. Janet Draper, despite polio on her teens, tuberculosis in her thirties, and cancer in her forties, has managed to give birth to four children, and run a multimillion-dollar engineering business at the same time. Her explanation of how she managed to cope with all that was simple: a busy life. 'Sometimes I feel like I deserve a nervous breakdown. Everyone seems to have one these days. But then on second thoughts I would like it to last only two days, Saturday and Sunday, so that I could be in the office Monday. I just cannot afford to take the time off to be sick.'

One medical history after another disclosed a body that was propped up by will power. Sally Harper, with her excessive weight, blood pressure, and stomach ulcers – she had also had her gall bladder removed – was a doctor's nightmare. But despite all this and her susceptibility to flu – 'I have always got flu. When it is going around I am the first to get it, and when no one else gets it, I still get it' – she did not let her body control her life. 'I come to work with the flu and a temperature, until I have to be taken home.' She considered herself 'a strong, fit person'.

Will power and a purpose in life were not unique to businesswomen in the survey; other high achievers, including men, have displayed a similar resistance to disease. Yet, without wishing to make out that the business Amazons are superhuman, it must be remembered that when they were ill, they did not have wives to look after them. Instead they had husbands and children who continued to need looking after themselves.

14 | **Life Is Not All Work**

People who are not career minded imagine that there must be a trade-off between the enjoyments of leisure and of hard work. They like to think that although workaholics achieve more at work, they miss out on other aspects of life. By any standards the business Amazons would be classified as workaholics. What do they do then after six in the evening when the telephones stop ringing, the secretaries stop typing, and their top executives start looking at their watches? Are they left high and dry, like generals without soldiers to command? Do they yearn for the new day to start and restore them to glory? Or do they perhaps enjoy their role of ordinary citizens, wives, and mothers?

The Change-over

The switch from commander to soldier was not easy for the women tycoons, and many of them did not really manage to separate their private lives from their business lives. The greatest difficulty was encountered by the married businesswomen who worked independently of their husbands. For them the change-over was abrupt and unconditional. One moment they were engrossed in one world, and a moment later they had to forget it existed. For the 39 per cent who worked with their husbands the conversion was less traumatic though not easy, especially when it was not they who wanted to separate their private life from their business life, but their husbands. For Rachel Shapiro, who started her cosmetics business from scratch and within seven years reached a sales volume of $7.5 million, it was her most important creation after her children. 'I don't mind talking about the business at home. I actually want to, but my husband does not.' For Claire Smith, too, who like Rachel started her fast food business before her husband joined her, the business meant much more to her than to him. 'I am usually the one who starts talking about the business in the evening. I have sworn that I will reform, but it is very difficult.'

But it was not always this way round. Sometimes, as in Delia Lewenthal's case, it was the husband with the less glamorous occupation who was eager to share his wife's experiences as a toy magnate, and it was she who felt the need to switch off. What women like Delia found most difficult about the change from the role of a boss to that of a mere woman was to stop laying down the rules when she returned home:

> I want to be able to talk to him when I feel the need, but not otherwise. Sometimes I say, 'Please, I don't want to talk about it,' and within five minutes I will be saying, 'By the way, what do you think about . . . ?' He will say, 'I thought you didn't want to talk about it,' and I stop myself and realise that I am dictating the rules of the game.

Bad experience with their first husbands prompted Frances Roberts and Lesley Trance to exclude business talk from their second marriages. Frances succeeded: her second husband was a theatrical producer who had no interest in her advertising business. She says, 'I do not talk business at all. I have learnt my lesson. For three minutes we ask each other about work and then we go on to the next thing.' But Lesley was not so lucky. Although, like Frances, she was determined not to discuss her travel business at home, her husband was keen to. She asks:

> What do you do with a husband who is sincerely keen to get involved with your business, when you know it can lead only to trouble? I have always said that when I get married again I shall keep business out of the bedroom. Yet unfortunately my husband is very interested in my business and he enjoys talking about it. He will first read his newspaper and then he will come into the bedroom and start, and I will say, 'I want to read my book.' It is very difficult to have to shut him off like this, but I had bad experiences in the past.

Inappropriate as it might seem to exclude one's spouse from a large part of one's life, it can and has been done. Men have always done it.

They have never found it to be a problem. Wives however feel uneasy about excluding their husbands this way; but, as has been proven time and again, when it comes to making this decision women are no different from men. When Amelia Jaeger decided that keeping her public relations business life to herself was the best formula for sustaining her marriage, she did not hesitate: 'The mixing of business and social life, is totally unnecessary for both men and women. I keep my social life totally separate from my business life.'

Publisher Lucy Curtis, too, whose husband is a scientist and knows nothing about business, thought it best to keep her work out of their life together:

> If he actually asks I will tell him about the business, but otherwise
> I never discuss any problems and never ask his advice. Like that,
> he cannot get hurt and be offended if I don't listen to his advice.
> Because, knowing myself, at the end I do what I want.

Few of the businesswomen were as self-sufficient and self-disciplined as Amelia and Lucy, who managed to move from one world to another with the chime of the clock. The majority did not live in such well-defined time zones. For them their business and private life were a continuum; but, surprising as it might seem, most of them loved it and could not imagine or wish it different. Where the couple worked together they took it for granted that their private lives and business lives were one and the same. Jay Simpson, the female half of a wife and husband team, remarks: 'I could never switch off, but then most business people can't.' Susan Willards, also teamed with her husband, says: 'My husband likes talking about the business. Also I like it. You know, it is our life. Both of us.' And Nancy Lennon, who used to work with her husband in the construction industry, but is now widowed, remembers: 'We used to sit up till two in the morning talking about what we were going to do and what we had done that day.'

Wives who worked with their husbands were not the only ones who let their business spread into their private lives. For Julie Karr, a childless divorcee with no one to await her return home, the film business was all she had. She had no wish to change over from one life to another. 'I don't really have any private life. The business is my life and I love it.'

Lack of private life is not the automatic outcome of dedication to one's business. Sonia Kaplan claims that her mail order business activities have actually enriched her private life.

We have a small family, and my only chance of meeting people is through the business. As a result nearly all our friends are business friends. I would also find it difficult to spend an evening with people with different interests. It is so contrived. What am I going to ask the doctor about his patients? Or the artist about his latest exhibition?

Outsiders to the business world can stop feeling sorry for the poor tycoon who either has no private life or does not know how to enjoy one. There are those who are loath to relinquish their day-time power base – especially married women who have to adopt a subservient role at home – but generally there are few complaints.

Free Time

One of the attractions of being one's own boss is the flexible working hours. In theory one can work when one chooses and eventually, when the business is established and successful, have lots of free time to pursue other interests. The image of the jetsetting business millionaire who knows how to enjoy his wealth is one that has lured many entrepreneurs into business. But how real is the image? Do successful business people manage to have free time? As for the business Amazons, although they have not produced any gurus of good living in the mould of Hugh Hefner, Bernie Cornfeld, or Victor Lownes, most of them have managed to find some free time for themselves – and know how to spend it.

The majority of them, with typical optimism, insisted that they had more free time than they did. More often than not this 'free time' turned out to be a fortnight's vacation with the grandchildren, or a day's shopping expedition to London. The inevitable conclusion is that although in theory these women could have had all the free time they wanted, in reality they took little advantage of their business owner's privileges. To gain such humble luxuries one did not have to be a millionaire. Most employees can manage better than that.

The realists were honest enough to admit that they did not really *want* any free time. 'I enjoy what I am doing. So what do I want free time for?' was a typical comment.

Free time is a gift only to those who have a use for it. Seventy-one-year-old Valerie Reynolds, a childless widow, did not: 'I usually arrange it so that I do not have any free time. It is not much fun having dinner alone at home. So I keep myself busy. I work most evenings until ten to eleven.' Even for Janet Draper, who had a husband and four children to return to after work, free time was not a coveted goal.

> I try not to have any free time because I get what is known as a relaxation headache. People like me who are not used to it become ill from doing nothing. I cannot stand doing nothing. I either read or sleep, or I work. I could not sit and watch soap operas for a day. I would go stark raving mad.

It would seem that the joys of free time have been exaggerated by those whose working life was dull and unrewarding. Faced with the choice of having two much or too little, even those among the business Amazons who said they wished they had more free time did not want an excess of it. Radio station owner Rose Kraus is one of them: 'I wish I had more free time. But life is never exactly the way we want it. I would rather have too little free time than too much.'

It seems that the real reason why business owners have no free time is that reaching the top and staying there requires total dedication. After twelve years in the aviation business Julie Kitson did not allow herself even a few days' vacation. 'I had no holiday or a day off in the last two years. I don't envisage having time off other than going into hospital to have the baby.' And even after thirty-one years in the gift business Eileen Geermie could not prise herself free from her twenty-four-hour a day duties.

> The pressures are just as great as when I started thirty-one years ago. When you are up there and you are successful, you have got to watch it even closer because, although I have a president and many other people, the key decisions are mine. Unless you sell your business or unless you merge, when you know that all the responsibilities will be taken care of by someone else, you are married to it, twenty-four hours a day.

The mistake of believing that success will result in more free time was discovered by talent agent Genevieve Rouche too late, when she was already consumed by the bug of success and was ready to do without free time to stay at the top.

After twenty-one years in the business, I have much less time than I had at the beginning. After my first three or four years in business I took vacations and weekends off. The biggest disappointment I have in success is the fact that it is hard to stay on top. It is an enormous emotional strain, and you have to watch your back constantly. Once you are up there, you cannot ask anyone to help you stay there. There are many who are just waiting to replace you.

One need have no pity for the successful since they are pursuing their careers out of choice and, what is more important, out of love. If the business Amazons had no free time it means only one thing: that they liked it that way. The fact that all but a few were reluctant to attribute the lack of free time to their passion for work was not a sign of hypocrisy, but of their sensitivity to their families, whose interests they were supposed to serve before their own. No husband or child would want a wife or mother who admitted preferring her business to them. The only woman who had the courage to own up was construction magnate Lena Gouldwin; but then even among the Amazons Lena was unique.

I have no free time whatsoever. I carry my work with me. I load my head with it. But it is my choice, so I cannot complain. There are many nights that I spend sleeping on the couch in the office. I sleep three hours and work straight on through. It is not uncommon for me not to go home for two or three days. I would have liked to be able to say that it is necessary for me to work like this, but it is not completely true. If I wanted I could have delegated a lot of what I do, because I pay enough people to do these jobs. I cannot even complain about my staff; they are good. The truth is that I do it mostly because I am having a ball. I like it. Much as it is unfair on my family and guilty as I feel about it, I must admit that I work like this because I like it.

But one did not have to lack free time to be successful in one's work. By being extremely efficient and squeezing two lives into one, travel agent Ellie Leonard has managed to have the lot:

I am terribly well organised. I get up extremely early at five in the morning. I do forty-five minutes of yoga, and read something inspiring for the day. Then I get breakfast for my husband and myself, and walk to the office. I am always the first person to enter the office and the first to leave. I leave by three o'clock. I can accomplish an enormous amount of work in a day. I don't have any business lunches. I don't waste time. I don't waste any action, and I am in two of the most hysterical businesses in the world, advertising and travel.

Starting the day at five o'clock in the morning and working right through without a break for lunch is one way to be left with free time to enjoy. Another is to determine one's priorities and stick by them. For Lucy Curtis, business success was not the most important thing in life: 'Perhaps I am not that ambitious. If I wanted I could work all the time because the work is there. But I made a conscious effort not to, because I know I'll hate it if I do.' Nor was it for Sara Holt, the cosmetics millionairess who, as a single woman of thirty-four, was more concerned about finding a suitable husband than about being a top businesswoman: 'I have got to have a social life. Much as I love the work, being single I cannot be a twenty-four-hour business person. I want to get married and have a family. So I must circulate and meet people.'

Although the majority of the business Amazons had very little free time, lack of leisure is not a condition of business ownership, but a conscious choice. Those who knew what to do with their free time managed to create it, while those who did not, allowed their work to prevent them from being burdened with it.

After-work Activities

In the little free time they had, the women tycoons could not be found lying around on beaches. Nor could they be found at ladies' tea parties indulging in trivial gossip. Because of their high energy level, their free time too was packed with endless activity until it was difficult to distinguish between what they called work and what they called free time. Apart from the fact that one was money-making and the other was not, there was little difference between their commitment to and efficiency in their work and their after-work activities.

Voluntary work

A hangover from their middle-class background was their involvement
with voluntary work. But unlike many of their non-working sisters,
they were not content to lick envelopes and wrap lottery prizes; they
planned campaigns and organised events. With their experience and
resources they managed to avoid the most frustrating aspect of
voluntary work, relying on volunteers for results. PR success Jackie
Sayer says, 'Rather than discuss everything with five people I tell my
secretary to do it and it's done. Saves time and money in the long run.'

Since they were able to contribute more than their own labour,
charitable organisations also counted on them for patronage. Consequently it was easy to get elected to leading posts in the organisations
and following the tradition of male business owners, they used this
facility to gain power and influence in the community. For instance
Barbara Carpenter, owner of a yarn factory, was the treasurer of one
charity and the secretary of another, and this without getting involved
in the detailed work herself. Her book-keeper looked after the finance
of the first charity and her personal assistant after the daily affairs of
the second. But it was she who attended the monthly meetings and was
invited to the mayor's inauguration.

The involvement of the businesswomen with voluntary work was
much more widespread in America than in Britain. While 60 per cent of
the American business Amazons were actively involved, only 22 per
cent of the British ones were. There was a similar disparity in charitable
donations. All the American businesswomen donated regularly; but
only 11 per cent of the British ones did, and not generously at that.

There were two reasons for these disparities; different tax laws
regarding donations to charities, and a different structure of governmental welfare support of the needy. The American tax authorities
recognise donations to charities as business expenditure, but the British
authorities do not (although they do make certain smaller concessions
regarding deeds of covenant). This meant that the same donation cost
the Americans much less than it cost their British colleagues. At the
same time, in Britain, where the government takes responsibility for the
nation's welfare, voluntary organisations have a much smaller role to
play.

Without making judgements as to which of the two systems is better,
and for whom, it is a fact that where the community relies on private
donations and voluntary assistance, the donors and the volunteers gain
a higher social status than where the government is in charge of such

functions. Thus, besides the personal satisfaction gained from helping the needy, the reason for the American women's greater role in their community was that it enhanced their social standing.

But social approval was not the reward all of them were after. Even in the USA, 40 per cent did not want to get involved with voluntary organisations. Ulrike Jameson: 'I am not Miss Goody Two Shoes.' Lois Jane Apple: 'I have no time and no patience.' And keep fit expert Lisa Collier: 'I disapprove of charites *per se*.'

Reading

Reading habits reflected their interests: 66 per cent did not read much apart from business publications and women's magazines. With regard to the women's magazines, the Americans and the British both read them regularly, and for both it was a form of relaxation. It was the business publications that showed their different reading habits. Without exception, all the Americans kept themselves informed about developments and trends in their industries through trade and business journals; but only a few of the British businesswomen relied on these sources of information.

There were three reasons for this difference: the higher educational level of the American businesswomen; their greater professionalism; and the bigger influence of trade publications in the USA. One would expect business people to be avid readers of the *Wall Street Journal* and the *Financial Times* but this was not the case among the women. Only those whose businesses related to finance read these publications.

The reading tastes of those who managed to read more than women's magazines and trade journals varied considerably. One read four books a week regularly, but for the majority reading was reserved for holidays. Although a few enjoyed philosophical works, detective stories headed the list. Next in popularity were bestselling biographies of successful people, which were referred to as 'true and inspirational stories' and with which these women could identify. These criteria also applied to their choice of fiction. Restaurateur Claire Smith declared that although she was not 'into romance' her 'favourite book', and one which she had read many times, was *Gone with the Wind*. 'I adore Scarlett O'Hara. She did not have any scruples and she was a good businesswoman. I always take strength from reading it.'

The type and quantity of their reading showed no correlation with their success or with their type of business. A political PR woman whose work brought her into contact with the high and mighty preferred to read whodunnits, while a children's wear manufacturer, whose work involved her with less elevated company, read philosophy for recreation. It also emerged that those who in their former incarnation as housewives used to be avid readers did not regret no longer having the time for it and at least one considered it had just been an escape from the drudgery of housework.

Hobbies and pastimes

Comments on this subject included Rachel Shapiro's curt dismissal: 'No, I do not have any hobbies. Work is my hobby.' Joan Sheldon's evenings were spent in a most unleisurely way: 'My only hobby is investment. I am not good with my hands. I have also not got the patience to collect and I'd rather use my spare time profitably. So I got a home computer and I chart my investments in the evenings, so that I can instruct my broker in the morning.'

This lack of hobbies was typical of one third of the business Amazons and was at least partly because they associated hobbies with the life of a housewife from which they were glad to have escaped. Hardware millionaire Ellis Rosen put it like this: 'I used to enjoy cooking. I used to enjoy flower arranging. I enjoyed a lot of these things, which I no longer like. I was really majoring in being a good wife and mother.' And Juliette Marlon, travel organiser:

> I used to be a real homebody. I used to do needlepoint, design and sew my own clothes. I no longer do any of these. It's not just that I don't have time, which I don't, but I have also got accustomed to driving in the fast lane and I like it.

Of the two thirds who pursued after-work interests, none was a collector; 29 per cent made a hobby of gourmet cooking (the British just referred to it as 'cooking'); 23 per cent gardened; 20 per cent pursued handicrafts such as sewing, needlepoint, knitting, and crochet; and a further 7 per cent had pets.

Many Amazons extolled the pleasure of working with their hands which demands a high degree of activity with no mental strain. Travel tycoon Lesley Trance is one: 'After a day in the office I find working with my hands so very relaxing. I do tapestry. I do soft furnishings. I do lampshades. I do summer clothes, pretty clothes for holidays. I sew for my daughter. I make things for charity. I keep myself occupied the whole of the time.' Of the 21 per cent whose pastimes did not involve activities with their hands, 10 per cent regarded travelling as their hobby and 7 per cent engaged in self-improvement. Two studied languages, one philosophy, and another was in the final stages of her business studies degree.

True to their generally low-key image, the business Amazons' hobbies and pastimes were not showy. Only the aerobatic flying of employment agent Denise Philips and sponsorship of polo teams by Eileen Geermie, the giftshop millionairess, were exceptions and required money.

Socialising

Most managed to have some kind of social life, except when they were mothers of young children and except in the case of some unattached older women who, like sixty-year-old Eva Helsing, found it difficult to initiate social contacts. The reason Eva Helsing had no social life was not due to her age, because she looks at least ten years younger than her sixty years. Nor was it due to her looks, because she is an extremely handsome woman. the cause was her work as a financier which demanded much travelling. She ruefully admits:

> My social life leaves a lot to be desired. I move around so much that it is hard to develop a meaningful relationship. There is not much glamour in my travelling. Although I stay at the best hotels I don't get much out of it. I wouldn't dream of going alone to the theatre or to a restaurant so, when I finish the lecture, I order room service, have a bath, and go to sleep. The only parties I attend these days are our office parties. Whenever someone has a birthday I give them a party after office hours. We get some wine and some cakes and it is really lovely.

Eva was the exception. On the whole, once their children were out of the house, the businesswomen managed to pick up the strands of their social life. PR Amelia Jaeger says: 'I entertain my friends, I go to the theatre and museums. I am in a creative business and I need external stimulation. I need to have other things so that I do not sit here from eight in the morning until twelve o'clock at night. I need a break, a change of scenery.'

The social circle of the women magnates differed from that of their male colleagues, for it consisted almost exclusively of friends rather than business colleagues. And, when they were obliged to entertain business colleagues, they preferred to take them out to restaurants or to the theatre rather than invite them to their homes. Both the British and the Americans excluded business associates from their social life, and it is not hard to see why.

When a businessman wants to bring six people home unexpectedly for dinner all he has to do is telephone his wife and announce their arrival. He knows he can trust her to have everything ready on time, including a new hairdo and a welcoming smile. A businesswoman would not dare to expect the same from her husband. There were three other reasons why the women in the survey kept business entertainment to a minimum. The first was that they believed it was a waste of time; the second was the difficulty of developing cordial but formal relationships with their business acquaintances, who were mostly men and, most important of all, they were anxious not to upstage their husbands.

The difference between the effects of a businessman's success on his social life and that of a businesswoman's on hers is tremendous. While he flaunts his, she has to underplay hers. A wife basks in her husband's success; a husband is diminished by his wife's. The more visible a businessman's success, the higher his standing in the eyes of his wife, while a businesswoman's success has just the opposite effect.

The married businesswomen were not the only ones who found the mixing of business and social life impractical; the unattached, who did not have a husband's ego to consider, also tried to avoid it. Being single and having to entertain male clients and suppliers, they had to be extremely diplomatic in their efforts to reject their amorous advances without ruining their business relations with them. Travel agent Lydia Eastern states: 'I have made it a golden rule never to date a client, a vendor, or a competitor. You can easily lose a customer without gaining a lover.' Financier Elizabeth James, although she does not have Lydia's long experience of being a single woman in business, has reached the same conclusion. It did not take her long to learn that lunching and dining male associates could develop into a tricky situation.

I would say that taking them to dinner has got me business half the time, and maybe the other half of the time it has worked against me. When they sit with you in a dim lit restaurant you stop being a businesswoman for them and become just another girl they are taking out. I must pick up the tab, otherwise they forget that they had a business meeting. It establishes the relationship as a business one and not a private one.

These three reasons – husbands who could not be overshadowed; male colleagues who had to be kept at bay; and the overall waste of time – made the business Amazons exclude business friends from their social circles. Instead they chose to spend their free time with their families and friends and of the two, wherever their families lived nearby, they took priority.

Small dinner parties were their most usual method of entertainment. These they would organise on average about eight times a year. Sometimes, on grand occasions such as a spouse's birthday or a family reunion, they would throw a bigger affair. Iris Williamson boasts: 'I have just had a huge party the other night for ninety people and cooked it all myself.' But she is, after all, in the catering business and such occasions were not frequent.

Between being guest or hostess, the women tycoons preferred the latter. Sue Heathcote reckoned that if she was not to waste her precious free time in boring gatherings, she had better organize them herself. 'We are much more hosts than we are guests; partly because when I am the host I can plan my timetable and meet the people I want to see.' Taking the initiative and playing the host paid the highest dividends for those who were unattached, such as Barbara Carpenter, who was widowed at the age of forty-four. She explains:

> I usually invite people for dinner because being a widow and single, most people have a hard time inviting me, as they find it very difficult to have seven at the table, but I don't mind: I don't think that everyone has to be paired. It is basically their problem, not mine. To overcome it I invite them and I don't wait to be invited.

After entertaining friends and family at home and business associates outside, there was not much left of these women's limited free time. As a result their excursions to the theatre, opera, and concerts were very infrequent. On average they did not manage to see more than three plays a year, and attendance at concerts, opera, or ballet was restricted to a handful of dedicated followers.

Following the stars

What is one to make of the fact that all the business Amazons knew their Zodiac sign and a majority of them (53 per cent) took an interest in the subject? Could it be a manifestation of their deeper feelings about their success and their entitlement to it?

Whatever one's own personal bias may be, in western culture business and the occult are simply incompatible. Business people are expected to be rational, dogmatic, and self-reliant, all of which are antithetical to a belief in the power of fate. The belief that one's fate has already been determined can have two effects on a person's attitude to the future. Either one becomes fatalistic and cynical about the worth of trying to improve oneself, or one believes in one's destined success and sets out to achieve it. The women in this study belong to the second group and almost without exception seemed to believe in their predestined fate to become successful.

It is useless, of course, to try and correlate their birth signs with their actual success, because the signs differed without any significant pattern – not that the women could have known this before the present survey was carried out.

As for the degree of their faith in the stars, this varied from unquestioning to doubtful. Deirdre Bovis, with a £1.5 million haulage business, states: 'I never come out in the morning until I have read my forecast.' Sally Harper, with an employment agency worth £1.5 million, says: 'I totally believe in the Zodiac signs.' Daphne Glover, whose market research firm is worth £1 million, admits: 'Whenever I get my hands on the *Standard* it is the first thing I look at.' Frances Roberts, owner of a $55 million advertising agency, says: 'I look every day at the reports and I think of it.' Rachel Shapiro, with her $7.5 million cosmetics business, is a little more circumspect: 'I do not believe what it says in the papers but I believe in the sign characteristics.' Barbara Carpenter, with $5.5 million in engineering, allows: 'I don't check it up every day, just once in a while.' And Iris Williamson, with $5.5 million in fast foods, remarks prudently: 'Whenever I get hold of a newspaper that has a horoscope I read it. When they forecast what suits me I believe them, but when it doesn't suit me, I don't pay any attention to it.'

Faithful followers of the occult expect to be guided by it, but the uncommitted expect it only to confirm their beliefs, not to change them. It was apparent that the women were not occult addicts whose daily life was guided by their horoscope forecast, so their interest in it

---

246

can be explained as a search for confirmation of their entitlement to success.

If the group under survey had consisted of businessmen instead of businesswomen, it is doubtful whether a majority would have taken such an interest in their horoscopes. It ought, however, to be remembered that one important reason for this is circumstantial: most of the handy sources of horoscope predictions are either in the popular press or in women's magazines which even the most highbrow business Amazons could not entirely avoid, if only at the hairdresser's.

A final reason for their interest in horoscopes was the newness of their success. Any sign, even of a horoscope in a women's magazine, that could be seen as a validation of this success was welcomed by them as reinforcing their claim to it, and assuring them that it would last.

15 | Regrets, Ambitions, Dreams

What does a mountaineer do when he has reached the summit? Standing on what can now be seen to be no more than a lump of rock, does he eagerly survey the surrounding mountains, looking for new peaks to scale? Or does he merely feel disappointment that the climb is over? Like mountaineers, the business Amazons have reached the summit of their climb. For most of them it was a long and tough haul and, despite their success in achieving it, some have wondered whether the effort was justified.

No Regrets

Despite the severity and length of the climb, 84 per cent had no hesitation in stating that if they found themselves at the bottom again they would start up once more rather than enter paid employment. Sonia Kaplan: 'I would start again the next day, even if I had a small wool shop, but I could not work for someone else.' Julie Kitson: 'I would not just fold up and go to pieces. I would immediately start again and if I didn't have any money whatsoever, and had to get a job, I would get one, make myself indispensable, command a good salary, and would start again the minute I had accumulated the minimum of capital.' Lois Jane Apple: 'I would not get a job. I would start again in business. I have so many businesses in mind that I wouldn't think of being employed. The opportunities in business are limitless. Business is merchandising. Business is people.'

There were, however, a few who could not see themselves starting all over again. Nine per cent were doubtful whether they would have the mental and physical stamina, and 7 per cent would have entered employment rather than tried once again to become their own masters. By any business criterion 84 per cent is a very high percentage of satisfied customers, but in effect this figure is even higher because the 9 per cent who were hesitant and the 7 per cent who said no did not actually regret having been owners. Thus although a few felt that they did not have it in them to do it again, none regretted having done it once.

The main reason given by the 84 per cent who stated that if for one reason or another they lost all they had, they would restart in business rather than enter employment, was that they considered themselves unemployable. Having tasted the power of being their own boss, they felt they could no longer work for somebody else. Employment agent Denise Philips says: 'After having been my own boss, made my own decisions, taken my own risks, and paid for the consequences for better or for worse, I don't think I could go back to work for somebody else.' But being one's own boss is not only a matter of freedom from accountability but also of security of tenure. Anne Liddie, running a London tourist centre, explains:

> I have girl friends who are top executives in bigger organisations than my own. They are much more frustrated than I am. They actually envy me. Their job might seem more interesting than mine. They whiz over to New York and all that, all expenses paid. But basically they say: 'Anne, you are lucky, being your own boss. At least you know where you stand. No one can give you the push.'

The verdict was loud and clear: not only did the business Amazons have no regrets about their chosen way of life but, faced with a situation in which they lost their business and needed to gain a livelihood, they would restart in business rather than be in employment.

Ambitions

Eighty-three per cent of the millionairesses expressed a wish to be bigger and more successful businesswomen. Even the biggest of them all, fifty-five-year-old Sonia Kaplan, the owner of a $100 million mail order business, was not content with her present size and was straining to expand: 'I'm not worried about not being able to cope with a bigger business. In ten years they have projected that we shall be doing $500 million a year. I am awaiting this day anxiously.'

Despite the popular portrayal of business people as restless and always on the look-out for new ventures, and given that the business Amazons would not have reached the top if they had deviated greatly from that image, it is still baffling that women who did not yearn for diamonds and furs, for wildlife safaris and lavish parties, who did not indulge in gambling or in expensive young gigolos, should have had one overriding ambition, to be bigger and more successful business-women. For what? For whom?

It was definitely not for money. For their modest needs they all had enough. But nor was it for power: the very word was taboo among these women. So money and power, the two chief motivators of the male tycoon, were not theirs. Their reasons had more to do with the business itself than with their own self-image.

Three reasons prompted their expansionist ambitions: a fear that not to expand was tantamount to regression; a strong wish for continuity; and a concern for their workers. The unjustified fear that unless they expanded, their business would evaporate was a fear they had caught from their male colleagues who had been raised on the postwar business philosophy that big was beautiful. Margaret Bryant, in children's clothing, admits: 'I would be happy with this size. But I cannot stay at this size because if I stand still I slip back.' Dorothy Simmonds agrees: 'I would like the business to grow only for one reason, because business, like a child, has to grow, it cannot be static.'

Continuity was the second reason. Hardware magnate Jenny Kin-nock Trafford states forthrightly: 'I want this business to be around for another hundred years.' It was not that they were out to create dynasties but that, as with their children, they looked on their business as their contribution to posterity.

If the first reason, 'expand or perish', is misguided but understand-able in the context of the business community, and the second is accepted as a bona fide if sentimental explanation, the third reason, that of wanting to become bigger and more successful in order to benefit their employees, seems suspect. Was it a genuine concern for employees or was it disguised self-interest?

Supermarket owner Doreen Hartman's justification for her growth ambitions was a mixture of the two, her workers' benefit and her own:

'I don't have that personal need to be bigger. But we will lose some good people if we don't grow – because there are people who are store managers and they want to climb to become supervisors. If I don't expand they will go somewhere else.' Although Doreen probably had no personal need to be bigger, and although it could not be denied that her top employees would have benefited from the business's growth, her expansionist ambitions could not be attributed only to her concern for her employees, but also to her own. It was the fear of losing her top people and being reduced to a smaller and struggling business without competent personnel that forced her to expand.

Expansion is not the only alternative open to the owner of a large private business. Among the business Amazons' male counterparts, going public and selling out are other popular options. There are obvious advantages in going public. Rachel Shapiro states: 'I might be a wealthy woman, but all my money is tied in the business. If something goes wrong I'm left with very little. Floating the business will enable me to separate my money from that of the company. But for this I have to go on expanding.' The fear of losing their independence was a reason for caution: only a few of them had floated or contemplated floating their company's shares. Lois Jane Apple re-counts: 'Back in 1969 we considered it, but we pulled back. The thought of having to sacrifice my freedom of decision-making, and most probably also my style of management which is a most caring one, stopped me from going through with it.'

For most business persons, selling out and converting book assets into cash that can be deposited in the bank to accrue sufficient interest to retire to the French Riviera was the dream of their life, but not for the business Amazons. Hotelier Tricia Bishop says, 'Sometimes I feel that if offered a deal I would consider selling the hotel. But I am sure that after having sold it I would have just gone on to start another one, because I wouldn't know what to do with myself. So I might as well stay put.'

Although selling out a business meant the availability of money with free time, for those who did not know what to do with either it was not an alluring prospect. Sonia Kaplan was offered millions for her mail order business. She could have left the hassle of the business world, retired to a Caribbean island, and enjoyed the sun and sea for the rest of her life. But she rejected the offer and chose to get up at six in the morning, lose her temper at least five times a day, spend one third of her time in and out of airplanes, hotels, and suitcases, and worry about the last or the next sales figures of the company. The reason why a reasonable and intelligent person like Sonia would opt for such a seemingly less enjoyable style of life was the fear that without the status that the business conferred on her she would be a nobody, an invisible has-been:

> Without the business I am nobody. Today, because I head a large corporation, I am invited to talk to trade associations and women's groups. I am asked to attend functions and I was invited to sit on a governmental committee. Why? Not because I am Sonia Kaplan. Sonia Kaplan is just a plain little woman. But because I am the owner of Avenmore Incorporated. If I sell out I become a nobody. I shall become a has-been overnight, and I have no intention of becoming that.

Wanting to expand and head larger corporations also requires the characteristic abilities and temperament that go with the job. The 17 per cent for whom expansion was not an ambition confessed that they lacked some of these requirements. Eva Helsing was not against expansion *per se*, but realised that for her it would not be the right thing: 'Directing a large group of people is not my cup of tea. So I dare say that I will not go national. I shall keep to my present size. I would like to be known as a financial expert. That would be pleasing to me.'

Like Eva, restaurateur Sue Heathcote felt more comfortable with the tangible shopfloor management style than with the more detached boardroom one. And although she realised that this was an obstacle to further growth she could afford to ignore it because she had proven her success. A few thousand more pounds at the end of the year were not going to change her life: 'I am a close-to-the-ground manager. I have to do things myself. I realise that it limits my growth, but I am happy as I am and the business is doing well, so why bother to change? Is there only one correct way to run a business? It is like bringing up children. There is not one and only one right way.'

An insatiable appetite for territorial expansion is not a requisite for becoming a business Amazon, but there is a direct correlation between such an appetite and the size of one's business. All of the 17 per cent who denied having expansionist ambitions were among the smallest owners of the whole sample.

Dreams

One may have realistic ambitions about the future; one may also have dreams. Although dreams are seldom realised they may be the preliminary stage that precedes a practical ambition, but it takes more than dreaming to move on to the next stage. Let us take the analogy of a fat person who has never been an athlete and a wiry person with plenty of running experience. They can both aim to win a marathon but the fat person's aim is in the realm of a dream while that of the wiry person is an ambition. Yet if the fat person slimmed and trained, this aim would cease to be a dream and evolve into an ambition.

Because an ambition is closer to materialisation than a dream, practical people tend to have ambitions while impractical ones have dreams. So it was a surprising revelation that 64 per cent of the women in the survey should have had aims which had not evolved beyond the stage of a dream.

Avoiding trouble

If dreams are about what one does not have, and the business Amazons had more than most, what was it that 64 per cent of them yearned for and could not attain? Was anything beyond the reach of these supremely talented women?

In fact for 89 per cent of the dreamers (57 per cent of the whole sample) the dreams were very much more down to earth. Reacting to the result-oriented life they had led, they dreamed about one of the few things that had eluded them: a less harassed life. The thing that most people had in abundance, time, was what they lacked and were unable to buy. Rose Kraus says: 'I would like to have more time for friends. I suppose lurking way down inside me I envy the women who go to Bonwit Tellers and buy a blouse and have lunch together. I never do it.'

Most of the businesswomen's dreams revolved around the same theme. They dreamed of time for themselves, time to relax and pursue ungainful occupations: time for lengthy stops on remote islands (11 per cent); time to acquire further knowledge (6 per cent), including languages, literature, and archaeology; and time to write (14 per cent). In some cases writing was more than a dream. Advertising tycoon

Frances Roberts had several novels, children's, and poetry books to her name. Eva Helsing was a veteran of four financial books. Linda Bailie had earned her livelihood by writing TV scripts before she became a lingerie manufacturer, but she had not rid herself of the writing bug. 'My dream is to be able to write what I want to write, not just for money. The business has enabled me to think in these terms.'

As Virginia Woolf so wisely observed, 'In order to write a woman needs money and a room of her own.' Money the women magnates had, and rooms in plenty; but not the time to seclude themselves there, or the courage to take it. So for most of them writing remained no more than a dream. After several unpublished plays and novels Genevieve Rouche was too realistic to give up her Los Angeles talent agency and adopt the precarious life of a full-time writer, so she settled for dreaming about it instead: 'Ideally what I would like more than anything in the world would be to be able to write like Dorothy Parker. That would be my ideal, to write well.'

Among those who had not yet tried their hand at writing but still dreamed about it were Marion Little who wanted to write a sexy novel à la Erica Jong, and Julie Kitson who was going to recount her experiences as a stuntwoman. Iris Williamson the fast-food organiser, giftshop owner Eileen Geermie and hotelier Susanna Barnes all hoped to write their autobiographies.

The search for a more inward life repeated itself in other dreams. Babywear manufacturer Hilda Bergdorf would have liked to concentrate on horticulture, and caterer Claire Smith on learning the piano. Even those whose dreams were more commercially orientated dreamed about smaller businesses which would allow them more time to themselves. Jenny Cox, who had a thriving chain of fashion shops in London, dreamed about running a small hotel in the Caribbean, and Laurie Richards was ready to exchange her $20 million marketing business with its 150 employees for a small restaurant where she and her boyfriend would stand behind the counter and serve homemade food.

The incredible thing was that, while dreaming about reverting to being the small business owners they had started out as, Jenny and Laurie continued planning the expansion of their present businesses. As far as they were concerned the two were not contradictory. One was an ambition, the other a dream. And being the practical persons they were, they were not going to sacrifice an ambition for the sake of a dream. Leisurely shopping and lunch with girlfriends are humble dreams which do not call for a great deal of money or supernatural intervention for their realisation. So are stays on remote islands or learning a language. What they do require to come true, however, is free time, which the business Amazons could have obtained only if they had abdicated at least some of the duties and responsibilities that went with their titles. But this they could not do.

In the public eye

Of those who allowed themselves to dream, only 11 per cent had fantasies which would have brought more rather than less trouble and public exposure. These were the ones who dreamed of careers in politics and public service. Had it not already become evident that the majority of them were in essence private persons, one might have expected more of them to harbour political ambitions, for on the face of it, with their capacity for hard work and managerial skills, they seemed naturals for public office. So why did they not hold such office? And why did so few of them even dream about it? Hilary Waldorf, chemicals expert, explains:

> Politics is aggravation. It is nothing but aggravation, you never have a free moment. Politicians must have egos that are never satisfied. I have a woman friend in her early fifties who has been the mayor of our town for four years, and early this year she had a stroke from all this aggravation. Yet she is running for another term, another four years of aggravation. She knows that a second stroke will kill her, but she said she cared for the city. I believe her, she is a sincere person; but I also think that she is addicted to it, she likes the confrontation.

Strange as it might seem, the business Amazons shied away from confrontation. Their toughness was of a different kind from that of politicians. Although they possessed the ideal qualities for politicians, such as the ability to function under physical and mental strain and be decisive and responsible for their actions, they were also sensitive to personal rebuke, felt uneasy about shifting alliances, and found it difficult to compromise, all of which are essential requirements for politicians. Financier Eva Helsing admits:

> I could not be a politician. I couldn't take the criticism. If they wrote only half about me that they write about some of them I would just cry. I would not be able to take it.

Barbara Carpenter, in engineering, also feels doubtful:

> I am interested in politics, but I'm not sure I have the character it requires. There is no loyalty in politics. An interest group supports a politician only until they get what they want, and then they drop him and support another. As soon as people get elected everybody is waiting to throw them out. I am not naive, but none the less I don't like it.

Janet Draper, also in engineering, takes a firm stand:

> I am very involved in politics but I would not run for office because I will not compromise or prostitute my ideas. If I believe in something I believe in it.

For most women a political career is in the dream category. But then for most women so are many other things. It remains surprising that where politics was concerned, the business Amazons' record was as disappointing as that of other women. In the UK only two of the women tycoons have held a political appointment. One was a Conservative councillor (a local government post) for eleven years and another a Conservative parliamentary candidate. In the USA only one of them tried to narrow the gap between her dream and reality by taking steps to secure a Republican nomination for governorship, but she failed.

It is in the nature of dreams that the fact that others have not managed to fulfil them does not stop other dreamers from keeping them alive. On the contrary, the less effort the dreamers made to realise their dreams, the more convinced they became of their feasibility. Not having tried to get involved in politics, electronics expert Stevie Frederick felt that her dream of a political career was closer to materialisation than it actually was: 'I think that those who are qualified should serve, and I feel I am qualified.' Little did she realise how many others there were who believed that they too were the right people for the job.

The same naivety applied to Lydia Eastern, the remarkable $80 million travel agent, who had no political experience whatsoever but dreamed about becoming the first woman president of the USA: 'I want to be the president of the USA. Why not? An actor got there. A peanut farmer got there. Why not a woman? I feel that I can do anything, that is my motivation. Keep looking forward and you are what you are. You are your own destiny, and if you have goals you can reach them.' A goal is one thing, a dream is another. Despite Geraldine

Ferraro's nomination as Mondale's prospective vice-president, in today's political climate in the USA a woman president is a dream. But then five years ago so was a female prime minister in Britain. Dreams, against all the odds, do sometimes come true.

Envoi: Why Not You?

The Business Amazons is not an exclusive club. On the contrary, its aims are to increase its membership and it welcomes newcomers. That is the reason why a hundred women, otherwise very private persons, forsook their privacy and exposed their ambitions, dreams, and ultimate success to anyone who cares to know. They did it in the belief that, by explaining how they function, they can help other women follow in their footsteps. They were not bothered by the idea that once they had revealed themselves they could no longer be seen as super-women. None of them had ever claimed to be anything other than ordinary, with a few extras that any woman could acquire if she were determined enough.

The difference between them and many other talented and remarkable women (civil servants, doctors, academics for example) is that they joined the right club: the Business Club where women can make their way as easily as men. Business disregards social barriers. If you have a product to sell and somebody wants it, they will not take exception to your sex, your religion, or the colour of your skin. And, at the end of the day, it is that initial choice that counts for more than the abilities of the individual.

A choice which could be yours. It worked for them. It could work for you.

The key to the Business Amazons' Club is the key to every success story: ambition. The urgent desire to do better. Frustration which is so common among women, dissatisfaction with their status and opportunities, could be ambition's greatest spur. Channel it the right way, and instead of bogging you down it can start you on your way to the top.

The other extras that can help to turn dream into reality are hard work and tenacity. And this is where women have an inbuilt advantage, because these are qualities in which they have always excelled. It is ironic that women still need to be reminded of their potential when even in Biblical times it was clearly recognised. Remember the description in Proverbs of the virtuous woman:

> . . . her price is far above rubies . . . She riseth also while it is yet night . . . and her candle goeth not out by night . . . She considereth a field, and buyeth it: with the fruit of her hands she planteth a vineyard . . . She maketh fine linen, and selleth it, and delivereth girdles unto the merchant . . .

The only difference between then and now is that *then* her qualities caused a man to pay for her, whereas *now* they can enable her to pay most handsomely for herself.

Select Bibliography

Books

BADINTER E. *The Myth of Motherhood*, Souvenir Press, London 1981.

BASIL D.C. *Women in Management*, Dunellen, New York 1972.

BLUMENSTEIN P. and SCHWARZ P. *American Couples*, William Morrow, New York 1983.

CHESLER P. and GOODMAN E.J. *Women, Money and Power*, William Morrow, New York 1976.

COOPER C.L. *Executive Families Under Stress*, Prentice-Hall, New Jersey 1982.

COOPER C.L. and DAVIDSON M.J. *High Pressure: Working Lives of Women Managers*, Fontana, London 1982.

DOWLING COLLETTE, *The Cinderella Complex*, Fontana, 1982.

HALL F.S. and D.T. *The Two-Career Couple*, Addison-Wesley, Reading, Massachusetts 1977.

HARRIGAN BETTY LEHAN, *Games Mother Never Taught You, or Corporate Gamesmanship for Women*, Warner, New York 1977.

HENNING M. and JARDIM A. *The Managerial Woman*, Marion Boyars, London 1974.

HERTZ L. *In Search of a Small Business Definition*, University Press of America, Washington D.C. 1982.

HOSHINO-ALTBACH E. (ed) *From Feminism to Liberation*, Schenkman, Cambridge, Massachusetts 1971.

KENDSIN R.B. (ed) *Women and Success*, William Morrow, New York 1974.

KINZER N.S. *Stress and the American Woman*, Ballantine, New York 1980.

MYRDAL A. and KLEIN V. *Women's Two Roles, Home and Work*, 2nd edition, Routledge & Kegan Paul, London 1968.

OAKLEY ANN, *Subject Woman*, Fontana 1982.

OAKLEY ANN, *Housewife*, Allen Lane, London 1974.

RAPAPORT R and R.N. (eds) *Working Couples*, Harper & Row, New York 1974.

RIVERS C. BARNET R. and BARUCH G. *Beyond Sugar and Spice*, Putnam, New York 1979.

SEAMAN B. *Free and Female*, Coward, McCann & Geoghegan, New York 1972.

SHERIN E.H. *Career Dynamics: Matching Individual and Organizational Needs*, Addison-Wesley, Reading, Massachusetts 1978.

SINCLAIR DECKARD B. *The Woman's Movement*, 3rd edition, Harper & Row, New York 1983.

STEAD B.A. (ed) *Women in Management*, Prentice Hall, New Jersey 1978.

SWAYNE C.B. and TUCKER W.R. *The Effective Entrepreneur*, General Learning Press, Morristown, New Jersey 1973.

WILLIAMS M.G. *The New Executive Women*, Chilton, New York 1977.

Articles and Reports

BAILYN L. 'Career and family orientation of husbands and wives in relation to marital happiness' *Human Relations* 23, 1970, p 97.

BAYES M. and NEWTON P.M. 'Women in authority: a socio-psychological analysis, *Journal of Applied Behavioural Science* no 1, 1978, pp 7–29.

BEM S.L. 'Androgyny vs the tight little lives of fluffy women and chesty men' *Psychology Today*, September 1975, pp 58–62.

BOYD D.P. and GUMPERT D.E. 'Coping with entrepreneurial stress' *Harvard Business Review* vol 16 no 2, March/April 1983, p 45.

DENMARKE F.L. and DIGGORY J.C. 'Sex differences in attitudes towards leaders' display of authoritarian behaviour' *Psychological Reports* 18, Southern University Press, 1966, pp 867–8.

FRAKER S. 'Why women aren't getting to the top' *Fortune Magazine* 16, April 1984, pp 36–41.

GOVE W.R. and GEERKEN M.R. 'The effects of children and employment on the mental health of married men and women' *Social Forces* 56, 1977, pp 66–7.

HARLAN A. and WEISS C. 'Moving up: women in managerial careers' *Third Progress Report* Wellesley College Center for Research on

Women, Wellesley, Massachusetts, 1980.

HISRICH R.D. and O'BRIEN M. 'The woman entrepreneur', in Vesper K.H. (ed) *Frontiers and Entrepreneurship Research* Babson College Center for Entrepreneurial Studies, Wellesley, Massachusetts 1981.

HISRICH R.D. and BRUSH C. 'The woman entrepreneur in management skills and business problems' *Journal of Small Business Management* vol 22 no 1, January 1984, p 33.

KORN FERRY INTERNATIONAL 'Profile of women senior executives', New York 1982.

KORN FERRY INTERNATIONAL 'Executive profile: a survey of corporate leaders' [American] by Sussman J.A., New York 1979.

KORN FERRY INTERNATIONAL 'British corporate leaders – a profile', a Korn Ferry International Study in conjunction with the London Business School, London 1981.

KRAVETZ D. 'Sex role concepts of women' *Journal of Consulting and Clinical Psychology* 44, 1976, pp 437–43.

LIPMAN-BLUMEN J. 'What shapes a woman's wish for a career or to be a full-time housewife?' *Scientific American*, May 1973.

LUTHANS FRED 'The female leadership dilemma' *Public Personnel Management*, May-June 1975, pp 173–9.

O'LEARY V.E. 'Some attitudinal barriers to occupational aspirations in women' *Psychological Bulletin* vol 81, 1974, pp 809–26.

PENDLETON B.F., POLOMA M.M. and GARLAND T.N. 'An approach to quantifying the needs of dual-career families' *Human Relations* vol 35 no 1, 1982, pp 69–82.

ROSEN B., TEMPLETON M.E. and KICHLINE K. 'The first few years on the job: Women in management' *Business Horizons* Indiana University Graduate School of Business, vol 24 no 6.

ROSEN B. and JERDEE T.H. 'The influence of sex role stereotypes on evaluation of male and female supervisory behaviour' *Journal of Applied Psychology* 57, 1973, pp 44–8.

ROSEN B. and JERDEE T.H. 'Sex role stereotyping in the executive suite' *Harvard Business Review*, 1974, pp 45–58.

SCHERIN V.E. 'The relation between sex role stereotype and requisite management characteristics' *Journal of Applied Psychology* 57, 1973, pp 95–100.

SCHWARTZ E.B. 'Entrepreneurship: a new female frontier' *Journal of Contemporary Business* vol 5, Winter 1976, pp 47–76.

STAINS G., TAVRIS C. and EPSTEIN T. 'The queen bee syndrome' *Psychology Today*, January 1974.

TERBORG J.R. 'Women in management: a research review' *Journal of Applied Psychology* 62, 1977, pp 647–64.

VAN DER MERWE S. 'What personal attributes it takes to make it in management' *Business Quarterly* no 4, Winter 1978.

VANEK J. 'Time spent in housework' *Scientific American*, November 1974, p 160.

WATKINS J.M. and D.S. 'The female entrepreneur: her background and determinants of business choice – some British data' in Hornaday J.A., Timmons J.A. and Vesper K.H. (eds) *Frontiers of Entrepreneurship Research* 1983, Babson College Center for Entrepreneurial Studies, Wellesley, Massachusetts.

WITTE R.L. 'The new working dynamic: men and women in the work force' *Business Horizons*, August 1980, pp 57–60.

'The Bottom Line: Equal enterprise in America', Report of the President's Interagency Task Force on Women Business Owners, 2nd edition, Government Printing Office, Washington 1978, p 5.